T0304704

Digital Infrastructures for Business Innovation

Digital infrastructures are the commonly used technologies, systems, products, and platforms which businesses use to conduct commerce, partnerships, and transactions. Chief among these infrastructures is the Internet – an infrastructure which is remarkable for its all-pervasive presence in our daily lives – while others include cloud computing, social media, mobile technology, blockchain technologies, and cryptocurrencies.

This book introduces the key concepts and models to help you understand digital infrastructures, their technologies, their dynamic evolution, and the ways that businesses can exploit them. The primary focus is on processes of innovation and change that are embodied in new digital infrastructures. The book takes a balanced approach, presenting easy-to-understand technical information and pragmatic business analysis. The book's concise chapters develop the topics carefully, with clear language and many real-world examples.

The intended audience includes management students on advanced undergraduate and postgraduate courses, as well as business professionals and entrepreneurs. Readers at all levels will value the book's explanation of the technical elements of digital infrastructures and will find insights they can use in developing their own business ideas, in start-ups or existing enterprises.

Magda David Hercheui is Professor (Management Education) in Project Management and Innovation at the UCL School of Management.

Tony Cornford recently retired as Associate Professor in Information Systems in the Department of Management at the London School of Economics and Political Science.

Business and Digital Transformation

Digital technologies are transforming societies across the globe, the effects of which are yet to be fully understood. In the business world, technological disruption brings an array of challenges and opportunities for organizations, management and the workplace.

This series of textbooks provides a student-centred library to analyse, explore and critique the evolutionary effects of technology on the business world. Each book in the series takes the perspective of a key business discipline and examines the transformational potential of digital technology, aided by real-world cases and examples.

With contributions from expert scholars across the globe, the books in this series enable critical thinking students to excel in their studies of the new digital business environment.

Digital Transformation in Accounting
Richard Busulwa and Nina Evans

Demand-Driven Business Strategy
Digital Transformation and Business Model Innovation
Cor Molenaar

Navigating Digital Transformation in Management
Richard Busulwa

Smart Business and Digital Transformation
An Industry 4.0 Perspective
Sándor Gyula Nagy and Tamás Stukovszky

Data Analytics and Digital Transformation
Erik Beulen and Marla A. Dans

Consumer Behaviour and Digital Transformation
Ayantunji Gbadamosi

Digital Infrastructures for Business Innovation
Magda David Hercheui and Tony Cornford

For more information about this series, please visit www.routledge.com/Routledge-New-Directions-in-Public-Relations--Communication-Research/book-series/BAD

Digital Infrastructures for Business Innovation

Magda David Hercheui and Tony Cornford

LONDON AND NEW YORK

Designed cover image: Getty © byakkaya

First published 2025
by Routledge
4 Park Square, Milton Park, Abingdon, Oxon OX14 4RN

and by Routledge
605 Third Avenue, New York, NY 10158

Routledge is an imprint of the Taylor & Francis Group, an informa business

British Library Cataloguing-in-Publication Data
A catalogue record for this book is available from the British Library

Library of Congress Cataloging-in-Publication Data
Names: Hercheui, Magda David, author. | Cornford, Tony, author.
Title: Digital infrastructures for business innovation / Magda David Hercheui and Tony Cornford.
Description: Abingdon, Oxon ; New York, NY : Routledge, 2025. | Includes bibliographical references and index. | Identifiers: LCCN 2024032196 (print) | LCCN 2024032197 (ebook) | ISBN 9781032473185 (hardback) | ISBN 9781032473178 (paperback) | ISBN 9781003385578 (ebook)
Subjects: LCSH: Information technology—Economic aspects. | Technological innovations—Economic aspects. | Infrastructure (Economics)
Classification: LCC HC79.I55 H474 2025 (print) | LCC HC79.I55 (ebook) | DDC 338/.064—dc23/eng/20241010
LC record available at https://lccn.loc.gov/2024032196
LC ebook record available at https://lccn.loc.gov/2024032197

ISBN: 9781032473185 (hbk)
ISBN: 9781032473178 (pbk)
ISBN: 9781003385578 (ebk)

DOI: 10.4324/9781003385578

Typeset in Times New Roman
by codeMantra

Contents

Acknowledgement

The authors want to thank the London School of Economics and Political Science for authorising the use of material previously produced for a study guide used by the institution.

Preface

In the three decades since the opening of the Internet for commercial activity in the 1990s, large-scale digital connectivity has changed how all manner of organisations and businesses operate; how they fit into their markets, address their customers and deliver their products or services. Along the way, a new set of digital infrastructures based on the Internet evolved and have changed how digital technologies are conceived, and consequently how they impact our personal and professional lives.

This book presents concepts and models to help you understand these digital infrastructures and the scale and scope of the changes they bring: their underpinning technologies, the dynamics of their evolution, and the ways businesses exploit them. The focus is on processes of innovation and change embodied in and achieved using digital infrastructures. As with any book, we could not cover all that we would like. Indeed, we would need a collection of books to try to cover more. Instead, we have focused on key conceptual pillars, with a critical perspective in pointing out pros and cons, advantages and challenges, risks and opportunities. From this solid foundation on digital infrastructures you will be able to explore more.

Our intended audience includes management students and business professionals interested in having a comprehensive introduction to the topic of digital infrastructures for business innovation. The book's short and sharp chapters develop topics carefully, with clear language and selected examples, presenting both the technical elements of digital infrastructures and their role in supporting business innovation or driving change. The book considers new modes of business that digital infrastructures have fostered including digital business platforms and diverse digital business models, balancing a theoretical understanding grounded in concrete descriptions of digital technologies and their business applications. The book takes a balanced approach, presenting easy-to-understand technical information, pragmatic business analysis, and essential theoretical underpinnings. But we never infer that these add up to simple recipes for success or that digital infrastructures are an unalloyed benefit to us all. There are hard challenges to be faced.

We hope you enjoy the journey.

Acronyms

AGI – Artificial General Intelligence
AI – Artificial Intelligence
API – Application Programming Interfaces
AR – Augmented Reality
ARPANET – Advanced Research Projects Agency Network
AWS – Amazon Web Services
BCG – Boston Consulting Group
BMC – Business Model Canvas
BYOD – Bring Your Own Device
CCPA – California Consumer Privacy Act
CERN – European Organization for Nuclear Research
DARPA – Defense Advanced Projects Research Agency
DBP – Digital Business Platform
DDOS – Distributed Denial of Service
DNS – Domain Name System
DOI – Diffusion of Innovation Theory
DSL – Digital Subscriber Line
FM – Artificial Intelligence Foundation Models
GANs – Generative Adversarial Networks
GCP – Google Cloud Platform
GDPR – European Union's General Data Protection Regulation
HPC – High Performance Computing
HTML – Hypertext Markup Language
HTTP – Hypertext Transfer Protocol
HTTPS – Hypertext Transfer Protocol Secure
IaaS – Infrastructure as a Service
ICANN – Internet Corporation for Assigned Names and Numbers
IETF – Internet Engineering Task Force
IGF – Internet Governance Forum
IMP – Interface Message Processor
IoT – Internet of Things
IP – Internet Protocol
IPV4/IPV6 – Internet Protocol, versions 4 and 6
ISPs – Internet Service Providers
ITU – International Telecommunications Union
LLM – Large Language Model

ML – Machine Learning
MMOs – Massively Multiplayer Online Games
MOOCs – Massive Open Online Courses
NFC – Near Field Communication
NFT – Non-fungible Token
NIST – National Institute of Standards and Technology
NLP – Natural Language Processing
PaaS – Platform as a Service
RBV – Resource-Based View
RPA – Robotic Process Automation
SaaS – Software as a Service
SEO – Search Engine Optimisation
TCE – Transaction Cost Economics
TCP/IP – Transmission Control Protocol/Internet Protocol
UDP – User Datagram Protocol
URL – Uniform Resource Locator
VoIP – Voice over Internet Protocol
VR – Virtual Reality
W3C – World Wide Web Consortium
WWW – World Wide Web (or just the Web)
XML – Extensible Markup Language
XR – Extended Reality

1 Infrastructures

Something old… something new

Introduction

Infrastructures are old, evolving, and enduring.

All human communities, societies, and civilisations rely on shared resources. These may be physical resources, but they need to be accompanied by shared understandings and practices that sustain them. History often tells the story of earlier civilisations in terms of their use of shared resources – be it the shared fire of a neolithic clan, the shared knowledge of metallurgy in a bronze age community, the shared roads that the Romans built across Europe and the Middle East to sustain their empire, or the shared fields and granaries of a mediaeval village. We call such shared foundational resources infrastructures.

The establishment and evolution of specific infrastructures are central to how historians explain economic and social development. For example, the establishment of railways and telegraphs in the USA in the 19th century, or the constructions of separate fresh water and sewage systems for European cities in the same century, are both important infrastructures shaping these societies. In both cases, the infrastructures (shared resources) were fundamental to enabling many profound changes in social and economic life. In the 20th century it was perhaps the road system in support of motor vehicles, as well as telephone networks and electricity grids that are identified as fundamental infrastructures driving or enabling change. In each case – roads, telephones, electricity grids – we need to include the organisations that managed and sustained these shared resources alongside the physical plant and equipment. Indeed, most infrastructures are some mix of physical plant and equipment and the organisational and intellectual resources needed to keep them working – a neolithic clan had a fireplace, wood store, and the knowledge of how to create fire from stones and tinder, for instance.

Some of our important infrastructures are less physical and more institutional. These might include the banking system, mass media, education, or healthcare. For these infrastructures to work, there need to be rules, norms, procedures, and best practices together with shared understandings which are respected and reproduced across social groups. For instance, without a shared understanding of the banking infrastructure and how to use it, we could not have global trade. Institutions such as banking, education, or the legal system help to bind society together and achieve goals. The potential for social achievement (robust economy, a skilled work force, a good level of healthcare, clean water, etc.) depends on how efficient, robust, resilient, and aligned these different infrastructures are.

In our own era, in the third decade of the 21st century, digital technologies and the services they provide are understood as fundamental infrastructures for our society and powerful potential enablers of new social arrangements, changed economics, delivery of high-quality public services, and new business models. And our digital infrastructures are, as ever, in part physical

DOI: 10.4324/9781003385578-1

and engineered, in part evolved over time, and in part institutional as they are managed and coordinated over time.

But even 'new' digital infrastructures are not so new. They 'build on' what came before – a process we call 'exploiting the installed base' (see chapter 7) – and they carry forward many assumptions and characteristics from the past, a legacy for good and ill. The first draft of this chapter was typed on a laptop in rural Italy, using software (Microsoft 365) delivered over the Internet and up a hillside using mid-20th-century copper wire originally designed and installed for voice telephones. The text was typed on a QWERTY keyboard designed in the mid-19th century to slow down typists and stop their complex mechanical typewriters from jamming up. Just as railway lines were built along the routes of canals in England, and later roads were built along the routes of railways, so new infrastructures build on and adapt what is to hand at the time – the installed base.

Conceptualising infrastructures

We can start defining infrastructures from the explanations in the Cambridge and Oxford Dictionaries.

> *Infrastructure:* the basic systems and services, such as transport and power supplies, that a country or organisation uses in order to work effectively.
>
> ('Infrastructure', n.d.a.)

> *Infrastructure:* the basic physical and organizational structures and facilities (e.g., buildings, roads, power supplies) needed for the operation of a society or enterprise.
>
> ('Infrastructure', n.d.b.)

Both definitions say that infrastructures are basic systems, physical or organisational structures, which support the organisations and society in their endeavours to work properly and effectively given defined goals. In this direction, roads, transport systems, water reservoirs and pipes, electric energy stations and cables, and buildings are all physical infrastructures, which rely on the counterpart organisational and institutional infrastructures to work well. Evidently, the roads without the laws for using the roads would not serve the purpose of safely and efficiently moving people and goods around.

These two definitions concur well, based on core concepts of the base for the operations of a given organisation, society, or country, and the enabling of particular ways of doing things. Sometimes different infrastructures compete as a means of achieving the same thing – for example, railways (the railway infrastructure) may compete with air travel (in Europe at least). The definitions also highlight that infrastructures are a bundle of systems, services, and facilities, including both physical and organisational structures. In other words, infrastructures are resources that create a base for operations, and they include the social and organisational arrangements that allow those resources to support useful activities.

These dictionary definitions also give examples of things that are considered to be or are often described as infrastructures, such as transport systems (roads), power supplies (electricity), and buildings (airports, power stations, schools). Infrastructures also have the characteristic of generating benefits because they are shared among multiple users or multiple uses. People or businesses will choose to use infrastructures which are, from their perspective, more efficient, reliable, secure, cheaper, easier, or safer than alternatives. Scale matters too when thinking about infrastructures, as does the ability to be shared by different types of users and for different uses – what we call scope. A large-scale, general-purpose infrastructure will often be preferred by potential users than a smaller and more specialised one. The more the variety of potential users and potential uses, the stronger the economies of scale and of scope will be (see chapter 6).

While the concept of an infrastructure can be quite widely applied to the way our world is organised and operates, this book is focused on the specific domain of digital infrastructures. This can be exemplified by the Internet – the infrastructure that underpins so many aspects of our lives via the ubiquitous mobile phone, laptop, and many other devices we use to communicate digitally and the myriad services and functions that the Internet supports. Therefore, in this book, we mostly use 'digital infrastructures' as a plural term and to include many kinds of shared digital services. The Internet is certainly fundamental to most digital infrastructures, and many other infrastructure-like things can be identified as using the Internet. The World Wide Web (WWW) might be described as an information infrastructure that sits on top of the Internet. In the world of user-facing digital services, we often use the word platform, as in social media platforms, e-commerce platforms, e-banking platforms, etc. The word platform is not exactly a synonym for digital infrastructure (it has its own specific characteristics as discussed in chapter 8, when we consider digital business platforms – DBPs), but in everyday speech it may be used as a proxy for the idea of digital infrastructures. Thus, in the book we also use the word platform in a more flexible way, differentiating its generic meaning vis-à-vis the more restricted concept of DBPs.

The emergence of Internet-based digital infrastructures

The Internet started as a means for the exchange of data files, and then emails – a clear improvement over communication channels such as letters and memos or mailing bulk data stored on disks or tapes. It also soon became used for the publication and distribution of information – via the early versions of the World Wide Web (WWW). At that time, in the mid-1990s, the Internet was an interesting technology spurring on interesting applications, but it was not (yet) an important national or global infrastructure. The situation changed over quite a short period of time, as the Internet and in-company Intranets became major channels of communication (email, online chat, discussion boards, and more general information sharing on the Web). Significantly, it also started to become a place to transact all kinds of business (e-commerce, e-government).

The more the Internet gained scale, speed, and capacity (broadband), the more it could accommodate interactions between people, organisations, and governments. This led to electronic commerce online. It also came to support more kinds of communication (such as Voice over IP, VoIP, and video-conference calls) and the diffusion of content (websites, blogs, videos, etc.). As these uses – all of which we take for granted today – expanded, reinforcing each other as more of one led to more of others. The Internet became more and more important and more visible, and became in a few years a fundamental infrastructure for economies and societies across the world.

The Internet became a commercial technology available for all to potentially use in the 1990s. Before then, only some groups of academics, scientists, and researchers had access to the Internet itself although some services were available from other commercial carriers and phone companies. But once the Internet was set free it did not take long before entrepreneurs, companies, governments, civil society organisations, and individuals realised its potential, e.g., in terms of supporting lots and lots of useful things for all types of tasks and activities serving a mass user base. In other words, it became an important infrastructure.

However, infrastructures have their feet in the past. The Internet could become commercially viable only because it made use of (or we might say was 'built on top of') the existing communication infrastructure of the telephone network and the telephone company. As ever, infrastructures are physical and institutional. Most infrastructures emerge partly from de-novo design and planning and partly from borrowing/building on existing systems or services and adapting them to new purposes – a process we call cultivation (see chapter 7).

The origins of the Internet in the 1970s (see chapter 3) was a need to transfer digital data through the then existing communication networks (the installed base – the systems 'inherited' from the past). By linking together diverse networks and resources the Internet became a bigger network with more individual connections. More connections and more people create more (potential) value for all. However, when digital infrastructures evolve from previous legacy systems, this legacy will almost inevitably create some constraints. This occurs when an infrastructure cannot change because it is dependent on legacy elements, for example, if it must accommodate older or slower technologies. Change in digital infrastructures is expected as infrastructures take up new technologies and improve their performance, but it can be difficult to achieve because of this kind of path dependency, when the decisions we need to make in the present and facing the future depend on the decisions we have made in the past, even if the circumstances which defined previous decisions are not there anymore (see 'path dependence', on Wikipedia, 2024).

On the basis of the ideas introduced so far in this chapter, we can identify a fundamental set of characteristics that we expect to find in any and every kind of digital infrastructure, following a conceptualisation developed by Hanseth and Bygstad (2015). These authors emphasise that infrastructures are an 'installed base' which depends on the previous systems, as per the idea above of the path dependency. This installed base has a multitude of 'heterogeneous elements', some technological, some organisational and institutional, some simply users which give life through their agency. The only way of putting together all these elements, to work harmoniously, is through creating a 'standardised system' of integration of parts, by establishing technical and institutional standards. These infrastructures are 'shared' among different users, who will appropriate them to serve different goals. Thus, they are by definition expected to be 'open' to new users and new forms of use. And finally, they are 'evolving' constantly: as needs change, it is necessary to adapt physical, organisational, and institutional structures and standards to allow the digital infrastructure to keep serving the objectives of its users.

In chapter 4, we discuss the layered model of digital infrastructures, and having these characteristics in mind helps to understand the unique potential of digital infrastructures as enablers of innovation. In chapter 7, we consider the role of standards to put together all the elements of a digital infrastructure.

Examples of digital infrastructures

This section introduces a short summary of the digital infrastructures discussed in this book. The limitations of space mean the book cannot cover all digital infrastructures. We have made choices, considering mature digital infrastructures that we know well and some that are exciting interest for their potential in the next decade.

The Internet

In 2023, the Internet was used by around 67% of the worldwide population, 5.4 billion people (International Telecommunications Union – ITU, 2023). Every day, more people get access to the Internet so this number is growing. However, this number also shows that 2.6 billion people do not have access to the Internet, with all the negative consequences of being on the wrong side of the digital divide; in high-income countries, 93% of people use the Internet, in low-income countries it is 27% of the population.

Readers of this book will probably have a good understanding of the Internet from the user perspective as well as of the other infrastructures that we briefly introduce below that use the Internet. One way to express this is to say that these other digital infrastructures are 'layered on top' of the Internet. You could also say that they are created out of the Internet and that the Internet is part of their installed base. We come back to this idea of one infrastructure 'sitting on top' of another more formally in chapter 4 and explore the idea of an 'installed base' in chapter 7.

The Internet is a network of networks that connect digital devices, big and small, extending across the world. This network of networks is made up of:

- physical hardware and software – computers, cables, satellites, phone masts, programs, devices, etc.;
- a common set of rules or standards that it operates by, in particular the protocols for the exchange of data between devices (e.g., TCP/IP protocols); and
- a complex set of businesses, organisations, and institutions that govern and manage the service and help it to develop further.

What makes the Internet special and distinguishes it from other digital communications services is the way it connects devices. Using an open standard (TCP/IP) allows *any* connected device to communicate with *any* other. Closed computer networks allow communication within defined boundaries – for a government, a particular firm, or a sector of industry. But the Internet is open: as a network, it offers universal and unlimited access, provided that the user is in a country which does not block content through firewalls and filters. Anyone can add new computers or other devices to the network, as long as the standardised communication protocols are used. Moreover, the Internet itself, as a technical infrastructure, has no concern with the content of the messages it transmits.

However, what really makes the Internet unique and fundamental is the willingness of people, businesses, governments, charities, non-governmental organisations, and all sorts of organised groups to pass messages and digital content through the network, to look for content across the network, and to communicate via the network. The Internet has become the world's preeminent digital infrastructure because all these social actors have decided to communicate through the same network. The more people and devices there are using the network, the more dominant the Internet becomes. Today it is the most important digital infrastructure, because of its reach, relevance, and capacity for wealth creation. What would happen if the Internet were not available for, say, one month?

In chapter 3, we discuss the history of the Internet and the relevance of Internet Protocols in detail.

The World Wide Web (WWW)

The World Wide Web (WWW or just the Web) was an innovation led by the computer scientist Tim-Berners Lee in 1989. In its first conceptualisation, the Web was a system for identifying and displaying documents and other resources held on Internet-connected computers. It uses URLs (uniform resource locators) as addresses of objects such as web pages, photos, images, forms, and videos. As a metaphor, one could think of the Web as an information space in which pieces of content can be located because they have a unique address. The Web embodies the hyperlink concept to navigate from one piece of content to another using an embedded link.

The link https://www.bbc.co.uk/news will connect to the BBC news page on their website and their news pages will contain additional links to related content. This simple mechanism of hyperlinks facilitates easy access to information and quick and direct navigation from one kind of content to another.

We can retrieve and read/listen/look at this content, or respond to it in a published comment, or an edit of a file, or by filling in a form. The presentation of all content uses standardised languages and conventions which other computers or devices can identify, such as HTML (Hyper Text Markup Language), XML or JavaScript standards used on web pages, or the PDF format for documents. In order to make this library (information infrastructure) useful we need to have ways to find relevant content including text, images, or videos. The Web would have far less value for us all if it was not possible to search and find *specific* content easily.

The solutions to finding content that have emerged include search engines such as Google, Yahoo, Bing, Baidu, or DuckDuckGo. Search engines use the page content (words and phrases), and also hyperlinks – those embedded in a page and those that refer there – to define the relevance and importance of a particular page. In this way, search engines decide if a particular page should 'rank' high and be shown to you on the first page of a search or rank lower and be on a later page.

The World Wide Web is often conflated with the Internet, as if they are one and the same. For everyday users they may seem to be. The confusion comes because these two digital infrastructures work so well together, like two pieces of a bigger mechanism. However, they are indeed different with different histories and different purposes, as explained in chapter 9.

The cloud and cloud services

The cloud is the provision of computing services (broadly understood) through digital infrastructures. These services include data storage, software, or a platform on which to run your own software programs. By sharing computing resources among a large user base, cloud-service providers promise a more professional and efficient computing experience. People and organisations adopt cloud computing primarily because it is a better solution to their needs. It may also be cheaper.

The potential of cloud computing and cloud services is clear if you understand it as an infrastructure. Just like electricity or water, it delivers services piped to your door – data storage, information processing, software as a service, programming platforms, cybersecurity services, and many more. As with electricity or water, the key concept is that users do not want to be concerned with managing these needs. Both the suppliers and their customers reap benefits from economies of scale and economies of scope. So, where once we bought software such as a word processor and installed it on our own device, today we probably subscribe to a provider that offers word processing services – such as Google or Microsoft.

Delivering services on demand and pricing them by the unit consumed suits many users big and small. Gone is the chore of maintaining software on your own device, doing updates and backups, and so on. The service provider will usually ask for a fee, but in some markets, they may offer services at no (direct) cost to the user. But remember, if something is free on the Internet then you and your data are the product.

The cloud and cloud services are discussed in more detail in chapter 10.

Mobile technology

Mobile technology represents the computer in your pocket, on your wrist, or in your car. Wireless connections allow such devices to connect to the Internet (e.g., via Wi-Fi, mobile data, or

Bluetooth). This allows access to services of all kinds almost anywhere, but also allows other people to keep tabs on you and what you are doing, where you go, and who you are meeting.

The most important enabler of mobile infrastructure has been the development of smartphones. By allowing access to the Internet in a very easy way, through touch screens, smartphone technology has fostered the creation of an infinity of apps, each of which reinforces the value of our smartphones. It is a kind of virtuous cycle in which the innovation in hardware and networking enables the development of apps and related services, and because of the diffusion of apps and services there is stronger demand for better hardware and networks.

The diffusion of mobile infrastructure has brought some unexpected benefits. If we go back in time, to the 1970s, 80s, and even 90s, a major concern for the economic development of poorer countries was how to provide effective communication through telephone landlines. At that time, people wondered how to make the enormous investment needed to establish the infrastructure for the widespread use of landline telephones. When mobile technology was first developed, it was not clear that it would quickly diffuse in the developing world. However, history shows that with mobile technology, even the poorest people in the poorest countries quickly understood the benefits to them of better communication, and once people experience the benefit, they convince others and the demand develops strongly.

In 2023, the number of mobile subscriptions was 8.9 billion, more than the world population, (ITU, 2023). This number shows the pervasiveness of mobile technology. Many people had more than one mobile. In similar research, in 2023, ITU found that 78% of the world population over 10 years old owned a mobile phone. Ninety-five per cent of the world population have potential access to a mobile broadband signal, even if some do not have access to the service itself. In low-income economies, the mobile-broadband service was judged to be 20 times less affordable than the same service in high-income economies. The mobile broadband Internet subscription rate was 87% in 2023 (with 4.6 billion users). But still, a large gap remains between more developed countries and the developing countries (ITU, 2023).

Fixed broadband (cable in the ground) is still responsible for 83% of Internet traffic (ITU, 2023). But the number of homes with a fixed landline has gone down from its peak in 2006 (1.261 billion) to 862 million lines in 2022 (ITU, 2023). We can infer from this that many individuals and families do not feel the need for fixed landlines anymore, emphasising the growing importance of mobile infrastructure for access to the Internet and all its services.

In chapter 11, we return to the topic of mobile technology and discuss not only the devices, but how they support innovation through new apps and services.

Social media

Social media is a term used for a diversity of digital services which allow people and organisations to easily communicate and exchange content including text, voice, photos, images, and videos. The best-known social media platform is perhaps Facebook, which had more than 3 billion users in 2023. This is a massive number and it appears that Facebook may become even more pervasive in the future, despite the Chinese government blocking the service in the country. However, there are services similar to Facebook in China, such as WeChat, which had around 1.3 billion users in 2023 (in China, the app is called Weixin).

Humans have always been social beings immersed in social networks – families, villages, workplaces, clubs, societies, etc. Social networking is not new. What is new is the capacity for doing this through digital means and at a new scale (read more in Standage, 2013). In the first generation of Internet tools, social interaction was not easy. The early services allowed for publishing content in files (similar to paper), with some level of interaction available through email and web chat-type services.

Around the turn of the millennium came what are called Web 2.0 technologies. Web 2.0 allowed the general public to go online and publish their own content, share the content they found interesting, and comment on the content of others, both individuals and organisations. Changes in software interfaces and in how social interaction occurred allowed the creation and rapid growth of what we call social media. Today, services such as Facebook, WhatsApp, X (formerly known as Twitter), Instagram, TikTok, WeChat, Tumblr, Pinterest, YouTube, and LinkedIn make this kind of interaction easy and pervasive. They all make use of the Internet and WWW infrastructure for data communication in order for billions of people to enjoy their social media.

Smartphones allow access to social media from any place, and the tools to create instant content which has increased the use of social media and made the mobile device a more interesting communication channel. This process is also connected to the improvements made on the Internet as a whole and particularly to the offering of wireless broadband services through mobile phone infrastructures. Once again this shows digital infrastructures supporting each other's growth.

Social media is so pervasive that it has changed the way we interact, but it is our decision, our choice to use the social media that creates new or distinct social networks. Every time that we connect to a new person, send a message through social media, publish content, or read the content of others or subscribe to their channels, we are acting to create or shape the social network. In other words, social media services are only as important, useful, or positive as our efforts to make interesting and relevant contributions. But not all social media interactions are positive or relevant, and many people worry about the negative outcomes we observe.

In chapter 12, we consider how social media has become a digital infrastructure.

Metaverse

The metaverse is an emerging idea for a new digital infrastructure. The metaverse aims to be a 3D (three-dimensional) digital environment, running on top of the Internet and bringing strong elements of the logic of social media – connection, interaction, and sharing. The metaverse is different, however, because it presents itself as an immersive 3D digital space, made possible by your 3D headset. We sometimes use the term more loosely to encompass other forms of extended reality experiences, which overlap layers of digital information with layers of physical reality (e.g., augmented reality). The proponents of a metaverse see it as providing services in areas such as e-commerce, e-education, e-government, e-health, and e-entertainment, among others.

The idea of creating a digital immersive environment in three dimensions is not new. You can, for instance, read about the history of Second Life (see 'Second Life', on Wikipedia, 2024), one of the first social media platforms to present the concept of 3D interactions through avatars. But evolving from observing 3D objects moving on a screen to having an immersive experience through a headset is different. Relevant technology has recently developed, and big players such as NVIDIA, Facebook, Baidu, and Tencent are investing in the area. Digital companies are creating more focused platforms in which users can have a more immersive experience for gaming, socialising, purchasing products, attending gigs, participating in conferences and classes, or consulting doctors and health professionals. The bigger ambition is to have all these kinds of services hosted on a single platform, although it is also possible that the market will evolve into a more fragmented space with many providers.

The COVID-19 pandemic demonstrated people can operate online in many areas of their lives, including office work. But many found the experience challenging. The promise of the metaverse is to enhance the online experience and bring it closer to the physical experience, although it will not be exactly the same because there is no absolute need to reproduce reality as it is. Even if the visual and sound aspects become more sophisticated, the images are mainly cartoon-like, and smell and touch are absent – your body is not there! One key success factor of these new platforms will be to find the right products and services to attract users and which they find valuable. For gaming, the addition of immersive experiences has been shown to be very effective. In situations which require meeting online, the metaverse may add a layer of engagement. So too for some educational applications where detailed information and 3D interactions might be highly relevant.

Despite all the promises of bringing a 'revolutionary experience' to users, the metaverse has two key obstacles. First, it is extremely expensive to build and to maintain such a platform. Second, the hardware is still expensive for users and content creators. Companies would need to invest massively in a kind of service which does not have many users. If users are not there, companies do not have further incentive to populate the metaverse with digital content. To build momentum, the metaverse probably needs to be experienced by users and companies as a coherent collection of related places and activities – which is hard if the various elements are based on different platforms. On the Internet, we easily move from one website to another, but on social media your friends on Facebook are not necessarily present on WhatsApp. Can the metaverse be a metaverse if it is fragmented into many platforms?

In chapter 13, we discuss the emergence of the metaverse, considering technical and business aspects.

Artificial intelligence infrastructures

Like the metaverse, we can also say that the artificial intelligence (AI) infrastructures are emerging rather than fully formed. The speed of innovation in this area, the scope of current and possible applications, and the expectations for a strong impact mean this new digital infrastructure may have a level of relevance which is revolutionary. This statement may appear to be too strong, but it is based on the technology demonstrated in the last few years and the attention being paid to AI by experts across many fields. There are serious discussions about how many jobs will be lost in mainstream industries once AI starts to rapidly diffuse, and how to manage the resulting shifts in labour markets and the implications for our educational systems. We certainly do not need to add expectations that one day we can create an artificial general intelligence (AGI), rather than today's focused large language models (LLMs). This also does not mean AI is the magic wand to solve all humankind's problems. However, knowing when and how to apply AI and how to assess the subsequent change will bring competitive advantage to companies, and potentially do good in many fields, such as healthcare, greening the economy, and education.

AI infrastructures depend on fast and powerful data processing hardware. Greater computational power for individual machines as well as architectures to connect machines to process more data at faster speeds are a core part of any new infrastructure. NVIDIA, for instance, is a leader in producing powerful hardware for AI. At the level of software, we see a new infrastructure emerging around foundation models (e.g., OpenAI's GPT), which create complex mathematical and statistical models to support the development of more targeted applications (such as ChatGPT-3.5 and ChatGPT-4, and others to come in this series), and similar models such as Google's Gemini and Microsoft's Copilot.

These foundation models can be applied to different types of tasks, such as image recognition or voice recognition or the generation of text. Based on a foundation model, a more specific model can be created for a specific task. For instance, a foundation model such as ChatGPT can be the basis for a customer-service agent trained to respond to questions from customers complaining about delays in delivery. AI infrastructure is not then one piece of technology or one service but many technologies operating in layers to deliver final products and services (see the layered architecture of digital infrastructures in chapter 4).

The emerging AI infrastructure will increasingly be integrated (layered) with the other digital infrastructures introduced above. Amazon, Microsoft, and Google, for instance, are leaders in this approach, creating foundation models and application models to speed up the adoption of AI by their customers, and delivering these through their cloud services. This architecture and this business model can speed up the adoption of AI, overcoming limitations such as the lack of technical knowledge by users. For companies with more resources, an alternative approach may be to create their own foundation models and provide services in-house, develop their own products with unique characteristics, and share the resources with their business partners.

All these developments in the field of AI are accompanied by concerns and challenges. Many people around the world, including people who work within the AI field, have expressed concerns about the risks of AI if humans are not wise enough to keep the technology under control. One primary concern is whether AI tools could attain a level of independence, including generating new code. In the hands of groups with evil intent, naïve experimenters, or poorly briefed workers, this could cause catastrophic harm. Some even talk about AI as an existential risk for humans, an equivalent to the atomic bomb. We do not need to reach this level of concern to already have enough potential problems deriving from AI.

There are other more mundane risks and challenges which are already here to be faced now. AI models have a degree of complexity that even the smartest people do not understand. We may see that an AI tool is delivering a service well, but we may not be able to explain how it does it. If there are hidden flaws in the system, we cannot see them, unless or until they appear as an output. For instance, a model trained for selecting candidates for recruitment may have a 'hidden' bias against a certain group of people, and it may be difficult to identify this before many cycles of use. This implies that additional safeguards may be needed with humans deciding when and where AI solutions are safe enough to be used and rejecting the technology when not convinced. This kind of debate is playing out right now in California where some driverless cars were banned from the roads in October 2023 on grounds of public safety.

In chapter 14 we consider the architecture of artificial intelligence infrastructures, some business applications, and relevant business models.

References

Hanseth, O. and Bygstad, B. (2015). 'Flexible generification: ICT standardization strategies and service innovation in health care', *European Journal of Information Systems*, 24(6), pp. 645–663.

'Infrastructure' (n.d.a). *Cambridge Dictionary*. Available at: https://dictionary.cambridge.org/dictionary/english/infrastructure (Accessed: 16 March 2024).

'Infrastructure' (n.d.b). *Oxford Dictionary*. Available at: https://www.oed.com/search/dictionary/?scope=Entries&q=infrastructure (Accessed: 16 March 2024).

International Telecommunications Union – ITU (2023). *Measuring Digital Development – Facts and Figures*. ITU Publications. Available at: https://www.itu.int/en/ITU-D/Statistics/Pages/facts/default.aspx (Accessed: 16 March 2024).

'Path dependence' (2024). *Wikipedia*. Available at: https://en.wikipedia.org/wiki/Path_dependence (Accessed: 16 March 2024).

'Second Life' (2024). *Wikipedia*. Available at: https://en.wikipedia.org/wiki/Second_Life (Accessed: 3 August 2024)

Standage, T. (2013). *Writing on the Wall*. London: Bloomsbury Publishing.

2 Innovation ... something new

Introduction

Innovation is an overused word. The general sense conveyed is that innovation is good, it is what we need. It can build competitive advantages, power our economies, and make life better for people. In this sense, innovation means new things (products and services), new ways and new places for doing things (processes and places), and new ways for people to think (perceiving) and act (behaviours). New or changed aspects of our world are expected to improve lives by creating economic value, promoting human wellbeing, and helping to secure collective prosperity.

The more globalised and competitive the world becomes, and the shorter product lifecycles are, the more relevance being able to innovate is seen to have for individual businesses and wider economies. Making profits, holding market share, and sustaining the capacity for generating wealth in an environment of globalization and climate change seem to demand that we keep up the innovation process. This is understood at the level of national or regional economies as well as for individual firms looking for a sustainable and viable future. We expect other positive benefits from innovation too. These may include things such as environmental benefits (innovation in green technologies), social wellbeing (innovation in education), healthcare (innovation in medicines, diagnostics, and treatments), and happiness and safety (innovation in social and cultural norms).

A very simplified definition of the concept is provided by the UK Department of Trade and Industry (Innovation Unit) (2004, cited in Tidd and Bessant, 2013), which links innovation to the implementation of new ideas which reveal themselves as successful for a period of time (we cannot expect anything to be successful forever). Across studies in the domain, it is widely understood that innovation is not principally about having new ideas or inventing something; rather, innovation is the process of 'growing' new ideas into practical use; in other words, the proof of the pudding is in the eating (Tidd and Bessant, 2013).

Following this line, innovation starts from an interesting pool of ideas and resources and some process for filtering and selecting those which seem most promising, practical, and value-adding. It is this last phase, arguably, where innovation is really achieved. Filtering, selecting, and bringing to the market, in a general way, are what biotech industries and start-ups do and what governments and venture capital funds seek to catalyse. This view of innovation – a pool of ideas and resources, a stimulus and funding, and a practical application – fits quite well with the account of the emergence of the Internet as set out in chapter 3 and many of the other digital infrastructures we consider in this book.

But our focus on digital infrastructures also prompts us to consider the subsequent phases of innovation, the capturing of value from innovation and the cascade of subsequent changes it may imply. There is not always a simple and direct link between who leads innovation at the

DOI: 10.4324/9781003385578-2

start, who benefits from it, who gets rich, and who suffers. In this area of digital infrastructures one innovation may well beget others. The Internet, taken as an innovation in networking, has had many consequential innovations across many social and economic sectors. This 'generative' ability of the Internet is discussed further in chapter 4.

Innovation models

There is an overabundance of authors presenting their own definitions, models, or theories of innovation (we might say that there is over-innovation in innovation studies). But the many models found in the literature do offer us a range of conceptual lenses that broaden our understanding of innovation. We do not intend here to judge which models are better, but rather to reflect an array of distinctive perspectives, all of which may have value in defined contexts, but each of which encapsulates its own take on innovation (as summarised in Table 2.1).

Creative destruction

There is a common view that sees innovation – both change in how things are done and in how they are understood – as the essential driver of our economies; what Joseph Schumpeter (1994 [1942]) called the gales of creative destruction. Essentially a process of 'out with the old, on to

Table 2.1 Conceptualising innovation

Model	*Key idea*	*Elaboration*	*Author*
Proof of the pudding	Innovation is implementing new ideas successfully	Judge innovation by the outcomes and consequences (e.g., success)	UK Department of Trade and Industry (2004), in Tidd and Bessant (2013)
Gales of creative destruction	Innovation is change which releases energy into the economy and/or society	A positive and even necessary process of mutation	Schumpeter (1994 [1942])
The innovation space	Innovation is typed: process, product, position, and paradigm	The change potential is nurtured in distinct sub-locations	Tidd and Bessant (2013)
Ten types of innovation	Innovation is based in modules suitably combined	Configuration, offering, experience	Keeley et al. (2013)
Systems approach	Innovation derives from context, which fosters dynamics for innovation	Organisations organise and strategise for innovation	Karlsoon and Magnusson (2019)
Innovation ecosystems	Innovation occurs in environments that offer diversity and focus	Sharing and pooling knowledge and skills of multiple participants	Budden and Murray (2019)
Open innovation	Innovation is sharing/pooling knowledge and skills across boundaries	Drawing on many participants, crossing boundaries, giving, sharing	Chesbrough (2006) and Chesbrough and Bogers (2014)
Diffusion of innovation (back to the proof of the pudding)	Innovation is adoption	Adoption will happen if the product is right for the right user in the right moment	Rogers (2003 [1962])

the new'. Schumpeter argued that pursuing new or different things (products) or new different ways to do things (processes) created opportunities for more and different kinds of economic activity – a positive process of mutation in the economic structures. As new ideas and practices gain traction in the economy, inefficiencies or vested interests are swept away in the metaphorical creative gale. The result is a different, more productive, and perhaps socially more agreeable future.

This is not of course painless. The gales blow away some people's jobs and their livelihoods – how many typist jobs have been lost since the coming of the word processor and the personal computer? Today we see these gales in areas such as the move to a new greener and low-carbon economy, or the challenge that Fintech companies and banking apps pose to traditional banks and traditional bank staff. The recent emergence of powerful, easy-to-use, and general-purpose artificial intelligence tools seems to point to powerful new gales of creative destruction on the way (see chapters 14 and 16).

One example of creative destruction is the invention and spread of the digital camera. Kodak had a very long history as a major photographic company, selling their film across the world. Indeed they even pioneered the digital camera in the 1970s (Goodrich, 2022). However, the company did not embrace its own innovation, fearful of destroying its businesses of selling films and developing photographs. For sure, the first version of the digital camera was not user-friendly: too heavy, too expensive, and not connected to other digital devices and services. However, the company failed to perceive the bigger picture: Kodak was not able to block other companies from developing digital cameras, or from embedding digital cameras in mobile phones, increasingly integrated through cloud services with social media. The result was that in 2012 Kodak filed for bankruptcy, unable to keep up with its own invention in its own market.

From the Kodak example, we see that companies face a dilemma when offered the opportunity to innovate: should they lead the change even if that means sacrificing their current businesses, or should they protect their current businesses and accept the risks of being disrupted or swept away by competitors? Christensen (2016) discusses this question in depth, calling it the innovator's dilemma. The answer to this dilemma is never obvious, particularly when the decision is about being the first mover or not. It is very unlikely that any company or vested interest can stop broad trends of innovation. But an innovator needs to question when it is the right time for the innovation (Rayna and Striukova, 2009), as a particular market may not be (yet) ready for change.

Considering the long cycles of investment that may be needed for digital innovation, timing is an important question. A good example is the massive investment Meta (Facebook's owners) has made to lead the development of the metaverse digital infrastructure. At the time of the investment, their shareholders questioned whether Meta should lead at a very fast pace the development of a new and innovative digital infrastructure which would potentially challenge their current social media products (see more on the discussion in chapter 13). At such a moment, history is being made. Meta may lose fortunes in a market that is not ready for the metaverse, or may lose fortunes for not being ready to compete with other big players such as Microsoft, Apple, Google, NVIDIA, AWS (Amazon Web Services), and Tencent, or the hordes of hungry start-ups.

Typologies of innovation: Context, environment, ecosystem

Tidd and Bessant (2013) suggest that innovation can happen in four key areas, which together define the innovation space. The most obvious one they suggest is innovation in products and services themselves. The second is innovation in processes (i.e., changes in the way products and services are created and delivered). The third is innovation in position, when the innovation changes the context in which products and services are introduced and consumed. Their last area is innovation in paradigms, when the changes affect mental models – perceptions (including business models) which define the way organisations or social and economic systems work and how they are understood. We can connect this idea to shifts in the institutional understanding of change brought about by innovation. Each of these areas of innovation are relevant for understanding the dynamics of digital infrastructures, their innovative potential, and their consequences. And of course, a successful innovation almost certainly has consequences for more than one of these four areas, perhaps shifting over time – first a product, then process change, then position, and perhaps finally paradigms. For example, this might be a useful way to think about innovation in music technology and how it has changed many aspects of the industry in the decades since the first Sony Walkman was launched in 1979, up to current models of music streaming.

Keeley et al. (2013) develop a model elaborating 'ten types of innovation'. This model presents ten aspects of innovation within any given organisation referred to as blocks. These blocks fall into three categories: the organisational configuration that gives rise to innovation, the offering of services and products (the focal new idea), and the experience of users. The focus of configuration is on the organisation (company) sponsoring a new idea in its business systems. This is represented in four aspects: a profit model, the networks the organisations work with, the company's own organisational structure, and its processes. The offering is related to product performance (e.g., its value proposition for customers), and how the new product is combined with a broader set of products (the product system). For instance, any new Apple product is expected to be connected to other Apple products, creating a seamless experience within the family of products offered by the company. The experience focuses on the services associated with the innovation from the user's perspective, including their experience of the channels for the distribution of products and related communications, the brands, and customer engagement. Innovation may be spurred on in any subset of these ten blocks. To gain advantages from innovation the organisation will need to focus on changes in the right combination of blocks. Digital infrastructures and technologies might be important for each of these blocks, depending on the actual needs of each organisation and its business model. This framework may be combined with others in the discussion of business model innovation (discussed in chapter 8).

Karlsoon and Magnusson (2019) propose another systemic view for understanding innovation in business, covering a long list of debatable dimensions: context, leadership, processes, support and resources, direction, culture, structures, and evaluation – comprehensive but a bit of everything. This framework emphasises the relevance and complexity of the contexts in which innovation may happen, and hence the role of leadership, organizational culture, and the (strategic) direction. Digital infrastructures may support innovation in parts of the systems, such as making processes more efficient, building resources, changing organisational structures (e.g., facilitating network organisations), and evaluating change (e.g., facilitating measurement of improvement). Across this book, we emphasise elements of context, leadership, and direction in the discussion of digital business innovation.

There is another often-studied aspect of innovation: the significance of being co-located with others in an innovation ecosystem (Budden and Murray, 2019). This approach not only includes the clusters of like-minded firms, focused on a common sector or technology and sharing a pool of co-located resources (e.g., Silicon Valley), but also recognises the role of governments in sponsoring business innovation. From an innovation ecosystem perspective, a group of stakeholders (government, funding bodies, venture capital funds, entrepreneurs, large corporations, universities, cities, etc.) are involved in the co-creation of innovation. Although Budden and

Murray (2019) emphasise the idea of co-location. Because digital infrastructures are mainly global in nature, our emphasis in the book is more on the collaboration among stakeholders within innovation ecosystems independent of location. Chapters 3 and 15 discuss the development of the Internet and its governance structures, which is a good example of the interplay of stakeholders within an innovation ecosystem for developing the fundamental digital infrastructure at a global level.

From all these models, we can learn two main lessons. First, no one innovation framework is going to be comprehensive enough to accommodate all aspects of the phenomenon. Across this book, we draw upon one concept or another, emphasising the elements which are more important or revealing of a particular phenomenon. For instance, in chapter 8, we develop the idea of business model innovation to understand the impact of digital infrastructure on the way companies organise their business. Second, we can combine different perspectives to create our own, keeping in focus our objective in this book to investigate and discuss digital infrastructures for business innovation. As the argument is developed across the book, we combine the ideas of business innovation with the development of digital infrastructures as layered models (chapter 4) which may enable further generations of great ideas that find favour with the market and improve our lives.

Diffusion of innovation and open innovation

A scholarly discussion of business innovation could not omit two key theories which are relevant to understanding the development and success of digital infrastructures. These are the Diffusion of Innovation Theory (Rogers, 2003 [1962]) and the Open Innovation Model proposed by Chesbrough (2006).

The Diffusion of Innovation (DOI) Theory considers how innovation spreads across markets. Two key ideas in this theory are relevant to the argument in this book. The first is to understand the characteristics of an innovation itself, and the second is to understand the profile of those who adopt the innovation. These two factors are combined in the social system that innovation is embedded in, and can determine how fast and far an innovation spreads.

The first version of Rogers' book was published in 1962 and reflected studies of innovation in American farming technologies such as tractors, fertilisers, and farm machinery. DOI Theory has, however, been frequently updated and applied to all manner of diffusion of innovation case studies. Rogers (2003 [1962]) proposes that for an innovation to spread, it should demonstrate relative advantages in relation to alternative products or solutions, compatibility with existing technologies or solutions already implemented broadly in a domain of activity, a manageable level of complexity (the easier to use, the more likely fast diffusion is), trialability (the opportunities users have to try the innovation before full adoption), and observability (the opportunities potential adopters have of observing others using the innovation and the positive impact of innovation). This approach offers a potential way to assess how likely a new idea is to reach productive use. DOI Theory can be used to analyse, for instance, the characteristics of digital products and services, from broad infrastructure, such as the Internet and social media, to individual apps and interfaces, such as games and generative AI, in order to understand their speed of adoption.

The second part of DOI Theory is about the profiles and attitudes of (potential) users of an innovation, and the way users are connected to and influenced by social systems. Rogers (2003 [1962]) proposes that there are five categories of adopters: innovators, early adopters, early majority, late majority, and laggards. Innovators accept higher risks and often have higher financial resilience to try innovations as soon as possible. Because they can afford to lose resources, they adopt innovation with less concern about its performance. Early adopters have similarities with innovators in terms of financial resilience, but they are also more careful about using their knowledge to evaluate benefits in order to reduce their risks. They influence the decisions of the next group, the early majority, who require more time to adopt innovations and are influenced by seeing others go first. The early majority wants more reassurance of the success of the innovation, particularly because they rely on the knowledge of others to inform their decision. In the sequence, the late majority faces more financial pressure, adopting innovation only when well-tested and established. Finally, the laggards are the last group to adopt innovation, being more resistant to change or reflecting some other strong cognitive or social perspective that shapes their attitudes.

It is key to the DOI model that there is a social system passing information on and influencing behaviours across groups. There is no guarantee that a good idea will diffuse: the innovation may have the wrong characteristics (e.g., being difficult to use and difficult to integrate with previous systems), or a social system that fails to communicate the value of it. It may also be that the contextual conditions require the innovation to adapt to different groups, and the innovation may just stop after reaching innovators and earlier adopters. In this case, the market may not be viable. When we talk about digital infrastructures and their uses, a critical mass of users and positive network externalities are shown to be important aspects of success (see more in chapter 6).

The Open Innovation Model is the last model we look at in this chapter (Chesbrough, 2006; Chesbrough and Bogers, 2014). Chesbrough suggests that companies face difficulties when managing innovation: on the one hand they may not have all the resources they need, and on the other hand they may have created innovation which is not relevant to them. In sum, companies may face the dilemma of not having what they need and having what they do not need. How to manage the problem? Chesbrough proposes the Open Innovation Model, in which companies look for external partnerships to acquire the innovation they need (through strategic alliances, partnerships, licensing, purchasing, etc.), and sell or license to others the innovation they do not need to keep to themselves. In this fashion, open innovation is the process to manage innovation across organisational boundaries, allowing organisations to perform better either through acquiring innovation from others or through monetising the innovation they offer to others (Chesbrough and Bogers, 2014).

Open innovation can escape the boundaries of business organisations (to some degree), and be found in more varied communities of interested parties (with multiple motivations) who collaborate to bring a new idea into use – an approach that is well suited to digital tasks (writing code), and well supported by digital infrastructures. Examples of such communities include the well-known Linux operating system and the Mozilla Firefox web browser. The motto of Linus Torvalds, the creator and lead developer of Linux, captures one key idea of such open-source software innovation: 'Given enough eyes, all bugs are shallow'.

This Open Innovation Model is particularly relevant to our understanding of rapid changes in digital infrastructures. For instance, the spread of generative AI infrastructure requires many companies across many sectors to make agreements with fellow firms in the sector in order for them to be able to catch up. Even the likes of Microsoft have seen the need to reinforce their position in generative AI through strategic partnerships with OpenAI. Millions of businesses around the world are incorporating bits and pieces of artificial intelligence tools into their digital infrastructures, using either proprietary tools (from companies such as Microsoft, AWS, and Alphabet, the parent company of Google products), or open-source solutions, as they cannot afford themselves to develop mathematical models and to create the computer network to process data for such operations. For the companies acquiring innovation from others, this means a reduction of costs in R&D. For the companies providing innovation, this means new sources of revenue. Thus, the Open Innovation Model can be a win-win situation for buyers and suppliers in the market.

Business innovation driven by digital technology

We all know that the Internet and the various infrastructures that make use of it (WWW, social media, e-commerce, cloud services, etc.) are based on independent pieces of technology interacting with each other, and combined so as to enable something more powerful and probably different to happen (e.g., operationalising a new idea). For example, we would not have cloud services and social media if we did not have the Internet to support these services and the WWW to diffuse them. In a nutshell, we can say that these technologies support each other.

The emergence of innovative, useful, and consequential digital infrastructures is possible because each of these technologies works as a module/layer/component, providing specific services to the whole. Each of these nurtures the development of the others, while itself being able to adapt and upgrade. The emergence of mobile phone apps, for instance, makes mobile technology more necessary, the WWW more useful, and the Internet more important too.

Digital infrastructures are fundamental enablers of all kinds of business in contemporary economies. Many different layers of technology need to work together in digital infrastructures to allow efficiency, flexibility, and value generation. They enable organisations to create new products and services, reach new markets, and often to explore new business models – in short, they drive innovation. A few examples, as outlined below, can help to clarify some concepts about how digital infrastructures enable new products, services, and business models. They are all in some ways infrastructures, focused on distinct user needs and creating distinct business models. They thus demonstrate the relevance of innovating around digital infrastructures as a way to open possibilities for new products, new user communities, new uses, and new businesses.

Apple iPod is a good example to start with. When it first arrived on the market in the early 2000s, the iPod was a piece of new technology, with a strong value proposition: it allowed people to listen to their preferred songs in an MP3 format. The first change then is in the product and the way the product reaches the consumer. Instead of buying physical CDs with music 'manufactured' into them, the consumer would buy an electronic file to be loaded onto the iPod. The product changed from a material copy (the CD) to an electronic copy (a file). There is another difference: the iPod allowed consumers to buy their songs through the iTunes service, and only the songs the consumer wanted to buy. This was a huge new idea. The traditional model for selling music used by record companies was to bundle products together. For instance, an album with a collection of songs. The selection and bundling would be done by the record company. The consumer could either buy all or not buy anything. With iTunes, the consumer was empowered to choose exactly the songs they liked, and they paid only for these songs.

The service also changed: iTunes kept a record of the songs you had bought in a cloud service, and it restored the copies in case of loss. This was not possible when you bought CDs – a lost CD is a lost CD. We see here that Apple has created a new business model. Traditional electronic companies would sell electronic devices only. The recording companies would be responsible for making the CDs available (or before, the vinyl discs). But Apple entered the space of record companies, and electronic gadget companies, unbundling albums and making individual songs directly available for purchase. This story goes on. Of course, other companies have entered this market with other devices, other services, and other business models. Almost all mobile phones today can do most of what an iPod could do, and iTunes today is not the only player in streaming music provision – think of Spotify, YouTube, and Amazon Music. In 2022, Apple withdrew the last iPod model from the market. The lesson here is that innovation is about change and digital infrastructures promote change, and then more change.

A second example is Amazon's Kindle reader. Traditionally, books have been sold as paper objects for centuries. Amazon bet on an alternative view: books could simply be long digital messages, to be read on electronic readers. Advantages of this new model include: lower cost, no need for space at home for storing books, capacity for carrying a large number of books in a small device, and capacity for recovering files in case of loss. Again, we have a combination of a new product and a new service. Not surprisingly, some publishers and bookstores have opposed this novelty, understanding that Amazon was taking a slice of their business. Later, Amazon took an even bolder step by starting a self-publishing service. Through Amazon, you can now publish your own books without the approval or disapproval of a publisher. Definitively, this is another new business model allowed for by the pervasiveness of digital infrastructures.

A third example is Google Search. The value of the Internet would be much reduced if people did not have the means to search for and find the content they need. Google Search offers a solution to the problem: for free (or not?), people can use Google Search to find the content they need with an impressive degree of efficiency in precision and time. The massive value that billions of users get cannot be calculated. Google Search multiplies the value of the Internet and the World Wide Web. So, what is the catch? Is this a free lunch? Not exactly. Google makes money selling advertisements, promising to match the advertisement as closely as possible to the interests of the person who is searching for something online.

Google Search's business model is quite simple: users like you and me get the benefit of free search, but in doing our searches we give away data about our interests and concerns. Google collects and uses the data to make money by selling adverts targeted at the people who use their search engine. So, Google knows that somebody is looking for a winter coat, thus that person gets lots of 'coat ads' for a few weeks every time they go online. All three stakeholders, the searcher, Google, and the coat advertisers, win (we hope). Users are, however, providing something to Google – we are 'paying' with the information about ourselves. This allows Google to improve the algorithm of both their search tool and the advertising services they sell. So far, all three parties appear happy with this business model – we (almost) all use it!

These are just a few examples to conclude this chapter. We cover many more examples of business innovations driven by digital technologies across the book, with an emphasis on digital infrastructures. Concepts and theories on innovation are used across the chapters, integrating the conceptualisation of digital infrastructures with their impact on business change.

References

Budden, P. and Murray, F. (2019). *MIT's Stakeholder Framework for Building & Accelerating Innovation Ecosystems*. MIT Sloan School of Management, MIT Innovation Initiative Working Paper (April 2019). MIT's Laboratory for Innovation Science & Policy. Available at: https://innovation.mit.edu/assets/Innovation-Stakeholder-Framework.pdf (Accessed: 16 March 2024).

Chesbrough, H. (2006). 'Open innovation: A new paradigm for understanding industrial innovation', in Chesbrough, H., Vanhaverbeke, W., and West, J. (eds.), *Open Innovation – Researching a New Paradigm*. Oxford: Oxford University Press, pp. 1–14.

Chesbrough, H. and Bogers, M. (2014). 'Explicating open innovation: Clarifying an emerging paradigm for understanding innovation', in Chesbrough, H., Vanhaverbeke, W., and West, J. (eds.), *New Frontiers in Open Innovation*. Oxford: Oxford University Press, pp. 3–28.

Christensen, C. (2016). *The Innovator's Dilemma: When New Technologies Cause Great Firms to Fail*. Boston, MA: Harvard Business Review Press.

Goodrich, J. (2022). 'The first digital camera was the size of a toaster', *IEEE Spectrum*. Available at: https://spectrum.ieee.org/first-digital-camera-history (Accessed: 25 February 2024).
Karlsoon, M. and Magnusson, M. (2019). 'The systems approach to innovation management', in Chen, J., Brem, A., Viadot, E., and Wong, P.K. (eds.), *The Routledge Companion to Innovation Management*. London, New York: Routledge, pp. 73–90.
Keeley, L., Pikkel, R., Quinn, B., and Walters, H. (2013). *Ten Types of Innovation – The Discipline of Building Breakthroughs*. Hoboken, NJ: Wiley. Deloitte Development LLC.
Rayna, T. and Striukova, L. (2009) 'The curse of the first-mover: When incremental innovation leads to radical change', *International Journal of Collaborative Enterprise*, 1(1), pp. 4–21.
Rogers, E.M. (2003 [1962]). *Diffusion of Innovations* (5th ed.). New York: Free Press.
Schumpeter, J.A. (1994 [1942]). *Capitalism, Socialism and Democracy*. London: Routledge.
Tidd, J. and Bessant, J. (2013). *Managing Innovation – Integrating Technological, Market and Organizational Change* (5th ed.). Chichester, UK: Wiley.

3 The origins of the Internet

Introduction

The Internet is the world's most significant and ubiquitous digital infrastructure. This chapter considers its history from its beginnings in universities and science laboratories to its position today as the backbone of the world's digital economy and society.

The Internet emerged in the late 1970s and early 1980s as a way for scientists and academics to share data and information. A decade later, in the early 1990s, it opened for wider use, including for business use. Thus, in the last 30 years (we are writing this in 2024), the Internet has changed from a relatively small project with the aim of creating a network to help share resources for scientific research, to becoming a universal network at the centre of operations for all kinds of organisations, the lives of all kinds of people, and arguably the most effective driver of economic and social innovation across the world. This chapter introduces the story of the Internet and draws from that story some general characteristics of all digital infrastructures, including those that derive from and exploit the Internet.

As you see in the paragraph above, it is easy to use a language of superlatives when discussing the Internet. It has grown in size, scope, user base, and technical performance at a phenomenal rate as billions of people around the world have become connected. Growth became particularly strong once smartphones with data connections emerged (the first iPhone was launched in 2007) offering Internet access to anyone and everyone.

The Internet is indeed a stunning example of how rapidly technological innovations (a new idea and a new set of tools) can diffuse across the world in rich and poor countries. However, in this chapter we try to be a bit less excitable and identify the key ideas that underpin the Internet as we see it today and in particular its character as a dynamic, evolving digital infrastructure. In later chapters we discuss in more detail some of the uses (applications) that are built on the Internet – such as the World Wide Web (WWW), the cloud and cloud services, social media, the metaverse, AI infrastructures, and digital business platforms (DBPs).

A brief history

The Internet has a history of about 50–60 years. Pinpointing a date is almost impossible, so it may be better to just say that it emerged out of ideas about the fusion of telecommunications and digital computers that were gaining traction from the late 1960s. Perhaps you may not be very interested in history, but for the Internet, as for any infrastructure, the way it is today is because of its history – what we have identified in chapter 1 as the exploitation of the installed base and path dependency. We might even say that an infrastructure is its history. We meet similar and related ideas again in chapter 7 when we discuss further details of the installed base, path dependency, and the cultivation of infrastructures.

DOI: 10.4324/9781003385578-3

The Internet is not, and never was, something completely new that was designed by a specific team of people on the basis of some specific identified needs and implemented in a single coordinated effort. Rather, it grew and evolved over many years, and through many different design activities, starting with limited efforts to share data and computer access among science communities in universities and laboratories in the USA, Europe, and beyond.

Universities and laboratories at that time knew that they needed data networks in order to do better science, so they tried to build them by exploiting different existing communications facilities (installed base) and linking them together. The word 'inter-net' has its origins in this earliest phase when the work was very clearly seen as being about linking together then-existing networks that different universities and research centres had available. These original networks were diverse, mostly small in scale, local to specific universities or brands of computers, and were used mostly to move data or allow remote login to the mainframe computers of that era. The goal was to inter-link smaller networks to achieve a bigger and bigger set of connections, incorporating more and more computers at more and more sites, and thus more and more users would be able to share and transport larger and larger files of data and perhaps do better science. Today, with hindsight, we might see those inter-networking efforts in the 1960s and early 1970s as limited but at the time they were at the cutting edge of computer science and communications engineering. These networking efforts, often based in universities, also showed a strong sense of hacking, making the best use of what was available and fixing a few problems to get some kind of a better network up and running – agile and improvisational, we could say.

Looking back at this period we can see that the context these early developers faced, needing to borrow and build on different local facilities and figuring out how to make them work together to share data and send messages, has proved to be a core strength of the Internet that emerged. The acceptance of differences (different users, different uses, different brands of computers, different technologies, different devices, different types of data), and the goal of doing what was necessary to make diverse parts work together, can explain today why the Internet is still able to absorb new and different technologies, new and different users, and new and different applications along the way. It is also relevant that the originators of the Internet were motivated by solving their own problems, rather than solving somebody else's problems or pursuing business opportunities. They were of course lucky to have modest resources available from national governments' research programmes to allow them to work freely and creatively.

Ever since computers were first used in the late 1940s, people had wanted to network them – that is both to send data between computers and to allow people to access computers remotely (and remote could mean down the corridor or across the world). Up until the late 1960s, this was either a local affair (terminals connected to one computer in a single building), or slow connections using telephone networks. Only the best-funded organisations could afford dedicated data networks based on proprietary technologies. Still, scientists and researchers (and their funding bodies) were becoming big computer users and were increasingly interested in sharing data and providing a communications infrastructure in support of science and technology development programmes. Governments in the USA and Europe sponsored national initiatives to build such networks, as did the US military. As a result, many research projects and small-scale experiments in networking took place through the 1960s and 1970s.

When we discuss any history, there are usually multiple versions of the key events that shape outcomes. For example, some accounts of the origins of the Internet place strong emphasis on the role of the US military in developing the infrastructure, set against the tensions of the Cold War and the possibility of a nuclear attack on any centralised communications infrastructure (Ryan, 2010). Indeed the Internet's most direct ancestor was ARPANET (Advanced Research Projects Agency Network), a network sponsored by the US government's Defense Advanced

Research Projects Agency (DARPA) for use by their contractors including universities. Other accounts are more focused on how the scientists set out to solve their own problems, and along the way created a general architecture for communications facilities that others could easily adopt, adapt, and use. Similarly, there are national biases in how the story is told – for example, the contribution made by an early French national science network called CYCLADES is sometimes seen as central, and sometimes never even mentioned. It depends which version you read (see 'CYCLADES', on Wikipedia, 2023, to find more about this network).

The aim here is not to put forward a definitive version of how we came to have the Internet of today. Rather, it is to acknowledge that the Internet emerged out of multiple efforts by multiple groups in different countries, each with multiple motivations. If we sometimes read somewhat contradictory accounts in different places, we do not have to choose one over another. Rather, we can use the different emphases to tell us something more insightful about how this infrastructure, and digital infrastructures in general, emerged and developed.

The Internet Society (www.internetsociety.org) has a lot more information on the early Internet including accounts written by people who were there at the time – one particularly interesting perspective is that of Vinton Cerf (also known as Vint Cerf), who was a Professor at Stanford University in California at the outset and a key figure in the development of the Internet Protocols (Cerf, 1995; Leiner et al., 1997).

Internet evolution: From a scientific endeavour to a universal service

Table 3.1 provides an overview of the evolution of the Internet in its early years. It is presented as a timeline. The events and dates shown are based on Zittrain (2008), Cerf's (1995) brief paper on the origins of the Internet, Leiner et al. (1997), and the timeline on the Internet Society's website (see The Internet Society, n.d.).

Table 3.1 Internet timeline

Brief timeline of the Internet in its early years: 1969–2007	
1969	US funded ARPANET project launched: first message sent between computers at UCLA and Stanford universities in California. By end of the year, four universities (hosts) are linked, adding University of California, Santa Barbara and University of Utah
1973	First international host connection is made to UCL in London
1974	First versions of the protocol TCP/IP is presented
1978	IP separated from TCP so they can develop independently
1983	ARPANET moves to using TCP/IP as its core protocols
1984	The domain name system (DNS) introduced
1988	First chat programs (IRC) started to be used
1989	Number of hosts >100,000
1990	First commercial dial-up link to the Internet in the USA (commercial consumer ISP – Internet service provider)
1990	First World Wide Web site at CERN: see http://info.cern.ch/
1992	Number of hosts >1M
1995	Main backbone passed from US government to commercial suppliers
	Hosts >5M
	US Federal Networking Council, Internet definition published (cited below)
1998	IP version 6 (IPV6) launched – allowing for many more host addresses
2003	First Skype VoIP client
2005	Hosts >317M
2007	First iPhone

As mentioned above, one particular network is usually identified as the Internet's principal origin: ARPANET, a project of the US Defense Advanced Research Projects Agency (DARPA), which was initiated in 1967 and started to operate in 1968. The ideas and technology embodied in ARPANET demonstrated themselves to be superior in general to other initiatives as a way to connect heterogeneous computers and local and regional networks together (heterogeneous = many kinds, a mix). Zittrain (2008) describes the ARPANET project admiringly as a way to bring together a myriad of already existing research and government networks, in order to get the benefits of a smooth transmission of data from one to another. In coming together, they become one network. Developers based in universities and science research centres were so creative (or innovative) that, over time, competing commercial networks and their technologies and standards were unable to survive as the Internet grew.

Zittrain also notes that the motives or philosophy of the ARPANET/Internet developers was distinct, and in particular very different from the competing commercial network companies which existed at the time and who sought to exercise control over how their networks were used and make revenues from their users. The Internet pioneers had the objective to embed into the code of the digital infrastructures the means to control them without the need for defined management hierarchies. This philosophy, arguably, still underpins some areas of the Internet, which still has no single, central, formal management structure. It is also similar to the philosophy that is seen in open-source software communities, emerging around the same time, and more generally agile approaches to technology development.

One way to explain the success of the Internet efforts, and the relative failure of the commercial vendors' networking products, is to say that the Internet was from the start (and still is) *an infrastructure*, while the competing networks with their commercial sponsors were conceived as *products* or *services*. The Internet had a logic of '*use me*' versus one of '*buy me*'. One significant difference between 'buy me' and 'use me' was billing. Commercial data network services, following the logic of the telephone system, assumed that every message needed to be identified and billed to someone. The Internet developed without any such requirement, which among other benefits from a user perspective, made it much simpler to design and build, and also made it easier for potential adopters to start using it. Think of 'trialability' in Rogers' Diffusion of Innovation Theory (Rogers, 2003 [1962]) (as discussed in chapter 2).

Over time, most other networking projects and services were eclipsed or became integrated into the Internet. Across the world, scientific researchers, other technology users and network managers started to use network services connected to the Internet, as well as the Internet technology standards and protocols (e.g., TCP/IP) and other Internet services. These services included early versions of shared files, email, chat programs, and, later on, the World Wide Web (WWW) with its web pages, browsers, and search engines. The Internet even came to challenge the traditional telephone network as users moved to Voice over Internet Protocol (VoIP) services such as Skype. In 2005, the *Economist* magazine had a front page with the headline 'How the Internet killed the phone business' (think of Schumpeter's 1994 [1942] 'gales of creative destruction', as discussed in chapter 2).

Internet architecture

While digital infrastructures like the Internet are not usually the result of a single project or a single design, but rather evolve over time, they do need a coherent structure and design principles that they retain as they evolve. This is what we refer to as their architecture and reflects the regular structure and ground rules for their operation. To dig a bit deeper into the Internet's architecture, we need first to establish some vocabulary to use when discussing the Internet in technical and user terms.

In the most general terms, we speak of 'messages' being transmitted by the Internet, where messages are whatever users want or need to be communicated. This can mean any kind of digital data, numbers, text, video, or voice, the transmission of which from A to B will help somebody perform a useful task. And, of course, the Internet (as a technical assembly) does not care or know what the human purpose is – for the Internet, a message is just a string of bits to be sent from point A to point B. The Internet as an institution may, however, be very interested in the sorts of content that circulate.

As we get into more detail, we talk about these messages or 'strings of bits' in terms of other units of data. A bit is a binary digit (a 0 or a 1), enough to encode a *yes* or a *no*. A byte is eight binary digits, enough to encode one text character in the Western alphabet. A word is four bytes or 32 binary digits. A packet is a bundle of user data plus the address of the sender and of the receiver and other control information. We talk about packets when we discuss packet switching and the IP protocol the Internet uses to route a message from sender to receiver.

Figure 3.1 shows a simplified model of the Internet and its (technical) architecture. This figure shows a number of computers – hosts, shown as hexagons – that are each connected to some national or regional networks (shown as four clouds in the diagram – remember it is the 'inter-net'). Hosts can be big, like a university computing centre, a large company, or a cloud-service provider; medium-sized, like a single supermarket store; or small, like a smartphone. At the top left of the diagram is a cluster of small hexagon-hosts to represent smartphones or perhaps IoT devices.

Each host is connected to at least one network, some (the bigger ones) may be connected to more than one for redundancy and resilience. For the network to work (e.g., reliably deliver packets of data), each Internet host must have a unique and unambiguous address. The general

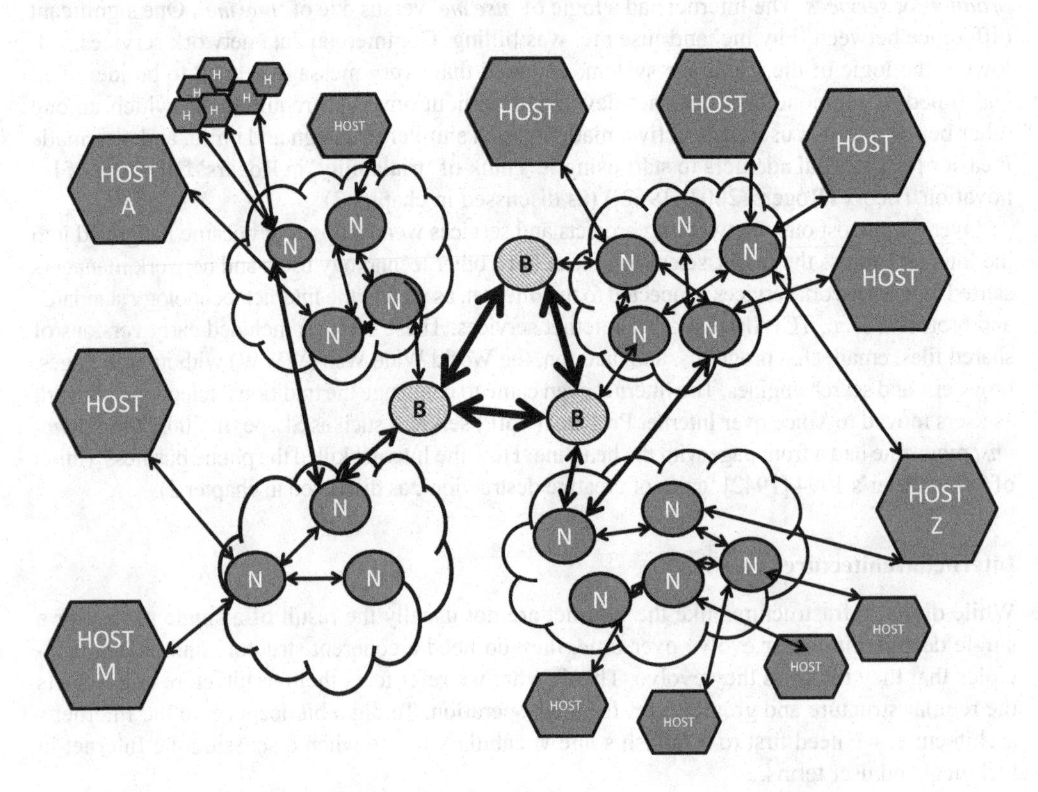

Figure 3.1 A simple schematic diagram of the Internet

name for the organisation that handles the host-to-node link is an ISP (Internet service provider), which could be a mobile phone or landline company, a cable network company, or other specialist providers.

Each network is shown as a set of nodes (circles with an N). The nodes are linked to each other by some communications medium – probably cables (copper or fibre optics), or perhaps radio or satellite links. Whatever the physical medium of the links, they all allow data (bits, packets, messages) to be passed. Nodes are the switching points in the network, and they are also sometimes called routers. As messages travel across this network in packets, each individual node they arrive at will decide which link to use to send the message on its next leg based on the destination address. Conceptually, this is exactly what a person employed as a post office mail sorter does (or did – today, it is probably done by a machine); they look at the address of a packet or letter, and put it in the appropriate bag (outgoing link) for its onward journey. A postal letter could potentially be sorted in this way a number of times before it is delivered, so too a message/packet travelling in our network.

In the centre of Figure 3.1 are nodes marked with a B. These represent the backbone of the network – the place where high volumes of messages will flow between different networks, and which needs higher capacity in terms of links and switches. The backbone links are shown with a thicker line to indicate their higher speed and capacity. The backbone is a bit like a six-lane highway with a very high speed limit and is itself a 'network of networks'. When this part of the Internet was passed from the US government into the hands of private companies in the 1990s, it was deliberately done in such a way that no one company could control it. The core backbone is still in the United States, although other regions and countries have their own backbone networks, e.g., in Europe, Asia, etc.

Consider a message from Host A (top left) to Host Z (bottom right). What route will it take, and how many hops will this include (if a hop is understood as traversing from one node to another)? Well, we cannot really give a definitive answer since there are many possible routes. It will depend on how each node chooses to route the message, and the best way may depend on how much other traffic is using the network. This is just like driving in a city, where at different times of day you may well choose to take a different route to avoid traffic. We call this approach dynamic routing.

So, the route for an email sent from England to Japan, for instance, will be made from the device in London to the local ISP (e.g., a mobile company, perhaps the university Wi-Fi), from there to a regional network in the UK, then up to the backbone. Then the message will traverse a similar set of layers from the backbone to, for example, a Japanese national network, and then on to an ISP to deliver the email to the inbox of the recipient, wherever the email is hosted (perhaps on Gmail in California even though the person lives in Japan). The message makes its way through such a complex set of interconnections (and does so in seconds), using packet switching and the TCP and IP protocols (more details on TCP/IP in chapter 5).

Defining the Internet

Figure 3.1 shows a simple schematic model of the Internet and one aspect of its architecture, and names the various parts. Now we can describe the Internet as a whole. A brief description in our own words is as follows:

> *The Internet is a global, shared public facility for sending digital data from one place to another in a fairly reliable way using standardised methods. This facility to transmit data is open to use by all and can be used to serve many purposes. All users receive equal treatment for their data as it is transmitted.*

The key elements of our definition can be teased out a bit and include:

1. Sends digital data: it does just the one task of sending digital data (e.g., anything coded in 0s and 1s, a string of bits);
2. From one place to another: data goes from point to point so we need consistent 'addresses' for these places so the data can be transmitted;
3. Network of networks: it is made up of multiple different communications facilities all linked together and adhering to some minimum common standards;
4. Global reach: it is big and operates (almost) everywhere, e.g., via smartphones, satellites, etc.;
5. Shared and public: it is available to all (billions of users) who share the network resources;
6. Fairly reliable: the policy of the Internet is described as 'best effort' and we cannot rely 100% on it so we need some backup procedures, security measures, etc.;
7. Equal treatment of all data: once data is in transit your data gets equal treatment to my data (but we need to discuss this issue more under the theme of net neutrality in chapter 15).

A more elaborated technical definition of the Internet was produced about 30 years ago by the Federal Networking Council (FNC), a US government organization. Their resolution of 24 October 1995 states:

> 'Internet' refers to the global information system that
>
> (i) is logically linked together by a globally unique address space based on the Internet Protocol (IP) or its subsequent extensions/follow-ons;
> (ii) is able to support communications using the Transmission Control Protocol/Internet Protocol (TCP/IP) suite or its subsequent extensions/follow-ons, and/or other IP-compatible protocols; and
> (iii) provides, uses or makes accessible, either publicly or privately, high-level services layered on the communications and related infrastructure described herein.
>
> (NITRD, 1995)

This is a more formal definition, but essentially says the same things, e.g., the Internet is a global system for communications, and can serve all manner of uses 'layered on it', reflecting a layered model (see chapter 4 for more on layered models). This definition stresses the central importance of the common rules of operation that the Internet uses – known as 'protocols'. Those TCP/IP protocols identified in 1995 as central are still central today. We discuss these protocols in more depth in chapter 5, but for the moment we should understand that:

- IP is concerned with the rules for addresses and for using them to get a message 'across' the Internet from its origin host, through switching nodes to its destination host on a 'best effort' basis.
- TCP is concerned with how messages are reliably delivered from a source host to a destination host and what to do if a part of a message is lost along the way (it does happen).

We can differentiate these two protocols by saying that TCP is an 'end to end' protocol while IP is a 'link-level' protocol.

The Internet today

By the 1990s, the Internet as we see it today was well established in academic and research contexts. For example, universities were among the first large organisations that gave all their staff and students email addresses. The Internet was also attracting more and more interest from commercial and business users. In theory, commercial (for-profit) use was banned, but still in the early 1990s it started to occur. To regulate the situation, the rules and governance were changed, the Internet was separated from the US government, and the US government research funding that had kept the Internet going was withdrawn. To achieve this the central management of the network traffic (the backbone) was redesigned and then contracted to a number of competing commercial companies (see Cerf, 1995).

From then on, the whole world was welcome on the Internet, and the millions of people with a home computer could connect via an Internet service provider (ISP) and benefit from web searches, email, and – slowly at first – e-commerce. At this time, the Internet was still a rather limited service for individuals, often still accessed using dial-up modems and telephone lines, but by the late 1990s in the developed world, almost any home computer could have full Internet connectivity using a much faster broadband connection, although usually still via the landline telephone cables (a system known as DSL, digital subscriber line), but without interfering with the normal telephone usage. For many people this remains the technology they use today. For others, a faster broadband connection is made via cable television networks, and in both cases these links are moving from copper cables to fibre optic cables for greater speeds and capacity. People in rural or isolated areas today may be using satellite connections or links via mobile phone networks. This diversity of access once again emphasises the Internet's ability to evolve and draw on multiple kinds of network technology.

And, of course, very locally in your house, school, office, or factory, connections to all manner of devices are today made via Wi-Fi linked to a local wireless router – a kind of mini-node. To offer even more choice of how to connect (and make it even more complex), smartphones, when away from Wi-Fi, link to the Internet via the mobile phone company's data services. Indeed, it is probable that the majority of users around the world rely wholly on their 4G/5G mobile phone network for their Internet connection.

It is not our purpose in this book to go any deeper into all these local connection technologies – what is often called 'the last mile' – in technical terms. But it is important to recognise that the multiple ways that we connect to the Internet as individuals, and how businesses and organisations connect too, are all based on a set of standards and protocols that ensure that, independently of the way we connect, we can all use the same digital infrastructure whatever our device or machine. From the largest corporate data centre down to a simple tablet or a network-connected video security camera, we can all 'speak the same language', or perhaps a better metaphor, we can all ride on the same roads and obey the same traffic rules.

References

Cerf, V.G. (1995). *Computer Networking: Global Infrastructure for the 21st Century.* University of Washington. Available at: http://homes.cs.washington.edu/~lazowska/cra/networks.html (Accessed: 16 March 2024).

'CYCLADES' (2023). *Wikipedia.* Available at: https://en.wikipedia.org/wiki/CYCLADES (Accessed: 16 March 2024).

Leiner, B.M., Cerf, V.G., Clark, D.D., Kahn, R.E., Kleinrock, L., Lynch, D.C., Postel, J., Roberts, L.G., and Wolff, S. (1997). 'Brief history of the internet', Internet Society. Available at: https://www.internetsociety.org/wp-content/uploads/2017/09/ISOC-History-of-the-Internet_1997.pdf (Accessed: 16 March 2024).

NITRD (1995). *FNC Resolution: The Definition of 'Internet'*. 24 October 1995. Available at: https://www.nitrd.gov/historical/fnc/Internet_res.pdf (Accessed: 25 February 2024).

Rogers, E.M. (2003 [1962]). *Diffusion of Innovations* (5th ed.). New York: Free Press.

Ryan, J. (2010). *A History of the Internet and the Digital Future*. London: Reaktion Books.

Schumpeter, J.A. (1994 [1942]). *Capitalism, Socialism and Democracy*. London: Routledge.

The Internet Society (n.d.). 'About the Internet'. Available at: https://www.internetsociety.org/internet/ (Accessed: 25 January 2024).

Zittrain, J.L. (2008). *The Future of the Internet – and How to Stop It*. New Haven and London: Yale University Press.

4 A layered model of digital infrastructures

Introduction

This chapter introduces a model of digital infrastructures – the layered model. By 'model' we mean a way of framing our view of the world to help us make sense of it. Such a model puts some order on our complex and messy world through schematic representations of reality to help us understand it (Wunsch, 1994). Classifying and framing phenomena in a model allows us to develop rational accounts to explain processes, events, and outcomes. This kind of modelling is the basis of most science, including social sciences such as management, economics, or sociology.

If we can test a model, drawing on data from the world, we may be able to confirm the plausibility of the model and generalise from it to propose a 'theory' – plausible explanations linking causes and effects between defined variables (Wunsch, 1994). In this chapter, we start at the level of a conceptual model, with the aim of better perceiving the complexities of digital infrastructures and how they 'work'. Using this model, we introduce the idea of generativity – a theorisation to explain the potential digital infrastructures have for innovation.

We start with Zittrain's (2008) hourglass architecture of the Internet, a very simple layered model. We go on to consider the layered model's application across a wider range of digital infrastructures using the model's concepts of modularity, hierarchy, and flexibility in the context of innovation. A short introduction to the layered model was given in chapter 1 when we discussed how the Internet and the WWW are related to each other, the one layered on top of the other. In this chapter, we develop these ideas further. In the following three chapters (5, 6, and 7) we add other important concepts to develop our model further, emphasising the dynamic architectures of digital infrastructures.

Zittrain's hourglass architecture

Zittrain (2008) describes the Internet as made up of layers and sub-layers performing specific functions. These layers interact with each other across well-defined and stable interfaces. The success of the Internet has come from both the independence of these layers one from another, and from the careful definition and standardisation of the interfaces between the layers. Interfaces and standards allow different parts of an infrastructure to 'plug' together.

This architecture allows flexible choice and independent development of each layer. They can be improved and amended in their own timescales as long as the interfaces between the layers are not changed. Furthermore, as an infrastructure adapts to new uses, more layers may be added. A simple example of a standardised infrastructure interface is the electrical plug and

DOI: 10.4324/9781003385578-4

socket and the voltage of the electricity supply. Standardisation of these allows us to plug in different devices to the same electricity infrastructure in our homes. You can move from a fan heater to a vacuum cleaner to an air conditioner, and the infrastructure does not need to know the purpose as long as you use the same plug and work on the same voltage. This standardisation of plugs and sockets is not universal or global, and many designs of plugs and sockets are used in different countries around the world. It is worth asking why this is the case and what forces drive towards a single global standard as with the Internet's TCP/IP, or against one.

Zittrain (2008) applies this model to the Internet, offering the simplest layered model with just three layers. At the bottom is the physical layer, in the middle is the protocol layer, and at the top is the application layer (see Figure 4.1). To do useful work, we need all three layers working together, e.g., through standardised inter-layer interfaces.

The physical layer represents all cables and wireless transmitters, the servers, routers, and other equipment which allow communications to take place and bit-strings to be transmitted and received. The physical layer may include many kinds of transmission technologies suitable for transmission in different circumstances. The physical layer is the foundation that enables other things to happen. In other words, a super-fast, high-capacity fibre optic cable between London and New York is of no use to anybody on its own. To be useful it needs to connect to other devices so it can serve the interests of some users. This idea was neatly expressed a century and a half ago by the American author Henry David Thoreau. In 1854 he wrote about technology in general, and information infrastructure in particular:

> Our inventions are wont to be pretty toys, which distract our attention from serious things. They are but improved means to an unimproved end … We are in great haste to construct a magnetic telegraph from Maine to Texas; but Maine and Texas, it may be, have nothing important to communicate.
>
> (Thoreau, 1854)

Thoreau's question of 'something important to communicate' points to the application layer. The application layer is where users do useful things and create value in ways that involve communication of data – for example, sending an email, updating a Facebook page, transmitting a large file of research data from a government department in Tokyo to a laboratory in Finland, WhatsApp

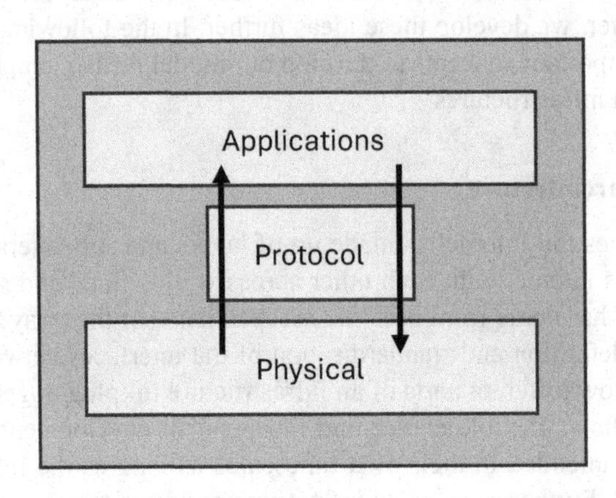

Figure 4.1 A layered model of digital infrastructures, inspired by Zittrain (2008)

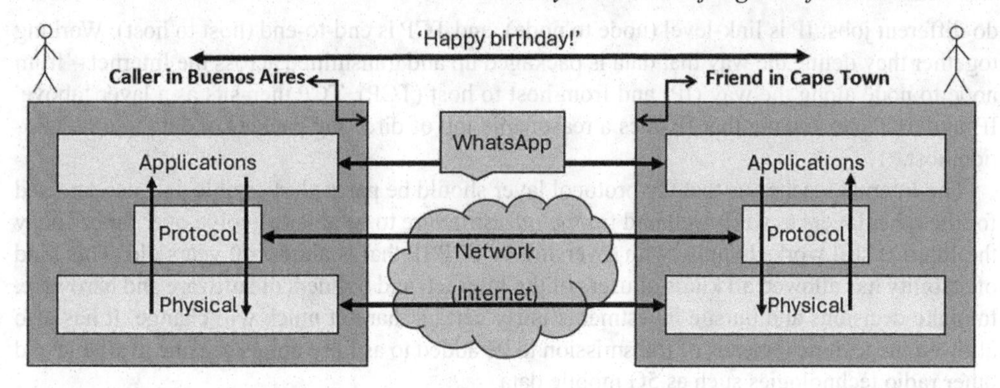

Figure 4.2 Example of application layer using lower layers

a friend in Cape Town from your home in Buenos Aires to sing them 'Happy Birthday', or perhaps even report the weather conditions in Portland, Maine to an airplane as it departs from Austin, Texas.

Each of these tasks, and the thousands and thousands more you could think of, require specific software to achieve the specific objective, but they all will use the physical layer to get their data (bit-strings) transmitted to the other end. Figure 4.2 elaborates the three-layer model for the case of a WhatsApp call occurring in matched layers with the network (Internet) shown as a cloud that links two locations.

The vertical lines in Figure 4.2 represent data moving down and up through the layers, from a microphone in Buenos Aires all the way to a speaker in Cape Town. The horizontal lines represent the way that the application at one end, WhatsApp on a phone, relates to WhatsApp on a phone at the other end. The other layers relate similarly to their own peers (their equivalents) with data that they understand and exchange – application to application, protocol to protocol, and physical to physical.

This still leaves the protocol layer – the jam in the sandwich – lying between the application and physical layers. What does it do? From the perspective of digital infrastructures, the protocol layer is the most interesting, bringing together the physical and the application layers and expressing the rules by which the infrastructure operates.

There are all manner of applications that users want, so too there are many kinds of physical equipment and devices that can support transmission of data. Each application wants to use a different mix of physical layer resources and in different ways. It is the job of the protocol layer to allow multiple different applications to access their required physical resources for communications. The WhatsApp program needs to access the physical layer to send a digitised voice to Cape Town. When voice data arrives in Cape Town it needs to 'find' the mobile phone app so the friend can hear the other friend sing. So, in Figure 4.2 the vertical lines go 'through' the protocol layer. The protocol layer directs data to the right place in the layers above and below and has responsibility for managing the passing of data from one place to another. 'Place' means the right host (e.g., a building if using a Post Office analogy) and application is the right port on the host (e.g., an apartment).

The Internet's protocol layer is based on two key protocols, the Internet Protocol (IP) and the Transmission Control Protocol (TCP). The two go together as the core standard of the Internet so people often write about the Internet as based on TCP/IP – and in our model here we bundle them together as belonging to the protocol layer. However, as we noted in chapter 3, they do different jobs: IP is link-level (node to node), and TCP is end-to-end (host to host). Working together they define the way that data is packaged up and transmitted across the Internet – from node to node along the way (IP) and from host to host (TCP). TCP then sits as a layer 'above' IP, and TCP can assume that IP does a reasonable job of directing packets of data to a destination host.

The Internet teaches us that the protocol layer should be particularly stable and standardised for the other layers to work well and for the infrastructure to be able to evolve over time. Today the Internet still works happily with a version of TCP/IP that is almost 40 years old. This kind of stability has allowed all kinds of users of the Internet, and builders of software and hardware, to make decisions and pursue investments fairly certain that not much will change. It has also allowed the technical means of transmission to be added to as fibre optics became available and other radio technologies such as 5G mobile data.

In general, as new technologies and possibilities become available, people will want to retain some backward compatibility. Thus, today the Internet works with two versions of the IP protocol – version 4 (IPV4) introduced in 1982/3 and still widely used, and version 6 (IPV6) introduced in 1998 and still slowly coming into use. As of February 2024, Google reports that about 40–45% of their users connect with IPV6, leaving 55–60% using the older IPV4, reflecting the slow and linear uptake of IPV6.

Zittrain (2008) names his model the 'hourglass architecture', with a broad application layer containing lots of different pieces of software available for use (e.g., WWW, websites, emails, games, apps), and a broad physical layer, with lots of different technologies to transmit bit-strings (e.g., servers, routers, cables, transmission devices). The protocol layer is necessarily smaller, and less varied – it expresses the common standard that defines the Internet functionality for all uses and all transmission means. Indeed, as suggested above, the Internet's protocol layer is found in just a few protocols – TCP, IP, and UDP (User Datagram Protocol), which we discuss in chapter 5. As expressed by Lyytinen et al. (2017), the protocol layer allows the flexibility of combining the upward applications with the downward physical layers of the networking technologies. All Internet users rely on this small and stable set of protocols which 'insulate' applications from physical data transmission. Applications can all share a changing set of physical layer connections, and connection technologies can develop as fast or as slow as technology, demand, and regulation allow without interfering with the applications we use.

A key advantage of a layered architecture with well-specified interfaces is that it reduces the need to comprehend complexity (Zittrain, 2008). Developers and innovators can work on individual layers or protocols and services within the layers without having to understand in detail the complexity of the whole structure, and without demanding that the whole structure changes because of their development. With communication between the parts (the interfaces) well defined, innovators can specialise in developing a particular protocol or element in a layer. And of course, the developers of new applications or business models can mostly just take the Internet's existence and the existing services it offers for granted.

An entrepreneur can develop a new app for a mobile phone just by knowing the communication interface of that device. For example, for an Android device, the programmer just needs to know the Android's API (application programming interface). The API is a set of standards to allow apps to access functions and procedures for the interchange of data from an Android phone. This architecture, using open and available APIs, fosters the capacity for developing new solutions that use the Internet in new ways. In a similar way, and in parallel, a country might be investing in improving the backbone of its broadband infrastructure (e.g., for 5G mobile data) without impacting the apps and the content providers using the network other than providing faster and more ubiquitous connectivity.

Generative architecture

Zittrain (2008) argues that the hourglass architecture demonstrates a form of organising infrastructures which is more 'generative', in the sense of being more flexible and welcoming of new elements being created on top of an existing infrastructure or refining the capabilities within layers. In other words: the architecture of the Internet fosters innovation. This characteristic stems from the limited interdependency of the parts, in the same way LEGO's blocks are interdependent. There are, of course, standards to be followed (we discuss standards further in chapter 7), but their purpose is more to allow innovation than to constrain it – although there are constraints implied in any standardisation (see the discussion of path dependency in chapter 7). These ideas of generativity have been developed further by other authors, including Yoo and Euchner (2015), and Lyytinen et al. (2017).

A layered architecture allows new users, new devices, or new protocols to join an infrastructure creating positive growth effects (a positive externality or network effect – see chapter 6). For instance, the more people want to use the Internet, the more ISPs (Internet service providers) will compete to provide connections. The more people have smartphones with apps, the more developers provide new apps or offer new online services. As explained by Yoo and Euchner (2015), digital technologies usually have architectures with embedded levels of malleability, allowing individuals, companies, and governments to adapt and recombine digital resources for their own purposes. This architecture is dynamic by nature and design.

Yoo and Euchner (2015) emphasise how new users innovate on top of the previous innovation, independently of the intention or approval of the original innovator. In the case of the Internet, the original innovators certainly could not have imagined all that would in the future sit on top of the Internet. It is clear, however, that such freedom has been available – think, for example, of the development of the World Wide Web (WWW) (see chapter 9). But it is not true to say that innovators in digital services will always be free to offer new services to the market, and that they do not need the authorisation of anyone to do so. Think of the tight controls that Apple and Google exercise over the apps that are offered on their mobile phone platforms or the strict rules that Facebook applies to services offered through its family of social media platforms. The Internet may be relatively free and thus generative, but other digital infrastructures operate by other rules.

Still a generative architecture for a digital infrastructure, even to degrees, is different from a closed and hierarchical architecture. In a hierarchical structure, developments are proposed and managed through the hierarchy, and any development needs to follow the guidance and the coherence defined by the hierarchy. For instance, Microsoft develops and sells proprietary software which is conceived, designed, and built by their employees. As a user, you can buy it, and you can change the configuration a bit, but you cannot change the program inside or borrow a bit of code for your pet project. Even making suggestions for changes or adaptations you want or need will be difficult and probably unproductive.

With a generative architecture, and assuming a certain level of openness of information, there can be freedom for individuals and organisations to create new things that draw on lower layers and interact with higher layers, without asking anybody's permission (Yoo and Euchner, 2015). The only limitation is that the new elements follow the basic set of rules of the system as a whole, including using standard interfaces. In other words, inherent in the layered architecture evolved for the Internet is a generative environment that fosters creativity and innovation, allowing people to adapt the infrastructure to their needs or business goals. To a degree, this generative quality has been inherited by other digital infrastructures and platforms that use the Internet.

Zittrain (2008) recognises that there are limits to generativity as expressed in different digital infrastructures, arguing that the generative potential of a digital infrastructure depends on five key factors. We can summarise these factors as: 'leverage' (inherent potential of doing things), 'adaptability' to new uses, 'ease of mastery' by users, 'accessibility' of use and information on use, and 'transferability' of insights from one user to another. We can see some similarities in this list to the concepts developed by Rogers (2003 [1962]) when proposing the characteristics of innovations which diffuse faster (Diffusion of Innovation Theory, in chapter 2): relative advantage, compatibility to existing technologies or solutions, ease of use, trialability, and observability are key aspects for the diffusion of innovation. Drawing upon both authors, we can conclude that digital infrastructures have more potential to foster innovation and to have this innovation diffused because they provide the resources for users to create new uses on top of the current structures. The infrastructure facilitates not only the innovation per se but also the means for its diffusion.

These features are individually desirable, but more importantly, they support each other. The more an infrastructure has of these features, the greater its chances of being generative, drawing in users, fostering innovation, and creating change. As Lyytinen et al. (2017) argue, digital infrastructures are generative *from within*, inherently fostering growth in diversity (scope), scale, and by the embeddedness of new applications. In summary, the concept of generativity suggests that digital infrastructures potentially have unique innovation dynamics if their architecture is right. These authors argue that key elements that make digital infrastructures more generative are: first, a variety of technologies forming the physical base; second, architectures which are modular and layered; third, autonomy in governing the way the infrastructure is used and developed; and fourth, the capacity of embedding the infrastructure in new sites as it expands. The Internet is an important example of a generative digital infrastructure matching these four characteristics. Before the Internet, there had been many attempts to build proprietary and commercial data networks. But they were controlled by a few people and organisations who sought to define how these networks would be used and developed – they lacked the ingredients for generativity.

The Internet successfully challenged the idea of a controlled and managed network. The Internet logic reflected a different understanding of the need for openness, where anyone can connect and disconnect and use it for any purpose. There is no need for a single management hierarchy defining what the Internet can be used for or who can innovate. Innovation comes more directly from user needs and visions, or identification of missing elements. When a problem or opportunity is recognised, it can be addressed within the layered architecture with new or improved protocols or physical equipment. For example achieving an appropriate level of security for banking data, or speed and reliability for video streaming have driven many innovations across all layers in the last decade.

Generalising the layered model

In this chapter we have focused on applying a theoretical perspective or model to the study of the Internet as a digital infrastructure. From the discussion, it should be clear that the Internet has a distinctive architecture which facilitates innovation, and history that seems to confirm this. Drawing on these insights, we can apply the concept of layers to other digital infrastructures. When it comes to the cloud and cloud services, mobile technologies, social media, the metaverse, and AI infrastructures (all discussed briefly in chapter 1), each deserves to be understood as infrastructures, each exhibits a layered architecture, and each can be seen as having high generative potential.

For example, cloud services work layered on top of the Internet. Anyone with access to the Internet can access cloud services. The cloud infrastructure of on-demand services, virtualisation (a way of better using servers), data storage, and sharable software, is itself generative, allowing in turn the development of other useful applications and new business models. A start-up company developing a new game can scale up to provide the game to millions of users by use of cloud services. More users will mean more processing power and more storage needed, all available on demand and paid for as a service. Without the cloud such a company would have a tough time getting enough capital to invest in their own infrastructure to launch the game. The cloud solution not only speeds up the innovation process, but also reduces the risk for the entrepreneur, who only pays for the software and the servers in the cloud if and when the company has revenues from sold products.

Similar generative patterns can be seen on social media. Social media services are successful because they operate on top of the Internet and thus have access to billions of people – exploiting the Internet's generativity. But they can take it a step further; for instance, Facebook makes its API public, allowing developers to design apps to work within Facebook including games companies. In this way, Facebook becomes a generative digital infrastructure as the company offers resources for further innovation on top of their own layer. When Facebook makes its API public and hosts third-party apps, it becomes a specific type of digital infrastructure – a digital business platform (DBP) which connects, for instance, gamers and game providers (see more in chapter 8). In a similar fashion, the metaverse potentially offers platform services to connect sellers and buyers in a three-dimensional marketplace, but with more potential in terms of developments (see more in chapter 13).

Mobile technologies show generative patterns too. Mobile phones have become pervasive because of access to the Internet and all that brings to the user via apps and data services. There is a symbiotic relationship between the Internet and mobile devices, in which one leverages the position of the other. Mobile technologies become themselves significant digital infrastructures with generative potential. At the heart of this are the APIs of the dominant iPhone and Android devices (Apple and Google, respectively). With APIs available, developers around the world have created millions of apps for mobile devices, innovating the way information services are provided in all areas, from games and entertainment to transport, education, and healthcare.

Artificial intelligence applications are also growing in layers, and some companies have themselves become platforms for further development. For instance, when Microsoft adds AI solutions to services such as Teams (in the case of Copilot), the company is enhancing other elements of their platforms through AI products. However, when or if AWS (Amazon Web Services), Google, and OpenAI sell access to their AI foundation models through APIs, other developers will be able to create AI-powered products and services perhaps on a scale similar to the mobile app stores.

These examples (the cloud, social media, metaverse, mobile devices, and AI) illustrate the relevance of the layered model and the concept of generativity for understanding the nature of digital infrastructures as channels for innovation. In later chapters we come back to each of these areas and discuss them in more depth.

References

Lyytinen, K., Sorensen, C., and Tilson, D. (2017). 'Generativity in digital infrastructures: A research note', in Galliers, R.D. and Klein, M. (eds.), *The Routledge Companion to Management Information Systems*. Abingdon: Routledge, Taylor & Francis Group, pp. 253–275.

Rogers, E.M. (2003 [1962]). *Diffusion of Innovations* (5th ed.). New York: Free Press.

Thoreau, H.D. (1854). *Walden (or Life in the Woods)*. Boston: Ticknor and Fields. Available at: https://www.gutenberg.org/files/205/205-h/205-h.htm#chap01 (Accessed: 17 March 2024).

Wunsch, G. (1994). 'Theories, models, and data', *Demografie*, 36(1), pp. 20–29.

Yoo, Y. and Euchner, J. (2015). 'Design in the generative economy', *Research-Technology Management*, 58(2), pp. 13–19.

Zittrain, J.L. (2008). *The Future of the Internet – and How to Stop It*. New Haven and London: Yale University Press.

5 Emerging architecture

Introduction

This chapter discusses the development of the Internet as a digital infrastructure. It focuses on the emergence of the Internet and some of the architectural decisions which shaped the network. The chapter explores how the Internet transmits data between hosts, with an architecture that is scalable, flexible, and resilient. The chapter is more technical, but the technical language is kept to the minimum, enough for us to understand the logic behind the emerging architecture.

The Internet is now the world's most important digital infrastructure. So, the obvious question to ask is why has the Internet been so successful? After all, as Zittrain (2008) explains, there were plenty of competing local or national networks under development in the 1970s. Many of these projects had more substantial financial and commercial backing than the university-based researchers working on the Internet. The answer we offer here is that this success has been based on the Internet's ability to evolve, meet the needs of new users, and add new functionalities, all of which were enabled by the basic Internet architecture established in the 1980s.

We focus first on three important design decisions that emerged in the early days of the Internet (the 1970s and 1980s), and that have been proven over the years:

1. Just transmit data: do just this one thing and leave all other things to other agents; any intelligence or value-adding activity can occur at the network fringes, e.g., in the hosts.
2. Use packet switching: optimise capacity and help build in scalability and levels of resilience.
3. Create a flexible addressing system: able to scale up from hundreds of hosts to millions (even billions).

Just transmit data: Do one thing (tolerably) well

At the outset, in the 1980s, computer scientists in many countries were working hard to link together (inter-connect) big mainframe computers located in businesses, universities, and research centres. These machines were built by different manufacturers to different technical standards with different objectives. Linking them together would require some kind of general purpose and adaptable solution that, looking ahead, could incorporate more computers and more variety in their design and what they were used for – not a solution optimised to the specific needs of the moment.

Given this context, the approach taken by the Internet's precursors (e.g., the ARPANET in the late 1960s) was to develop a general-purpose data communication capability, isolated from any specific make or model of computer, by creating a network access device (a small computer just dedicated to sending and receiving data). This device was called an Interface Message

DOI: 10.4324/9781003385578-5

Processor (IMP) (Cerf, 1995). To add a new computer to the network, the only work needed would be to reprogram the IMP to 'translate' that computer's data into the shared standard for transmission and receipt. The IMP from the 1970s world of mainframe computers evolved later to become a small segment of code present in all devices compatible with the Internet and working to the standards of the core Internet Protocols, TCP and IP (discussed in chapter 3).

One way to express this is to say that the Internet was (and still is) a deliberately 'dumb' network. It needs to know almost nothing about who sends or receives data or what the data is about: a bit-string is just that, a string of bits. The only thing that the network needs to know is the recipient's address, and perhaps the sender's too if they want to be told of successful or unsuccessful delivery. The Internet does not care what the data represents, and it undertakes to do nothing clever with the data while it is in transit. As mentioned in chapter 3, it does not keep any kind of detailed billing data to count bits and send out bills (unlike your mobile phone network!). Today our Internet service providers manage access to the Internet, and bill final users on the overall volume of data sent or received, but with no input from the Internet. Remember, at the outset in the 70s and 80s, the Internet was subsidised by the US government and did not need to account for specific usage in financial terms. We might say, reflecting ideas found in later chapters, that the original Internet had a very simple business model – it was free and subsidised (see chapter 6 and Quah, 1999, on patronage).

The genius of the Internet pioneers was to recognise that building a dumb network was easier than a smart or busy-body network, and more importantly helped to make a network architecture that could scale up and evolve and attract new uses over time. This means that any intelligence, specific services, or extra features have always had to be added in the hosts not in the network – for example, encryption of data can be done in the application layer. This decision to remain a simple carrier of bits has proved a very powerful driver of innovation based on *using* the Internet and augmenting it with upper-level apps and protocols.

Packet switching: Share bandwidth and build in resilience

The Internet is a 'packet switched network'. That is, messages (data to be transmitted) are broken up into separate chunks – called packets – and each packet is sent independently over the network. The file for this book in Word format is about 1,100 KB of data. If this file is sent to another person using the Internet, it will not be sent as one big chunk of data, but split up into about 1,100 separate packets (rough estimates in decimal numbers, not a precise technical reference), given that an Internet packet for the IP protocol is on average around 1,000 bytes (e.g., 1,000 characters). The maximum data in a packet is 64,000 bytes, but for sound reasons such large packets are seldom used.

The Internet Protocol (IP) is the direct successor to the original IMPs. It chops up the file and generates the packets. Each packet will contain a section of the file (a string of bits called the payload of the packet). It will also contain about 24 bytes of data for the sender's address and the destination address and other control data including a sequence number to help reassemble the file out of over 1,100 packets at the destination host end.

When the file is sent from Tony's computer to Magda's, packets will travel in both directions, bigger packets carrying data to the destination (Magda's computer), and smaller packets as acknowledgements sent back to the sending host for each arrived packet (Tony's computer). So, in practice, many packets travelling on the Internet carry only a few bits of data, just an acknowledgement of delivery. When Tony sends this file, he should not expect that these 1,100 packets will necessarily all travel along the same route, arrive in the order sent, or even arrive at all. But do not worry, between them TCP and IP – the core Internet Protocols – will sort this out, in what we call the 'reassembly' of the original stream of bits from the many packets arriving at the destination.

When a packet of data arrives at a node in the network, the node's principal task is to read the destination address in the header of the packet and to make a decision as to how to direct the packet 'towards' that destination. Perhaps it already knows how to reach that address in a single link, and it can dispatch the packet directly to its destination. But, if not, then the node must decide on the basis of a 'best guess'. That is, try to send it on to the node it can connect to which has the best chance of leading to the destination. This decision can be made based on the first part of the address which relates to the network that the destination belongs to. In other words, if the address is in 'Australia' then all it needs to do is to send 'towards' that network. If the switching node is not in Australia itself, then sending it towards the backbone probably is the best route to choose.

You might well ask why messages are sliced up into packets and sent independently through the network. It may not sound very efficient or reliable. In the early days the developers of the Internet were in a minority in choosing this approach and many thought it inappropriate. The alternative was a circuit-switched network, as used in older data networks and in the original telephone systems. In a circuit-switched network, the first task is to establish a circuit from one end to the other (e.g., dial a number and wait for the telephone exchange to go click-click-click as it sets up a solid copper wire connection from caller to receiver, and then hope that the receiver picks up). Remember, up to the 1960s, telephone exchanges were huge electro-mechanical devices that used physical switches to set up a line and make a call possible. Once that connection is made, the data (a conversation or a data stream) can flow, but not before.

Today, using packet switching for digital networks is almost universal. Put simply, if a network is used efficiently as a shared resource – a core characteristic of an infrastructure – the primary concern is with the best utilisation of the overall system's capacity to move data. By breaking messages down into packets, each node in the network, and each link between nodes, can be kept busy handling packets without needing to know if these packets are part of the same message – they are just packets of data to be sent on their way. Keeping each link busy (high utilization) equates to efficient use of the network. This is sometimes explained in terms of networks being designed for 'bursty' traffic – that is streams of data that include bursts of intense activity, and then periods of little or no data transmission (silence). In circuit switched networks, resources are held during periods of silence. But with packet switching, resources are not held for periods of silence.

Flexible addressing: Dynamic and distributed naming

The third core decision in the early 1980s was to adopt a very flexible way of giving hosts unique addresses, registering those addresses, and sharing that information across the network so as to support routing decisions. The early decision to use 32-bit words for IP addresses (host addresses) foresaw the potential for many hosts in a network. This 32-bit address is still used today in IP version 4 (IPV4) – the most commonly used version as we write this book. In IP version 6 (IPV6), to which the world is gradually moving, the size of addresses is increased from 32 bits to 128 bits giving a staggering number of possible addresses. Currently, IPV6 accounts for 40–45% of the Internet traffic (Google, 2024).

We usually type an Internet address in a textual form, for example we type www.wikipedia.org when we use our browser. Similarly, we send an email to sales@example.com. We call these URL (Universal Resource Locator)-style addresses. This way of writing an address suits us as humans but our computers have to find and use the actual IP address (the 32-bit or 128-bit number) that we refer to. To do this, the Internet uses a kind of online 'telephone directory' to look up a URL-style address, www.lse.ac.uk for instance, and retrieve the IP address as a number – usually written in the form 212.113.11.22 (called dotted decimal notation). An IP address is 32 bits, or four bytes, each of which can hold a number from 0 to 255. So, this notation uses four decimal numbers to stand for the 32-bit binary number. So, we could convert 212.113.11.22 into binary as 11010100.01110001.00001011.00010110.

To better understand IP addresses and URLs, we need to understand IP address domains. These are familiar to us as the last part of a URL:.com,.info,.net,.uk,.nz,.edu,.cn,.sg,.jp are examples of top-level domains. For the purposes of addresses, each domain relates to different parts of the Internet – and they may be geographic (.uk,.fr,.cn) or they may be thematic (.com, .info,.gov,.coop). Over time the Internet has authorised more of these domains – the list is now quite long (see 'List of Internet top-level domains', on Wikipedia, 2023). In an IP address, some of those 32 or 128 bits are used to specify the domain, and the rest to specify the host address *within* the domain. We call these two parts the 'network ID' and the 'host ID'. The network address comes first (even though the domain comes last in the URL) and is the most important part for routing the message.

An IP address will usually need to be validated before any message can be sent. Doing this is the job of the Domain Name System (DNS) which provides billions of IP addresses matched to URLs every day. It is core to the running of the Internet, and itself runs on the Internet. Your computer or smartphone uses DNS all the time to 'look up' the URL style address and find the equivalent IP address.

One big advantage of having the DNS online, and looking addresses up (almost) every time, is that address information can be kept up-to-date. So, if you change your company's name and web URL from www.tonymagda.com to www.magdatony.com, or if you change your IP address because you change the ISP where your website is located, you just need to update the directory (DNS) which everybody uses, and the world will still be able to find you.

The DNS can fail though. On Friday the 21st of October 2016, DYN (dyn.com), a company that offers DNS services to many US-based web users on the East Coast, experienced a failure of their system. The cause was a DDoS (Distributed Denial of Service) attack on the company by persons unknown. In a DDoS, a coordinated attack is made by sending a huge number of requests, updates, or amendments to a host such that computers are overwhelmed. In this case, the messages came from all manner of Internet devices including cameras and video recorders that had been hacked and were running malware under the control of the attack's initiators (botnets). The result of no DNS was that many web businesses big and small were out of action, including Amazon.com (BBC, 2016).

The role of protocols

This chapter so far has explored three key decisions made as the Internet was being developed and began evolving, and which we suggest help to explain the Internet's success – both as a functioning technical phenomenon and as a scalable and robust infrastructure that people and businesses have been drawn to adopt for their own purposes. We need now to look a bit closer at the role of the Internet Protocols, TCP, and introduce a third, the User Datagram Protocol (UDP) (see 'User Datagram Protocol', on Wikipedia, 2024).

The word 'protocol' means a guiding set of rules. The *Oxford English Dictionary* says, among many other definitions, that a protocol is an established code of behaviour – in other words, an agreed set of rules for doing something. In the same spirit, the dictionary also gives a definition specific to computing and telecommunication, in which the protocol is the standardised rules applied to exchange of data in the communication between devices. We may summarise by saying that a protocol is a set of rules, standards, and behaviours, and can be applied specifically to exchange of data – which is the business of the Internet or more generally of digital infrastructures.

The protocols we consider here, IP, TCP, and UDP, are certainly standardised across the world. These standards specify rules that are programmed into computers (hosts, nodes, routers, mobile phones, TVs, and dishwashers – indeed, any device with an Internet connection), and these devices will all obey common rules when exchanging messages.

The devices at the two ends of every link on the Internet (hosts, nodes, and routers) will 'run' the IP protocol – run a program that embodies the IP rules so as to forward packets towards their destination. The IP protocol is described as a 'link-level' protocol because it manages packets as they travel along individual links. IP embodies the rules for how a node will receive a packet and then send it on towards its destination host. Each IP program running on every node in the network will make its own routing decisions about which link to forward the packet to.

The TCP protocol, in contrast, is called an 'end-to-end' protocol and the rules are followed by the source and destination hosts. TCP's job is to prepare data for transmission, breaking it up into 'segments', and pass it to IP for the journey. On arrival at the destination host, TCP will reassemble the segments to create the original data. But if any part is missing (a lost or corrupted packet), or other problems occur, then the TCP program on the destination host can ask for a retransmission by the source host.

IPV4 and IPV6

IPV4 is a stable protocol that still operates according to the specifications set out in September 1981, and indeed is very recognisable in the original specification of 1974. The stability of these ideas over 40+ years once again indicates how insightful the original developers were. Of course, it has had a number of improvements and extensions over the period. IPV6 dates to around 1998, and was the response of the Internet Engineering Task Force (IETF) to foreseen address space limitations. As well as offering more bits for IP addresses, it also readjusts the way that IP addresses are assigned and makes it more efficient for a router to decode them. IPV6 also has more security features and makes it easier for a new node to share information (e.g., routing information) with other nodes around it.

The address space limitation and the need for more bits in addresses are usually linked to the coming of the Internet of Things (IoT) (see chapter 11), and the need to give IP addresses to vast numbers of devices and objects. Anything electronic from a toaster to a torch or a camera may need an IP address. Something like an airplane jet engine might have thousands of components each of which wants to send and receive messages, report data, receive program updates, etc.

Despite the very good reasons to develop a new IP protocol, extend the address space, and offer better security, IPV4 is still pervasive. Perhaps there are a few lessons here about innovation and infrastructures in general. Lesson 1: if it works for users then they have few reasons to change or move on. Lesson 2: the ability of IPV4 itself to adapt over time (a sign of its clever design at the outset) has meant that most significant problems found along the way have been addressed by add-ons and workarounds. Lesson 3: infrastructures draw on their installed base and march at the speed of their users, and while that base is not IPV6-ready, there will be little movement. As and when the installed base is IPV6-ready, the shift may come very fast.

TCP

The IP protocol defines the rules that allow packets to move across the Internet from node to node and thus allows messages to be sent and received. However, the Internet is not 100% reliable, as explained above. If you are sending a video image as part of a live conference call (e.g., using Zoom, Microsoft Teams, or Skype), you can live with a few lost packets of data. The image may flicker or freeze, but the conversation goes on. But, if we send the Word file of this book to our publisher over the Internet, we would be very disappointed if it did not arrive whole and as exactly the same string of bits that we sent.

We thus need to do something about the reliability of the Internet. We may also have the problem of the sender sending packets too fast for the receiver to process them – the problem of flow control. These are issues that TCP addresses, layered on top of IP. That is, TCP assumes IP to be working well enough, and then adds some more useful functionality 'on top' to make the network even more usable – or we might say to increase the utility of the digital infrastructure.

TCP is a host-to-host, end-to-end protocol, also sometimes called a transport protocol (for the transport layer). The Internet is a 'network of networks' seen at the IP layer, but once we get 'up' to TCP we are considering the Internet as one network and assuming that it mostly works to get packets from sender to receiver – to transport them. TCP is about the relationship between a sender host and a destination host. The network, e.g., IP and below, does not care about or do anything much with TCP. The switching nodes and routers are (mostly) unaware of any higher protocols being used.

So, what does TCP do to help get data across a network in a more reliable way? We can build a simple example, again using the transmission of a Word file:

1. TCP on the sending host accepts a data stream as an input (e.g., the Word file), splits it into chunks, and adds a TCP header to each chunk. The results, chunks of data plus a header, is what is called a TCP segment.
2. The segments are passed to IP (together with the destination IP address). The IP protocol puts each segment in one (or more) IP packet and sends it on its way across the network. It is generally best if the TCP segment goes in one IP packet – e.g., we can set TCP to make small enough segments to fit in one IP packet.
3. The IP packet header will contain the protocol code that says that this packet contains data related to a TCP connection. So, when it arrives at the destination host, the data (TCP segment) will be handed from the IP layer to TCP.
4. The TCP layer on the receiving host will acknowledge the arrival of the data by sending back an acknowledgement (ACK) to the sending host. This acknowledgement message can also set the 'window size', e.g., the number of bytes the receiver is prepared to handle at one time. In this way, the receiving host can indicate that 'I am busy and need less data sent at a time', or 'I am happy to receive more data', or even 'stop sending me data'.
5. The TCP layer at the receiving host will reassemble the original message (in our case a Word file) out of the contents of the many segments it receives, each with a sequence number, and then direct the data to the program designated in the 'destination port' field.
6. If the sender does not receive an acknowledgement message in a reasonable time (e.g., if the IP packets get lost on the way there, or ACK messages are lost on the way back), then the sender will retransmit the segments.

UDP

The UDP (User Datagram Protocol) is a much simpler protocol than TCP as each UDP segment (called a datagram) is independent of any other. The header, as with TCP, includes source and destination ports to identify the sending and receiving software of the two hosts, a checksum, and a length in bytes. Indeed, the source port and the checksum are optional, so UDP is the simplest way to send data. There are no acknowledgements, no set-up procedures for a connection, just some data delivered to a destination, and all that is known is the destination port that it is going to – even the source is optional.

As you may expect, this is a very efficient way to send small or urgent data if you do not need flow control or reliable transmission. For example, this might be the case for streaming video across the Internet. If it is 'real-time' as in a WhatsApp or Teams call, using UDP may help to ensure a faster link and a better user experience even if the video or audio quality is at times a bit rough. Much voice and video traffic on the Internet uses UDP for this reason.

UDP also suits simple small message exchanges. For example, the DNS system discussed above uses UDP rather than TCP. Efficiency is probably the main reason, given the billions of DNS look-ups that are made every minute of the day, which just consist of a simple URL sent and an IP address returned – in both cases around 10–20 bytes of data in total. Having two protocols for host-to-host communication with different characteristics offers the ability for users and the application layer software to make their own trade-off between efficiency, timeliness, and reliability. This is a good example of the generative capability that has been nurtured in the Internet, a network that offers a bundle of features but lets the user decide how or when to use them – and if need be, offers the opportunity to create a new protocol to serve specific needs.

References

BBC (2016). '"Smart" home devices used as weapons in website attack'. Available at: http://www.bbc.co.uk/news/technology-37738823 (Accessed: 16 March 2024).

Cerf, V.G. (1995). *Computer Networking: Global Infrastructure for the 21st Century*. University of Washington. Available at: http://homes.cs.washington.edu/~lazowska/cra/networks.html (Accessed: 16 March 2024).

Google (2024). 'Total use of IPV6'. Available at: https://www.google.com/intl/en/ipv6/statistics.html (Accessed: 25 February 2024).

'List of Internet top-level domains' (2023). *Wikipedia*. Available at: https://en.wikipedia.org/wiki/List_of_Internet_top-level_domains (Accessed: 16 March 2024).

Quah, D. (1999). *The Weightless Economy in Economic Development*. London School of Economics and Political Science (LSE), Economics Department. Centre for Economic Performance, Discussion Paper number 417. Available at: https://eprints.lse.ac.uk/2291/1/The_Weightless_Economy_in_Economic_Development.pdf (Accessed: 16 March 2024).

'User Datagram Protocol' (2024). *Wikipedia*. Available at: https://en.wikipedia.org/wiki/User_Datagram_Protocol (Accessed: 16 March 2024).

Zittrain, J.L. (2008). *The Future of the Internet – and How to Stop It*. New Haven and London: Yale University Press.

6 Economic perspectives

Introduction

This chapter introduces economic perspectives to help understand digital technologies in general, and digital infrastructures in particular. The chapter gives short summaries of key economic ideas that can tell us about how digital infrastructures create value – changing the way businesses run, how markets are organised, and the economic consequences of both digital infrastructures and digital goods and services. Our aim is to use these economic ideas to help explain the dynamics of digital infrastructures, not to expound in depth on the theories themselves.

We first present a main theory which explains the economic foundations of the growth of digital businesses: Transaction Cost Economics (TCE). We go on to discuss other relevant concepts such as network externalities, economies of scale, switching costs, and lock-in. Finally, we dedicate a section to discussing the characteristics of digital goods and services, and how these affect perceptions of the value of these goods and services, including increasing economies of scope.

The Transaction Cost perspective

Transaction Cost Economics (TCE) examines the different possible ways of coordinating the production and sale of goods and services. It focuses on the costs of placing a product on the market, matching it with a buyer, and completing a transaction (e.g. a sale). Without these kinds of transactions taking place all the time, we would not have much economic activity as we understand it. We define transaction costs as the costs of getting products and services transferred from the seller to the buyer, including the costs incurred by sellers, buyers, and any other third parties. TCE is concerned with the costs incurred when selling and buying, not with the cost of manufacturing or creating a product – materials, machines, labour, etc. The other costs are important, but not for the perspectives discussed in this chapter.

Transaction costs are not trivial for most producers or buyers and have a great influence on individual decisions and thus how economies work. For example, consider the classic 'build or buy?' decision. Do you make a birthday cake for your sister at home or do you buy one at a shop? Should a company hire people to take care of the payroll in-house, or look for a service company which handles payrolls – outsourcing? In both cases, cake or payroll, the decision will be influenced by the comparative transaction costs of 'build' versus 'buy'.

Transaction costs are associated with the information that economic agents need to make good decisions and the way economic agents organise the agreements to transact (contracts), e.g. to supply and to make payments. The contract is particularly important in situations where any one party is going to have to trust the other, i.e., the costs of risk of default. Of course,

DOI: 10.4324/9781003385578-6

information flows are what digital infrastructures do so they can change transaction costs; in this way, they can change the way that business is done.

The origins of TCE are found in the work of the economist Ronald Coase in the 1930s. He posed a big economic question, 'Why do firms exist?'. His answer was that they exist to help entrepreneurs to manage and mitigate transaction costs. Since then his ideas have been developed further, and in this chapter we also draw upon the work of Williamson (1981), Malone et al. (1987), and Cordella (2006).

Economists often start their theorising with the idea of a 'perfect market'. In this ideal market, all economic agents (buyers or sellers) have access to all information available to make their decisions about what to produce or what to buy. In this perfect market, the price mechanism coordinates production and consumption at the point where supply curves cross demand curves. On the one hand, suppliers are going to keep producing goods up to the moment that they are still making profits for each new item produced. On the other hand, consumers are going to evaluate the price of the good vis-à-vis the benefit that the good brings them (what economists call its utility). The price mechanism creates an equilibrium in the market in such a way that suppliers and consumers get what they need for a price that is good for both of them. In this way, the invisible hand of the market (Smith, 1776) does the work of optimising the allocation of resources in an economy, coordinating production through price mechanisms.

However, there is a problem. Economic agents (producers/suppliers and consumers) do not all have the same level of information (e.g., of prices from different suppliers, quality of competing goods, or the reliability of customers) – what we call information asymmetry. More than this: some economic agents try to get advantage in the market by adopting opportunistic behaviours. A traditional example is the market for used cars. The car dealer (seller) may not tell the whole truth about the vehicle on sale, for example its mileage, how many owners it has had, and any previous crash repairs. The buyer cannot pay the cost of researching this. Such opportunistic behaviour, in this case withholding information, on top of the overall lack of information available to the buyer, means that buyers of used cars face a high risk of buying a lemon (American slang for a dodgy car). And lemons can cost money so information asymmetry and opportunistic behaviour by the seller impose transaction costs on the buyer. Better buy a new bicycle. Additionally, the level of information complexity makes decision-making more difficult. For processing large amounts of information, humans use mental shortcuts, thus decision-making is more an exercise of bounded rationality than actual rationality.

In the face of such challenges, economic agents may try to coordinate production and flow of goods and services in other ways. For example, by doing it in-house and keeping it under control (think of the birthday cake or the company payroll), or by increasing the levels of trust and the flow of information in the market. Transacting 'in-house' (making your own cake) helps reduce opportunistic behaviour, as it is easier to control information flows and people's behaviours inside an organisation (or a family kitchen). But we still see vast numbers of economic transactions happening in markets where information flow is far from perfect.

Earlier we defined transaction costs as the costs for getting products and services transferred from the seller to the buyer (consumer). Thinking about transactions in a market we can divide transaction costs broadly into three categories: search costs, bargaining costs, and policing and enforcement costs, as explained below.

Search costs are the costs related to finding the information to allow an exchange to happen. These costs include finding suppliers or customers and the best price in the market. The supplier looks for the highest price a customer will pay and the customer looks for the lowest price any supplier will provide the goods for. This search effort varies in accordance with the value and relevance of a particular good or service. If a product is very cheap, such as a cup of coffee, customers may not care to research the cheapest price in the neighbourhood, as the cost of searching would be higher than the difference in price. Purchasing more expensive or enduring goods and services would justify a more thorough search and more information.

Bargaining costs are the costs required to negotiate the contract between the seller and the buyer. This cost involves the negotiation itself, in which each party tries to get a better deal, and the establishment of the contract which documents the terms under which the transaction is happening. Some authors call this the 'contracting costs'. Again, the amount of costs (in terms of time and resources used) for negotiation and contracting depends on the type of product and service. If a person is buying a house, the cost of negotiation is high, with imperfect information going back and forth from the buyer to the seller and involving third parties such as a surveyor or a mortgage lender. The buyer needs to protect their interests through a better contract, which depends on having the services of a good legal representative. For very cheap or standardised products, this contract may be very quick and informal – we ask for a flat white coffee extra hot, the barista nods towards the card terminal, we touch our card for payment … and the contract is made. There may be some laws, rules, or conventions that support this contract, but we do not expect to invoke them. Thus, the level of bargaining costs depends on the sort of product and the sort of regulation for that particular market in a given country.

Policing and enforcement costs are the costs required to be sure that all parties follow the contract, which may sometimes include the legal costs involved in taking the party to court in order to uphold the contract. Some authors call this the 'control and regulation' costs. This cost can occur in any transaction, but they are more likely to happen in transactions concerning higher-value goods and services, in which the opportunistic interests of parties may be more significant. They may occur less when negotiating low-cost goods and services, as neither suppliers nor buyers are interested in fighting for small amounts of money.

Digital infrastructures have, it would seem, reduced transaction costs in many retail markets – travel, music, clothing, eating out, but also in global markets such as iron ore, oil, wheat, or rice. In the next few paragraphs we give some examples.

Search costs are reduced when buyers and sellers use digital infrastructures to find more and better information in real-time. They can compare prices and features of products and services either by going to different websites or using Internet services that specialise in comparing prices. A person can compare the cost of airline tickets by visiting the websites of airlines, or go to a service like Expedia or Skyscanner which aggregate the information, allowing easy comparison of products and prices. Search costs for the buyer are lowered; there are no trips to the high-street travel agents or to airline offices to collect prices and details of baggage allowance, seat choice, meal options, etc. Meanwhile, airlines (suppliers) can find potential buyers via targeted online advertising, reducing the costs of finding customers.

Bargaining costs are reduced from the buyer's perspective by finding more information on the prices asked by competitors, the reputation of the seller, and the quality of the product they are interested in. This reduces the risk of opportunistic behaviour in the negotiation. For example, a buyer can check the customer feedback of a seller on e-commerce services such as eBay or Amazon and in online forums to check what previous customers are saying about the company and its products and services. The buyer can also check online the sort of contract a company offers, to see that the terms are acceptable, compared with the terms of other sellers; is it free to change the date of your flight or is there a hefty fee? The seller too can go online to check whether the buyer is genuine and has a good credit rating. This second option, to profile the customer, becomes easier and easier as the Internet and WWW create stronger digital footprints of us all. Indeed, one of the primary roles of platforms such as Uber, Airbnb, and eBay is to rate suppliers and buyers and thus reduce the informational asymmetry in their markets.

Policing and enforcement costs are also changed by online transactions. As mentioned above, many platforms offer a standard 'contract' to all parties which includes some enforcement mechanisms if there is a dispute. If a contract is respected and both parties are happy, the policing and enforcement costs are small, perhaps just taking the form of a check to see whether the expected product or service has been delivered on time and to the expected quality. In the past, when this did not happen, there would be a private dispute between the parties, and other customers, or other businesses, would never know. With social media, people can publish their disappointment online in relation to companies and products, and this information travels fast. Concerned for their reputation, sellers may be keen to sort out problems with customers as soon as possible.

The transaction cost perspective, as introduced here, helps us understand digital infrastructures and platforms in a number of ways. First it gives a strong role for digital platforms as information accumulators and conduits. Both buyers and sellers are attracted to this kind of market which is, in economic terms, more efficient. Transaction costs can also be seen as one of the main reasons digital infrastructures have become so pervasive. The more apps target transaction cost issues and reduce informational asymmetry, the more we can foresee markets being changed and the overall utility generated rising.

Network externalities and economies of scale

Why do people and companies come to agree on or adopt a particular standard or platform to use – e.g., TCP/IP protocols or Facebook? They do it because they want to facilitate a particular communication process, but it is more than that. Seeing an agreed standard with a critical mass of users means that even more people are likely to adopt the standard. If you want to communicate, transact, or connect then there is a strong argument to join a bigger group. Think of the kilo as a standard weight. Once this standard has been adopted by companies, consumers, and governments, it is easier to buy and sell products so others join in and the numbers using the standard grow.

In economics this is known as a network effect or a network externality (Blind, 2004). This expresses the idea that in a network (of almost any kind), all members benefit or lose from the addition of new members. This is called a network *externality* because it implies that external actors benefit (or lose) from a particular transaction (a member signing up for Facebook) even though they have not participated directly in the transaction. These effects are often positive – a positive network externality – for example, new members on eBay or WeChat increase the value of using these platforms for all members. Network effects can be negative too. More users on Facebook may mean an overload of information and more fake news and conspiracy theories. A common negative network externality for digital infrastructures is seen when cybercriminals choose to focus on the largest social media networks.

The idea of positive network externalities is often used to explain why successful digital infrastructures grow very large. The argument is that size (number of members, nodes) matters, and people recognise that belonging to or using a bigger network delivers more value to them. Better to be on Facebook (around 3 billion users in 2023) than a smaller social media platform. The argument applies to the Internet too. The Internet has become a dominant digital infrastructure by attracting a large variety of users and uses – where 'users' indicates numbers and 'uses' indicates scope/variety. The more people, organisations, services, and devices that use the Internet, the more benefits the network brings to each connected host. One version of this logic is found in Metcalfe's law, which relates the value of a network to the square of the number of devices or users in it, thus there is increasing value as more devices, people, and organisations join the network (see 'Metcalfe's law', on Wikipedia, 2024).

We need to be careful not to confuse economies of scale with network externalities. Economies of scale are about the costs of doing business; there may well be some such economies in operating on a large digital infrastructure versus a smaller one. For example, even very small businesses can have a reach around the world by using eBay – and benefit from the larger customer base. Economies of scale usually drop off at some point – a situation of reducing economies to scale. Bigger things need more management, adapting and changing slowly, and this can mean a lot of costs and a lack of innovation. Network externalities, in contrast, are about the value (positive or negative) that participants experience because of the size of the network. In economic terms, economies of scale operate on the supply side when bigger is better by producing similar outputs at lower cost. Network externalities operate on networks that link the demand and supply side – think how both Uber drivers and Uber users benefit from the addition of more drivers and more users.

However, it is not all about growth, size, and positive value. Negative network externalities exist, such as cybercrime, breach of privacy, fake news, and cyberbullying. These can be called negative because value is diminished when more people join the network. We can see the mental health issues of teenagers as a significant negative network externality as social media distorts their world. Or in Internet banking where if fewer people made use of it then criminals would not have the same incentive to go online trying to trick customers and hack sites where bank and credit card details are held.

Switching costs and lock-in

Digital infrastructures and digital goods and services offer many benefits in economic terms, but they have one more drawback we need to consider – switching costs and lock-in. Consider this example. Before Facebook became the dominant social network, other social networks offered a similar service. At one time, Facebook was competing with other social networks, such as Orkut (Google) and MySpace. There was a moment, however, when Facebook became so successful in terms of numbers of users and volume of traffic, that it became very difficult for other companies to compete. The more people join Facebook, the more the service locks in its users. Where do you want to be, with your friends and family who are on Facebook, or on another social network? If you switch you will need to think about another issue: what is going to happen to photos and interactions you had with your Facebook friends over a number of years (or decades)? What will switching cost you? Are you locked in?

Other technologies can create similar situations where it is too costly, difficult, or disruptive for someone to leave one network and join another – perhaps to shift from Android to Apple phones or vice-versa. Once upon a time mobile phone numbers were issued by the networks – to change networks meant to get a new number, a high switching cost. Newer technology and the intervention of governments changed this. In some markets, governments and regulators look closely at switching costs and try to drive them down and encourage an open market – for example, in gas or electricity supply or in inter-bank competition – and online comparison sites are part of this (see 'The Transaction Cost' section above).

Switching costs can create situations in which the winner takes all or at least keeps all. Perhaps it is better to say that the winner takes a big slice of market share, not necessarily the whole market. Facebook may be the most important social media platform around the world (not in China, where WeChat leads the way), but there are many other ones. Android has the biggest market share of the mobile devices, but Apple, with its more closed ecosystem, keeps a relevant slice of the market and makes substantial profits. Big companies are still fighting for the cloud and AI markets, including Amazon, Google, Apple, Microsoft, IBM, and OpenAI, but no player has come close to excluding the others so far.

In the end, lock-in may make the use of a particular infrastructure irreversible – think about the Internet today. This does not mean people could not choose otherwise. At any time, society may decide to not use a particular infrastructure. However, this may imply a huge cost (switching costs) which might be impossible to pay (financially or politically).

To abandon the Internet or our favourite platforms and services is an extreme scenario. But lock-in may be temporary, and new generations or social groups can change their perspectives on the use of a particular technology. For instance, social groups have migrated their preference from Facebook to WhatsApp as their main communication channel with closest friends and family, others to TikTok and Instagram. From a societal perspective, digital lock-in is not beneficial. People want to have the flexibility to change their digital platforms *and* keep the property of their own data over time. If and when data can be moved from one platform to another (data portability regulations), there may be more incentives for companies to be more innovative. Conversely, without the risk of losing users, platforms may not have strong incentives to innovate.

The digital goods and services

Digital goods and services can be defined as products or services that are made of bit-strings and that depend to a significant degree on digital infrastructures for their production, distribution, or consumption. The availability of digital goods and services adds value to digital infrastructures. Examples of digital goods could be music, a design for a sailing boat, a computer game, a book, or a video of keep-fit exercises. Economists have struggled to understand the nature of digital goods and the economic implications of a higher proportion of digital goods and services in the economy.

Identifying the economic characteristics of digital goods is not a trivial question. Economic theory is based on assumptions about scarcity of resources, from commodities, labour, and capital to final goods and services. It is because there is scarcity, a cost for raw materials and for production, that there is a limited supply of any physical good. This means market mechanisms can find a price for the goods, such as the highest bidder or 'marginal cost equals marginal benefit'. This leads to the price of a product tending to be the marginal cost of production: in principle, companies do not produce goods with selling prices below their marginal costs (although there are economic and business circumstances in which this may happen).

Digital goods challenge this logic of material goods for the simple reason that copying a digital good costs almost nothing in terms of 'production', raw materials, or distribution. What is the cost of copying an electronic book a million times for a million readers around the world? The answer is that the cost is so low that we can almost ignore it. In other words, the marginal cost of production would tend towards zero (or be very close to zero), and thus the price would tend towards zero too following the traditional economic perspective of relating prices to marginal costs in a competitive market. The problem is that there are no incentives for the producers of such a good. Why record music if it will be consumed by millions of people who will not pay a penny? This was not the case when a million LP records (physical goods) were made and distributed across the world.

But, of course, people still do record music and distribute it digitally, and they do make money out of it – Taylor Swift is a billionaire. So economists have developed new theories to understand the difference between physical and digital goods, and how digital goods are wrapped up in services and activities that we do pay for – think of a plastic DVD as a product (physical *good*) vs. the Spotify streaming *service*. Economists are also interested in how we can ensure incentives for companies and entrepreneurs to keep innovating and selling digital goods. We summarise here the properties of digital goods (nonrivalry, infinitely expansible, aspatial, and recombinant), drawing upon the work of Quah (2002) and Rayna (2008).

1. *Nonrivalry*: Digital goods are nonrival, meaning that when a person uses it, there is no degradation of the good for another person to use it too; there is no difference between the original and the copy. A paper book in a library can be borrowed by one person or another, but two people cannot borrow the same physical book at the same time. A copy of a digital book can be accessed by many people at the same time, without disturbing the reading of others. You can think of other digital goods or services like this: computer software, photos and videos, films, music, newspapers, electronic games, online educational material, or AI-based medical advice and diagnosis services. Once created, these goods and services can, potentially, be freely used by all.
2. *Infinitely expansible (almost)*: Digital goods can be copied at almost no cost. Although producing the first copy may be costly, the reproduction of a digital good is not. Ideas (intellectual property) have this characteristic of being expansible; being able to be thought and used by an infinite number of people. But the price of a product which can be reproduced infinitely tends to go to zero, in accordance with classic economics. In a situation in which the reproduction of the digital good is not regulated, innovators would not have monetary incentives to create something new. Two common solutions are found in intellectual property laws (patents and copyrights) which give a legal right to restrict and put a price on copies being made (copyright) or ideas being used (patents). However, there are other possible views on what constitutes motivation for the creation of new digital goods. The open-source software industry, for instance, relies on intrinsic motivation to make people want to contribute to a product that will be freely distributed. But it still uses copyright law as its basis as a way to keep the goods freely available – what they call 'copyleft'. Those who contribute to open-source projects may find their reward in the reputation they gain for writing good code; it looks good on the CV.
3. *Aspatial*: Digital goods are nowhere and everywhere at the same time – they are highly and swiftly transportable. Digital goods are inscribed into servers and physical devices, and in this sense, one can see their presence in a particular space. More directly we can see that while shipping physical goods around the world takes time and costs money, digital goods move easily, rapidly, and cheaply.
4. *Recombinant*: Digital goods may be recombined in different forms, in such a way that original works can be generated at a low cost. Recombination enables high levels of creativity, as the recombination of content is limitless (see the concept of generativity in chapter 4). The generative architecture of digital infrastructures is a good example of the ability to recombine parts. Any website is indeed a combination of multiple layers. On the content level, YouTube has plenty of these examples, in which people create new videos from existing films and songs.

The spread of digital goods and services has gone hand in hand with the growth of digital infrastructures and platforms. The characteristics listed above suggest that there is a great variety in digital goods offering economies of scope and increasing customers' choices even if just a small group of people are interested in any specific product. In marketing jargon, this phenomenon is known as the 'long tail' (see 'Long tail', on Wikipedia, 2024). In the traditional economy of physical goods and services provided in face-to-face interaction, the cost of providing a variety of products is high. Mass standardisation is the strategy used for providing lots of people with cheaper products: as the products are mostly the same, the cost of producing each product is lower (economies of scale) and stock holdings are minimised. In the era of digital goods and services, the cost of customisation is more affordable so companies can provide products tailored to individual customers. Companies can attend to customers who want some very specific services if the cost of production and customisation is low. The long tail of customers is served by digital goods and services, thus delivering economies of scope.

Economists are concerned about the characteristics of digital goods in part because it is necessary to provide incentives for people and companies to create new goods. Producers and innovators can be incentivised and protect their interests by using legislation on intellectual property rights (IPR), such as patents, copyrights, and trademarks. These legal protections create incentives for producers, mainly by stopping people from freely copying and spreading digital goods. Such laws guarantee the payment of economic rents to innovators for a period of time. However, it also brings a level of inefficiency for society, as the wide use of digital goods for a very low price might really benefit society – think of the IPR behind COVID vaccines. The protection of digital goods through IPR may also reduce the potential use of them for recombination, limiting the potential for further innovation.

There is then a tension between the interests of producers and of consumers of digital goods. The solution is to find the ideal level of protection of intellectual property rights for each case, considering on the one hand the incentives for innovation (economic rents), and on the other hand the benefits for society. This balance was addressed in 1787 in Article 1, Clause 8 of the US Constitution which said that the Congress would have power 'To promote the progress of science and useful arts, by securing for limited times to authors and inventors the exclusive right to their respective writings and discoveries' (American Constitution, 1787). The key point in the sentence is that the protection is expected to exist for a period of time only.

Beyond IPR, Quah (2002) suggests two other solutions to the innovation incentives issue: the use of procurement and of patronage. In the procurement stream, a government or benefactor pays a reward to a pool of innovators to find a solution to a problem. The solution is then distributed to the whole of society. This is a solution which is institutionalised already: the military purchases innovation in this way, paying a contractor to produce something new for the wider service of society. In the patronage stream, a government or benefactor gives research awards to competent professionals, allowing them to decide which innovations would be more relevant. So governmental research councils and medical charities give money for pure research in universities, allowing the researchers to decide on the best innovations on offer. These two models provide incentives for the innovators at the same time as protecting the best interests of society at large. They also limit the economic rents of innovators, creating new incentives for them to look for more innovation.

Another way to protect the value of digital goods and incentivise innovators is by associating a non-fungible token (NFT) with the digital good. The NFT is a unique code associated with a digital good (e.g., pictures, films, images, audios, etc.). The NFT certifies that a copy is authentic (instead of being a pirate copy), because each NFT certifies one copy only. It can also prove ownership of a digital asset, providing a unique code associating the digital asset (perhaps a drawing or a music track) to a particular owner. The control of unique identifiers and of ownership can be done through blockchain technology – a kind of secure digital infrastructure with a high degree of reliability. Blockchain technologies rely on peer-to-peer networks, so to change something in a fraudulent way needs someone with control of the network, which is unlikely (not impossible!) for large networks. NFT technology has thus generated the scarcity which is found in physical goods. This may create a trail of ownership of the asset (a provenance), from its creator to the final owner.

References

American Constitution (1787). Available at: https://www.senate.gov/about/origins-foundations/senate-and-constitution/constitution.htm (Accessed on 15th March 2024).

Blind, K. (2004). *The Economics of Standards: Theory, Evidence, Policy*. Cheltenham: Edward Elgar Publishing.

Cordella, A. (2006). 'Transaction costs and information systems: Does it add up?', *Journal of Information Technology*, 21(3), pp. 195–204.

'Long tail' (2024). *Wikipedia*. Available at: https://en.wikipedia.org/wiki/Long_tail (Accessed: 11 April 2024).

Malone, T.W., Yates, J., and Benjamin, R.I. (1987). 'Economic markets and economic hierarchies', *Communications of the ACM*, 30(6), pp. 484–497.

'Metcalfe's law' (2024). *Wikipedia*. Available at: https://en.wikipedia.org/wiki/Metcalfe%27s_law (Accessed: 16 March 2024).

Quah, D. (2002). *Digital Goods and the New Economy*. The London School of Economics and Political Science (LSE). Available at: http://cep.lse.ac.uk/pubs/download/dp0563.pdf (Accessed: 16 March 2024).

Rayna, T. (2008). 'Understanding the challenges of the digital economy: The nature of digital goods', *Communications & Strategies*, 71, pp. 13–16.

Smith, A. (1776). *An Inquiry into the Nature and Causes of the Wealth of Nations*. (Cannan ed.), vol. 1. London: Methuen.

Williamson, O.E. (1981). 'The economics of organisation: The transaction cost approach', *American Journal of Sociology*, 87(3), pp. 548–577.

7 Evolving digital infrastructures

Introduction

An interesting question to ask about any successful digital infrastructure or platform is how they have become what they are today. This chapter starts with this question, considering how digital infrastructures develop and are sustained over time. The chapter presents three linked concepts: first, the installed base; second, cultivation; and third, the sustaining institutional arrangements.

For other kinds of technological products, a good answer would often be that they are the way they are because of the work of analysts and designers. Creating a product or service within an organisation is usually done in this way under centralised control within a management hierarchy. The process is managed in terms of analysis (finding what is needed), design, and then creation and use. However, the logic of analysis and design that applies in an organisation focused on relatively discrete tasks of innovation does not apply to large-scale digital infrastructures. An answer to the question needs to reflect the idea of evolution over time, building on what went before, and accounting for the forces that shape what we see today. The concept of analysis and design in a holistic and discrete sense, as a single encompassing act of creative thinking, is not that useful. We need a different way to account for digital infrastructures.

This new account can be described as: first, choosing a modular layered architecture; second, cultivating what already exists – the installed base; and third, channelling wider processes of innovation. In this way, digital infrastructures are shaped and sustained by drawing on many people's needs and their creativity in using the infrastructures for new purposes. Zittrain's concept of generativity (discussed in chapter 4) expresses this in terms of an openness to unanticipated change by contributions from unknown people (Zittrain, 2008). There will of course be some design efforts at the start and along the way, aspects of all infrastructures can and are 'designed', but relevant design is more than a solution to a present need: it must be a viable seed for further (unimagined) developments. To extend the seed metaphor, we might say that it needs to be sown in fertile soil and carefully cultivated (Ciborra, 2002).

Installed base and cultivation

The early Internet relied on basic telephone infrastructure, a physical layer just about capable of sending low volumes of data, a message, small files, or low-resolution graphics. From an installed base of voice telephones and modems, the Internet has evolved to a state where vast amounts of today's traffic consists of streamed video watched on mobile devices. The original Internet was imagined and brought to life in one form (copper wires and big computers) and over time it has been cultivated to become something rather different in technical terms (wireless connections and handheld devices), but also rather different in its social and economic significance.

DOI: 10.4324/9781003385578-7

The same pattern of cultivation can be seen in other digital platforms and services. The World Wide Web (WWW), built on the Internet as the installed base, needed innovations such as search engines to grow its appeal to new users and allow new uses to bloom. With parallel innovation occurring in network technologies and data speeds, cloud services, and security, the evolved WWW now supports far more types of interaction and communication (see chapter 9). Such evolution of the Internet and the WWW infrastructure, occurring in all layers, in turn supports innovation in application areas such as social media, e-commerce, or online payments. We can also be sure that there is more to come. This process of cultivation will continue to deliver in unforeseen ways.

Start at the beginning…

The installed base is all the current elements of an infrastructure available and operational at the current time – what is installed and in use. Digital infrastructures are built by using existing resources and adapting them over time. This means that they are often first created on a modest scale, drawing on earlier technology and practices, but potentially their utility for a wider audience means that they might take off and develop scale and scope rapidly (network effects, as discussed in chapter 6). Of course, not all new digital infrastructures are successful, and of course we mostly only see the ones that do take off and fly, not the ones that fail.

It is the nature of digital infrastructures and the process of cultivation that it takes time for them to emerge from their early manifestation. In the beginning, nobody can be sure a particular infrastructure or platform is going to become useful, popular, or will be sustainable in the longer term. One problem can be that developments and evolutionary steps which become desirable or even vital are not compatible with the original installed base or the chosen architecture. In other words, the architecture or installed base may define a path dependency that constrains the way it can evolve.

To accommodate innovation means an ability to integrate new elements within previous practices, standards, protocols, operations, etc. It is often necessary to adapt layers or elements within them but still keep backward compatibility in mind. The need may also be met by generating new layers that operate on top of the existing layers. In these two ways, innovation may be able to incorporate new needs and compensate for limitations while leaving older functionality in place. For example, TCPCRYPT is a protocol for encryption, to increase the security of data sent by TCP. This could be achieved by replacing the original TCP so everybody gets security but everybody and every device must make the change. In the spirit of backward compatibility it could also be offered as an improved TCP that can operate with peers that are also TCPCRYPT-aware as well as those who are not. A third choice could be to add a layer of security on top of TCP for those who want more security. TCPCRYPT takes the second choice (see 'TCPCRYPT', on Wikipedia, 2024). See also the IPV4 vs. IPV6 debate discussed in chapter 5.

Another challenge to change comes from the proliferation of the number of elements in the layers of a digital infrastructure. The more elements, the more interfaces, the more difficult it becomes to negotiate changes. In the hourglass architecture discussed in chapter 4, each element of each layer has its own standards, with its own functionality, which are supported by different stakeholders with different interests. The larger the number of stakeholders holding different interests, the more complex the negotiation for change, especially if it is necessary to obtain agreement among social actors with contradictory interests. It is in part for this institutional reason that the ideal architecture for large digital infrastructures is based on maximum flexibility for how parts are developed and used, while also fostering interoperability through the use of stable standards to facilitate interactions and communication among the parts.

Considering these issues of retaining the evolutionary potential of an infrastructure, Ciborra (2002) suggests that strategies of 'going against the installed base' and relying on analysis and design are unlikely to succeed. His alternative is a principle of 'cultivation of the installed base'. This was a more controversial idea in 2002 when he wrote about it than it would be today. His idea of cultivation recognised that each part of a large infrastructure will evolve in its own direction and at its own speed. Given this, adherence to a formal design or the policing of digital infrastructure elements will not be successful. Instead, he argues for accepting the challenges imposed by the installed base and its potential for evolution. The installed base will, of course, impose its own limitations, but sustained attention to change (cultivation) over time will address this.

Ciborra (2002) argues, unsurprisingly, that the Internet is a good example of how digital infrastructures grow by cultivation. He also emphasises that the Internet evolved out of the perspectives of two strong stakeholder groups – what we sometimes call social actors. On the one hand, the military looked for a resilient communication network which could survive a massive attack from an enemy, and on the other hand, the academic community looked for a technology that would favour decentralisation and open exchange of data. These groups were joined in time by strong commercial interest focused on doing business online.

TCP/IP appears a good solution to bring together the property of resilience and an open decentralised network, although both the initial stakeholder groups would continue to have different ideas on the desired outcome and uses of this protocol set. Commercial interests were then added to this mix. TCP/IP allowed different networks to come together as a single digital infrastructure, but also different social actors. And it still does. In providing the gateway standards through which inter-communication is possible, the interests of many different groups of social actors are served. This kind of alignment of interests helped the Internet evolve the installed base, rapidly grow the user community, and sustain a vast array of digital businesses.

Ciborra (2002) proposes alternative approaches for managing the complexity inherent in the cultivation of digital infrastructures. He proposes strategies such as constructing gateways/interfaces and building adapters as the Internet pioneers did with their IMP (Interface Message Processor) device (see chapter 5). Adapters and gateways allow a part of an infrastructure to evolve in its own way. Internet features such as the backbone and the distributed DNS system reflect this kind of strategy. The approach can also support the inclusion of less relevant or well-resourced parts in an infrastructure, thus providing for groups who may require something very specific for their needs or within their budget. It also increases adaptability if new parts can be added without affecting directly existing services (see backward compatibility above).

Ciborra's cultivation approach is intended to shape a better interaction with the installed base. It recognises that there will be a diverse installed base and that new developments need to build on this now and in time reshape it. It also recognises that it is difficult, even impossible, to replace or bypass an installed base, either for reasons of costs or for political reasons (e.g., the different perspectives of stakeholders). In recognising that there is (always) an installed base which is not going to change easily or quickly, we accept that each part of a digital infrastructure will evolve in its own way and at its own speed.

The role of standards

All infrastructures, as shared resources, are based to a significant degree on common and understood standards. These affect the hardware and software aspects of digital infrastructures and how users connect with them. Standards may be embodied in a formal agreement, described in laws and regulations, or negotiated and legitimised more informally by social actors' wide acceptance. Standards also need some agreed and legitimate processes for their improvement or substitution over time. In the case of TCP/IP this is via an independent non-governmental body, the Internet Engineering Task Force (IETF). Other infrastructures may have similar non-governmental bodies such as the WWW Consortium (W3C). And, of course, commercial platforms manage their own standards – for example, Android or Facebook APIs.

Standards used in digital infrastructures usually seek to establish some communication pattern to be observed. This requires agreement which may only be achieved by complex negotiation processes in which social actors (professionals, civil society, business organisations, governments, regulatory bodies, etc.) come to a (perhaps minimal) consensus which will benefit all. The assumption is that all involved in the definition of a standard for a particular aspect of a digital infrastructure have an interest in the digital infrastructure working well. This is the starting point of the negotiation. Naturally, this conversation will not start from scratch: the established standards of the installed base and their proponents may well affect and limit the potential to propose new or revised standards.

Standards work for all of us. You buy a new tablet, you open the browser, and immediately you have access to the Internet and the WWW because your software adheres to standards such as Wi-Fi, IP, or HTTP, doing it the same way as billions of other devices. The strong adherence to a common standard means that the infrastructure services you use work and are shared with billions of other people, which increases the value of it to you (positive network externality).

But there are areas in which standards do not work so well. Think about your mobile phone charger and how many you have had in the past few years. Each mobile manufacturer wants to decide which standard they are going to use for their chargers or charger cables. If you need to charge your mobile, you need to have a charging cable which is specific to your device (voltage, plug, etc.). It would be easier for most of us if all small chargeable devices could be charged with a standardised charger and a common cable. We are not there yet! In this case, the industry players have not reached an agreement – and it may not be in their interests to do so. Meanwhile, some governments and the EU, concerned with the waste created by the profusions of charging devices, exert pressure on the industry, but not much. And we as users have also not exercised much pressure.

One significant aspect of technical standards found in digital infrastructures is whether they are open or closed. An open standard is one which is publicly available and allows different social actors to decide how to use the standard. Open standards are generally freely available and well documented, on which grounds they are more likely to be taken up and used. A closed standard either imposes a rule that limits access to it (as in proprietary systems), or only allows someone to use the standard in accordance with defined criteria (such as payment of fees, licensing of patents, etc.). Technology companies have many standards that they develop and use in their products or services, but which they carefully control and limit access to. On other occasions, they may choose to make a standard relatively open, and freely share it on the grounds that this helps everybody (and, we suspect, them in particular). Even open standards have various levels of openness. For instance, an Internet standard embodied in open-source software allows the code that expresses the standard to be seen, used, and amended. TCP/IP is an open standard, available to all to use, which is owned and managed by a non-governmental body (the IETF).

Standards are then enablers of communication and exchange, particularly in infrastructures that work on a large scale and include many players or stakeholders. There are benefits from all users having a clear standard to follow, facilitating the interoperability between the various parts and supporting flexibility and adaptability. At the same time, standards often constrain the things which can be done with or on the infrastructure. This property is inherent to any and all technology: in enabling a certain group of actions, a technology also inhibits or impedes others (see more in Hanseth and Monteiro, 1997).

For key digital infrastructures, the processes of standardisation happen at an international level, involving companies, governments, international standardisation bodies and professional associations, interest groups, and international institutions. The establishment of a standard is seldom a rational design and choice process; rather, it is a political and social process, which tries to get a number of social actors to align their interests around a particular piece of technology or way of doing things. The decision on a standard is only one possibility among many – and any decision will not be final if the alignment of interests is not strong. It is once a particular standard is agreed that the test comes. Will individuals, companies, and other institutions start using it? If they do, then the standard gets stronger and more and more difficult to change, and it may become the new constraint in the installed base, returning to the idea of path dependency as discussed above.

Application programming interfaces (APIs)

The acronym API refers to standardised interfaces between programs or online services – a software-to-software interface, as opposed to a software-to-(human) user interface, or a software-to-hardware interface. The term is used widely in discussions of business computing, in particular business computing that depends on linking to and using other providers of services, as is the case in most cloud services (see chapter 10). APIs are in many ways similar to formally defined standards, doing a similar job of offering a well-defined way of interacting with a particular cloud service.

In technical terms, an API is a standardised interface defined by the *provider* of the requested service or services (e.g., a software module or cloud SaaS provider). The API is published – made known to others who may wish to use it – and says as it were, 'This is what I can do for you … if you give me the right data' (not so dissimilar to what a protocol such as IP offers). Of course, the *requestor* of a service needs to know the specification of the API, so as to access the API in an appropriate way and with appropriate data. The requestor says, as it were, 'I understand that you can do these things … I would now like you to do this particular one … and here is the data you need' – which in the jargon is known as an 'end point'.

APIs are central to digital platforms such as Google's Android, Apple's iOS, Facebook, and Amazon Web Services (AWS). Their APIs allow third parties to develop software (apps) which run on top of these platforms. Without a defined and available open API, they would have to develop apps themselves or commission them, but by not integrating the work of others they would lose out on generativity. The API also serves as a barrier – it offers a service but does not say how that service is delivered or how the delivery may change over time – the 'how' is hidden. This is, of course, consistent with the layered model. APIs can also allow third-party apps to talk to each other, exchanging information. This adds another layer of potential innovation, when apps collaborate with each other 'via' the platform.

The APIs of companies offering online services are a kind of hybrid standard, both open and closed. User companies and individuals have access to the API and can develop apps to run on these platforms and use their services – in this sense, the standard is 'open'. However, the platform owner defines the rules of use of the API and thus their platform is 'closed'. For example, Steve Jobs, Apple's late founder, when announcing the launch of the App Store in 2008, set tight rules for creating apps on the Apple platform, with some sorts of content and functionality being excluded. In this way, the Apple platform retained the right to curate the content which is available in their virtual space and could take a cut of revenues generated by these apps. In 2024 (16 years later), the EU has legislated to break this tight control and issued Apple with a fine of €1.8bn for restraints on music streaming apps. As we write, this case is moving towards an appeal.

The key role of APIs is compatible with the layered model, and the wider role of interface standards supporting ideas of cultivation and generativity. As we have seen, these help to isolate the detail of specific functions or services (end points), and thereby allow the detail of how things are done to be changed (improved, we hope) without undue consequence elsewhere (again, we hope).

APIs we might say are the 'glue' that holds the application layer of modern digital infrastructures together, or perhaps the 'LEGO brick' is a better metaphor than the glue. APIs are created by service providers to establish a standardised format by which service users can connect to them. APIs in this way define the 'rules of the game'. As with any standard, APIs can be public or private. In the world of business platforms, digital commerce, cloud services, and social media, APIs are in between public and private – sometimes called 'partner' standards.

The importance of APIs is in the way they support a dynamic and evolving digital landscape. If a business offers services via a well-developed API, one that other people can understand and use as they solve their own problems, then you are 'open for business'. Other people/businesses/apps/programs are able to use your services and, one way or another, pay you for them.

Consider a restaurant chain which advertises on various social media platforms informing of locations, opening hours, and menus. They also want to allow people to book a table, order food for delivery, order taxis to take people to or from the restaurant, or give directions for driving or taking public transport. There is also a need to take payments from credit cards (payment for take-out orders, perhaps deposits for reservations). To do all of this you need a wide range of digital services. All these services can be accessed via the APIs of other firms offering relevant services. In London, it might be Uber (taxi), OpenTable (booking), Opayo (credit card payments), Deliveroo (delivery), and Google Maps (driving and public transport). In your hometown there is certainly a different set of possibilities – but the same principle applies. To use each of these services the restaurant chain probably needs to register as a user and pay to use the service – though some may be 'free' as in you pay with your data.

Even a small business may need to use tens or even hundreds of APIs to access needed services. The restaurant chain described above has more needs for digital services. For example, in their supply chain of food and other goods needed to run a restaurant, to run a payroll, to keep accounts, to recruit staff, etc. There is also a specialised set of service providers that sell API management services to big corporations to help them develop API for their services and keep track of all their other connections online.

A new concept of the 'API economy' has emerged to reflect the importance of APIs for digital businesses and their economic function in driving revenue for service suppliers and innovators. SaaS providers, for example Adobe, Microsoft, Salesforce, Dropbox, or Zoom, have products and services that are fundamentally expressed in their valuable API. This is what connects them to their customers and drives their revenue. Another important part of the API economy is intermediaries who 'match' transactions between two or more parties – for example, a taxi ride company like Uber that matches drivers with passengers via apps on the mobile devices of passengers and of drivers. Indeed, many of our familiar digital business platforms (see chapter 8) are manifestations of the API economy (see 'API', on Wikipedia, 2024).

Looking beyond technology: The institutional perspective

The discussion of standards and APIs has emphasised the technical role they play and the architectural benefits they offer. We now shift focus to how standards are created and more generally the institutional arrangements behind the emergence/cultivation of digital infrastructures. An institutional perspective is relevant to many aspects of information and communication technologies. Institutional analysis helps us to understand the role of digital infrastructures in contemporary societies and the reasons why they have become pervasive. The institutional view adds a perspective somewhat different to the economic ones (discussed in chapter 6) although Transaction Cost Economics is often described as institutional economics.

The institutional perspective focuses on social structures (Scott, 2014; Silva and Backhouse, 1997), and the way people individually and as groups come to behave in particular circumstances. Rules and norms may enforce a particular sort of behaviour, and so too can beliefs and cognitive frameworks which are internalised by people. Such frameworks will affect the way designers, developers, sponsors, and society as a whole understand what a particular technology can do and how it should evolve. In this way, the interplay between technology and society is intermediated by institutions, while technology itself may be an instrument of enforcing a particular behaviour – an institution.

From the institutional perspective, we can derive three conclusions which apply to digital infrastructures. First, institutional forces influence the way digital infrastructures are designed and organised. Second, the adoption of digital infrastructures is influenced by the collective interpretations of a variety of social actors. Third, digital infrastructures influence the way people behave in certain domains. These three statements are explained below.

Institutional forces influence the way digital infrastructures are designed and organised. Innovators may create any digital infrastructure they wish. However, if their innovation is going to thrive, it must align with relevant institutional forces and these forces will influence the structure and architecture of digital infrastructures. From this perspective, we can study the development of digital infrastructures through the aligned interests of those who fostered the development of particular services, protocols, or applications, rather than others. Think about the role of the US government in influencing the design of the Internet, and the institutionalised market and non-profit forces (e.g., open-source community) fostering the development of AI foundation models. So it is not cool technology and novelty for its own sake!

The adoption of digital infrastructures is influenced by the collective interpretation of a variety of social actors. The diffusion and use of a particular infrastructure or platform does not depend only on the technical characteristics, or the economic benefits it can bring. From this perspective, the most important influence is the way relevant groups of social actors (we could call them influencers), such as academics, consultants, vendors, consumers, journalists, politicians, etc., are able to form a coherent view of the infrastructure – its purpose and potential. If this collective view is positive, then society broadly is going to adopt or at least accept that infrastructure. In this view, the social interpretation of the relevance and forms of use of any piece of technology is the key aspect to understanding whether it is going to succeed (see Swanson and Ramiller, 1997, in particular their definition of the concept of 'organising vision').

An interesting representation of possible interpretations is provided by Gartner's Hype Cycle model, a graph which shows how a community of influencers is perceiving a given technology as time passes, from increasing positive perspectives and a peak of inflated expectations, to a trough of disillusionment, slope of enlightenment, and plateau of productivity (see 'Gartner Hype Cycle', on Wikipedia, 2024). This Hype Cycle developed by Gartner is a very realistic picture of the way a community of experts and users interpret technology, mostly starting with a too optimistic view (love at first sight), just to realise over time the limitations of the technology (reality bites back), but also its actual potential applications (a moment of wisdom). Depending on the stage in the Hype Cycle, the same technology will be perceived in different ways by the same actors. Indeed, we have discussed before the same idea that social networks influence individuals in their decisions to adopt innovation (Rogers, 2003 [1962]) (chapter 2).

Digital infrastructures influence the way people behave. Digital infrastructures are not neutral – even if they like to claim to be. The design/evolution process and institutional forces inscribe them with particular features, and these features frame the way people use the infrastructure. For instance, Facebook has a particular way of organising information. If you would like to organise the information in a different way, Facebook is not going to be helpful. Facebook decides through an algorithm who is going to see your posts. It is not possible for you to define either who is going to see your post or what you are going to see on your home page. Any piece of technology has characteristics for enabling some actions and constraining others. Facebook promises to show only relevant things of interest to you, but the cost of this 'benefit' is that Facebook also decides what is not relevant for you (you may disagree with the algorithm's choices). Overall, Facebook can influence what you see and thus influence the way that you behave, feel, and think. Digital infrastructures influence the way we frame and solve problems, the way we design organisations, and the way we understand politics and forms of working. It also influences the way we perceive others' behaviours and uses of technology as being legitimate and proper in defined contexts or not.

This institutional perspective challenges the view that technology is a rational, technical phenomenon. Rather, we need to understand digital infrastructures as institutional arrangements, defined by social interaction between stakeholders with some stakeholders being stronger than others and all having different sets of motives.

The Internet once again provides good examples to help to understand this institutional perspective. For instance, we all expect that companies of any size have a presence on the Internet, that airlines sell tickets online, and that companies communicate with us by email. These expectations frame the way both companies and individuals behave. If most of my friends and people in my social circle use social networks, it creates a pressure for me to use social media as well. It may even appear weird or suspicious in some social groups if I do not use social media. Another example: anyone looking to buy a new phone these days would think first to compare prices on the Internet, either from individual vendors or on comparison websites. The idea of going from store to store researching prices would be seen as a waste of time.

An interesting aspect of this institutional view of digital infrastructures, influencing our cognitive understanding, is that sometimes the 'new form of doing x' is not even as efficient as the old. However, the shared interpretation of how things should be done – i.e., using digital technology – influences behaviour. An example of an institutionalised behaviour is the habit of sending text messages through mobiles. Who could imagine that people would prefer to type long messages instead of calling a person on the very same device and sorting out the issue in a few minutes? One could argue that this choice is fostered by the difference in costs, which may favour messaging. However, many phone contracts offer unlimited calls and texts at affordable prices, and yet people keep writing messages. At some point in time, people have decided that asynchronous communication by messages is more acceptable than being interrupted by a phone call. This is a new social agreement with potentially enormous consequences.

A second example in the same direction is the diffusion of AI applications for recruitment (companies, schools, universities, etc.). The assumption behind these AI recruitment tools is that the algorithm will be smarter and less biased than human recruiters, and will process applications faster, delivering the right 'classification' of applicants. Although it is true that there are efficiency gains in the process, there is plenty of evidence that the AI algorithms may not only be very biased but also be a closed box which cannot be scrutinised because of the complexity of their mathematical and statistical models (Crawford, 2021) (see more in chapter 14). Yet, companies and educational institutions keep using the tools despite their limitations, trusting models which cannot deliver what they promised. In this example, there is an institutional arrangement of adopting a piece of technology, despite not only its limitations but also the known damage it can cause to individuals and social groups. Again, society and regulators have not added enough pressure to change the industry practices.

References

'API' (2024). *Wikipedia*. Available at: https://en.wikipedia.org/wiki/API (Accessed: 17 March 2024).

Ciborra, C.U. (2002). *The Labyrinths of Information – Challenging the Wisdom of Systems*. Oxford: Oxford University Press.

Crawford, K. (2021). *Atlas of AI*. New Haven and London: Yale University Press.

'Gartner Hype Cycle' (2024). *Wikipedia*. Available at: https://en.wikipedia.org/wiki/Gartner_hype_cycle (Accessed: 18 March 2024).

Hanseth, O. and Monteiro, E. (1997). 'Inscribing behaviour in information infrastructure standards', *Accounting, Management & Information Technology*, 7(4), pp. 183–211.

Rogers, E.M. (2003 [1962]). *Diffusion of Innovations* (5th ed.). New York: Free Press.

Scott, W.R. (2014). *Institutions and Organizations* (4th ed.). Thousand Oaks, London, New Delhi: Sage Publications.

Silva, L. and Backhouse, J. (1997). 'Becoming part of the furniture: The institutionalisation of information systems', in Lee, A.S., Liebenau, J., and DeGross, J.I. (eds.), *Information Systems and Qualitative Research*. Weinheim, New York, Tokyo, Melbourne, Madras: Chapman & Hall, pp. 389–414.

Swanson, E.B. and Ramiller, N.C. (1997). 'The organizing vision of information systems innovation', *Organization Science*, 8(5), pp. 458–474.

'TCPCRYPT' (2024). *Wikipedia*. Available at: https://en.wikipedia.org/wiki/Tcpcrypt (Accessed: 17 March 2024).

Zittrain, J.L. (2008). *The Future of the Internet – and How to Stop It*. New Haven and London: Yale University Press.

8 Business models and digital platforms

Introduction

This chapter gives continuity to the idea of exploring theoretical perspectives to understand the phenomenon of digital infrastructures, advancing into a more managerial approach, presenting key concepts related to business models and digital business platforms (DBPs). A substantial part of the impact of digital infrastructures in the last decades has been triggered by the way business professionals and entrepreneurs find opportunities for new business models leveraged by information technologies in general and digital infrastructures in particular. A segment of these business models is what has been called the digital business platforms (DBPs), which benefit greatly from the possibilities of offering digital goods and services, systematically collecting data from customers, and the growing network effects of having more economic agents connected.

Throughout the chapter, we present arguments to show that digital infrastructures are resources for competitive advantages, not only because they generate new capabilities, but also because they enable new business models. We end the chapter by reconnecting the idea of digital infrastructures with concepts of competitive advantage and digital business strategy, linking the managerial approach to the diffusion of these technologies.

Conceptualising business models

There are many perspectives on business models. Considering the objective of this book, we focus here on a few ideas which can be applied to the context of digital infrastructures. In a nutshell, we think about business models as being a collection of blocks which work well together to generate sustainable profits for an organisation. All businesses have a business model, from the small, local coffee shop with home-made cakes, to an international global business. The key point for a viable business model is to find the right combination of blocks which makes the business robust enough to face competitors and sustain profits in the long term. If applied well, these profits are converted into more resources and capabilities, preparing the company for a new cycle of competitive advantages.

Osterwalder et al. (2005) propose that business models are similar to blueprints, which aim to explain how the company conducts business to deliver value to customers and society. A business model is a process of translating the organisation's strategies into a conceptual model of how the business should function in order to deliver the strategic objectives. The business model should show how the company creates and commercialises value. This conceptual model contains elements and relationships which express the business logic adopted by the company – how the parts of the business fit together, forming a coherent system. The parts of

DOI: 10.4324/9781003385578-8

the business model should be understood in accordance with the whole, as they are interdependent. A successful business model will allow the organisation to have competitive products and sustainable revenue.

The logic of the business is the combination of elements in a particular form of relationship. From the idea of a business model, business professionals and entrepreneurs embed the logic of the businesses into organisational structures, business processes (workflow), and infrastructures and systems (such as the information system) necessary for the business to work. Naturally, the business model can change over time, and the organisation structure should be adapted to the new model. The business model should show how to provide value to customers while generating positive financial benefits for the provider of goods and services.

Focusing on this combination of building blocks and their relationships, one of the most well-known business modeling approaches at the time of writing is the Business Model Canvas (BMC), proposed by Osterwalder and Pigneur (2010), also drawing upon their previous work (Osterwalder et al., 2005). The BMC proposes to explain any business model based on the ways of arranging the relationships between nine building blocks. In the heart of the model you find the concept of 'value proposition', which is a way of presenting the offered products (goods or services) from a perspective of value created to the 'customer segments'. These two blocks are strongly related to each other. There can be no value proposition without an understanding of the needs of the customer segments.

Once there is an understanding of customer segments and the value proposition, the other blocks are arranged around these central ideas. For instance, the company needs to find means to deliver products and reach customers ('channels'), and to communicate with customers ('customer relationship'). For providing products and services, the company needs to have 'resources' and 'partners', and organise their 'activities' around the idea of generating the value proposition. These activities, resources, and partners define the company's 'cost structure', which is then balanced by the 'revenue streams'. As long as the balance goes well, profits are generated allowing the company to keep the positive cycle of creating more and better value propositions, supporting sustainable competitive advantage.

Despite the advantages of a simplified understanding of business models, there are some elements which are missing in the BMC. For instance, the model does not explore the differences in context, which trigger different arrangements between blocks. To cite an example, in a society with high levels of concern about protecting privacy, social media platforms would not succeed so easily. Neither competitors nor stakeholders are explicitly discussed in the BMC, nor the relevant social perspectives which can make or break an organisation. A very good business model launched by a start-up may easily be copied by incumbent firms with more resources. In countries with high levels of censorship, Western social media platforms are blocked by firewalls. Other sorts of red tape are regularly used against successful digital businesses which try to enter protected markets, many times with the argument of protecting national values (see, for instance, markets in which Amazon and Netflix cannot operate). These examples show that there are other complexities to be understood in the domain of business models.

Another view which is often missed in the discussion of business models is the idea of how organisations must evolve over time to keep their competitiveness. The dynamic management of business models may be implicit in many conceptual frameworks, but most times it is not incorporated into the model explicitly. This is a main contribution from Rayna and Striukova (2016), who developed a model very similar to the BMC from a perspective of blocks (although rearranged through a value perspective), but twist their framework to focus on how organisations innovate and evolve their business models. The authors understand that organisations may change the elements of their business models in accordance with their business needs in a changing context. The authors are particularly interested in digital business innovation, and they approach the topic trying to understand why some companies which are not so advanced technologically can still build competitive advantages through their business models.

Indeed, there is a broad literature on business models, with different emphases on how these elements or blocks work together, and the sorts of relationships they sustain. In a literature review, Perkmann and Spicer (2010) found four types of business models. The first model emphasises the transaction structure between stakeholders, including defining who the traders are, what is traded, and the governance structures for supporting transactions. Think, for instance, of Google Search, trading money from advertisers in exchange for links to individuals who search for their interests on the Internet. The second model focuses on the mechanisms for creating and capturing value. For instance, Facebook has found mechanisms to motivate people to generate content for the social networking platform, which brings value for users themselves but also for advertisers (network effects). The third model explores mechanisms for designing and structuring organisations. Think about Amazon Web Services (AWS) designing its cloud platform which enables a myriad of organisations to grow their businesses on this digital infrastructure, and to connect with other service providers who share the same platform (what we could call a business ecosystem, supported by the structure of a digital infrastructure). The last model is the most intriguing one: business models are cultural representations, allowing business professionals to tell convincing stories to investors, customers, and partners. Think, for instance, about the promise of a decentralised exchange unit (currency), not controlled by anyone, even central banks and governments, such as Bitcoin. What else could explain how millions of people joined a peer-to-peer digital network to invest their real money, despite poorly understanding the blockchain technology and its risks except for a convincing story of a new business model?

Digitally enabled business models

Discussions of business models are not always straightforwardly linked to the idea of digital infrastructures or digital business platforms (DBPs). This is because digital infrastructures have many layers, with a large variety of companies and organisations behind each of the layers. Each economic actor has its own business model operating as part of a large digital infrastructure. The frameworks on business models apply, however, to businesses that are part of digital infrastructures or are DBPs (discussed in more detail later in the chapter), and to businesses which are enabled by digital infrastructures and DBPs. The sub-sections below summarise a few business models of companies that offer digital products and services, linking their activities to digital infrastructures. The objective here is not to give an exhaustive account of each business model, but to link the key idea of the business model with digital infrastructures through examples.

Netflix: The emergence of streaming services

Netflix was created in 1997 around the concept of allowing people to rent DVDs by mail services (instead of using traditional retail channels in high streets). In 1999, the company changed to a subscription model, allowing customers to pay a fee for the right to see as many DVDs as they wanted. By that stage, the company was offering an innovative channel (mail) available through an innovative pricing model (subscription), changing its value proposition (convenience, unlimited access). With the increasing number of customers, the company learnt how to leverage their data, building an algorithm for recommendations of movies (customer relationship). A further step into business model innovation happened in 2007, when the company started its streaming service, using Internet broadband and cloud infrastructures. As per 2024, Netflix is the most important streaming company with around 260 million users, despite the intense competition from Disney+ and Amazon Prime Video, among others. The company uses its data on customer preferences to define its approach to the creation of original content, not only for fostering customer loyalty but also to add additional revenue from the sales of content to other non-competitors, such as TV channels. The rapid development of mobile infrastructure also served the expansion of Netflix, which offers content for all sorts of devices, thus allowing customers to watch their preferred movies on the go.

eBay: The customer-to-customer marketplace

eBay innovated in building a customer-to-customer marketplace. In order to make this possible, eBay has built a value network, in which sellers offer products through the digital marketplace. The company at first targeted very specific customer segments: sellers and buyers of used products. Before e-commerce, this market segment for used products was marginal in relation to retail companies. In intermediating the communication between sellers and buyers, eBay has provided an innovative value proposition for both segments. Interestingly, eBay only facilitates the exchange of information through the marketplace, and is not responsible for the logistics of stocking and delivering products, thus keeping needs for resources and the number of activities lower. The revenue model is based on commissions per sale. The communication channels are all through the Internet and the Web, using a proprietary app for use in mobile devices. The company uses complementary assets, such as the PayPal payment system, which improves the security of exchanges for both sellers and buyers, and has grown further by attracting retail companies selling new goods via the platform.

Airbnb: The sharing economy

Airbnb offers an e-commerce service to connect people who want to rent their home or a room in their home (hosts) to other people (guests) on short-term contracts (customer segments). The idea is to offer guests operating on a limited budget an alternative to hotels, and also an alternative for guests who wish to rent a place for shorter periods in markets where landlords impose long contracts (value propositions). Airbnb is a marketplace for renting property or rooms. The company has a revenue model based on commissions. The service is distributed through the Internet and also has a proprietary app for mobile devices. The service is an example of the so-called sharing economy, in which people share with others assets that they do not need at a particular moment. The target market segments are two: those who have something to share (in the case of Airbnb, hosts who have properties) and those who want to rent this something (in the example, guests who want to rent a place to stay instead of going to a hotel). The service includes a rating system, thus both hosts and guests may rate each other, generating valuable information for those on the platform and increasing the value of the interface for all users and for the good hosts and guests. Similar logic of sharing resources and connecting the two sides of a market through a digital platform is used by Uber and Didi (car transportation), and bike-sharing services across the world – other typical examples of the sharing economy.

Skype: The freemium model

Skype is a Voice over IP service (VoIP), running on the Internet from any computing device. In order to get a significant market share of the VoIP market, challenging the traditional telephone companies, Skype entered the market with a freemium revenue model. The company offers free calls for those who are online and can use the Internet, including calls between two individuals and conference calls with more people (value proposition). In addition, they offer a service for the same users for calling landlines and mobile phones using Skype. For this service, users need to pay, either through a model of pay-as-you-go or through a subscription. The fee is competitive in relation to traditional telephone companies. Skype uses the Internet as a distribution channel, but it also needs to connect to other communication channels when calling landlines and mobiles. The company has a value network with partners, for instance, to accept online payments (including payments from PayPal). The information on users and contacts is supported by a distributed model similar to peer-to-peer (cloud service). Skype was bought by Microsoft in 2011 and it is fully integrated into the Windows platform.

Facebook: The user-generated content and the third-party interest

Facebook is the most used social media platform in most countries, relying mainly on user-generated content to deliver value to users. The company offers a service of social networking, allowing people to connect to each other (value proposition). The user-generated content is the product delivered by Facebook (posts, photos, videos, memes, etc.). For the users, the service is free. The revenues come from the advertisers, who want to reach Facebook users (revenue model). This is a third-party interest model: Facebook intermediates the access to users, in exchange for a fee, paid by those who want users to see ads. In order to properly match users and ads, the company has developed a powerful algorithm (core competence). Facebook has complementary assets, such as the social games which run on its platform, and Messenger, which aims to be a substitute for other email services (to a certain degree only).

Wikipedia: The gift economy

Wikipedia is an online encyclopaedia accessible for free from any part of the world. Most articles on Wikipedia are in English, but increasingly versions in other languages are added. The content is distributed by the Internet on any device (channels). The audience is distributed around the world and could be any person who wants to know something from a reliable source (customer segments). Naturally, Wikipedia could not exist without a strong value network of partners: the contributors who add content for free, and who keep the content updated and free from vandalism. It is an anonymous community of knowledgeable people who dedicate their time to spreading knowledge (ethos and story). In spite of having voluntary contributions for the creation of content, Wikipedia needs money to run its basic managerial structure and to maintain the servers which host its content. This money comes from donors all around the world (revenue model), as Wikipedia does not sell ads. These donors are also interested parties in this business model: they donate money aiming to achieve a positive impact from knowledge diffusion in societies.

Wise: The challenger of incumbents

The banking and insurance industries have faced many challenges from fintech companies in the last decade. In some cases, challengers have been successful in taking businesses from incumbents. For instance, companies specialising in transferring money between countries have been able to attract customers to use their online platforms (channels), with the benefit of being cheaper and easier to use than banks (value proposition). An example in this group is Wise, previously known as TransferWise. The company offers an easy process to open an account online, and to send money to other countries in other currencies at a fraction of the cost of a regular bank. Wise's main value proposition is to transfer money easily and cheaply. The trick of the business model is simple. Wise has bank accounts in all countries it operates in. If John sends money to Mary from the United Kingdom to Brazil, indeed John's money goes to a Wise's account in the UK, meanwhile the company transfers their own funds in Brazil to Mary. In this way, the money is never leaving the frontiers of any country, which reduces the costs of exchange rates. All operations are done through Internet and cloud infrastructures, thus reducing the operational costs substantially.

Digital business platforms

We change our focus now to digital business platforms (DBPs), exploring their similarities with digital infrastructures, and their own business models. In the same fashion as digital infrastructures, DBPs evolve through time in layers, enabling other businesses to develop their products and services on top of these platforms. The key difference is that DBPs are mainly information systems specialised in particular goods and services, which run on top of broader digital infrastructures, and have their own business models, which are themselves enablers of business models of other organisations.

For instance, the Internet is a digital infrastructure, providing the environment for all sorts of digital products and services we have access to online. It is a very broad resource. It is the same when we conceptualise social media as a digital infrastructure. We are talking about hundreds of different applications which have similarities enough to be aggregated into a category of social technologies. These are very generic infrastructures, which bring together a large variety of layers. Differently, DBPs are more specialised technology structures, enabling a particular segment of digital products and services, and contributing to a well-defined value chain or business exchange among economic players.

For instance, Facebook is a service which has become a fundamental layer of the social media infrastructure. However, Facebook is also a DBP, as it provides the infrastructure for other businesses to be built on top of its service. Through APIs (application programming interfaces, discussed in chapter 7), Facebook allows companies to build complementary apps, such as games, to be used through Facebook. Similarly, Amazon is one of the most important e-commerce platforms of the Internet, and one of the most important cloud-service providers (Amazon Web Services, AWS), being thus part of the cloud computing infrastructure. However, Amazon and AWS are also DBPs, allowing companies and developers to create apps and business solutions on top of their services, increasing their capacity for reaching customers (thus adding value to the business chains which connect those companies and their customers).

From this introduction, we can see that DBPs are closely related to digital infrastructures. We use the term digital infrastructures to conceptualise the broader assemblages of information systems (hardware, software, people, processes, and governance layers), which enable a very generic and large number of applications. The term digital business platform is more specific for the intermediary layer which enables a particular set of more specialised products and services. DBPs are thus layers which operate on top of broader digital infrastructures, enabling other business and technical layers to emerge.

The concept of platforms is used in many industries, but in the last decade it has become more pervasive when discussing the nature of businesses which rely substantially on digital technologies to offer services to others. In this book, we refer to this group of companies as DBPs, as they specialise in enabling or supporting digital business. Companies like Amazon, Alibaba, Microsoft, Apple, and Google are examples of large DBPs that sustain ecosystems of innovation, putting together hardware and software layers, connecting to different devices, and creating networks of users – individuals and organisations – as creators/developers and as producers and consumers. There are, of course, many smaller and more niche DBPs too, often focused on a specific industry sector like travel, finance, and investment or transport.

To be a DBP is to enable others to do digital business in the most general sense. A DBP can be seen as an intermediate application layer in the layered model of digital infrastructure. DBPs conform to the six characteristics of digital infrastructure (as defined in chapter 1): shared, heterogeneous, installed base, evolving, open, and standardised. A DBP offers digital services and products which are used by (many) others, helping them enable and further develop their individual businesses. A DBP provides necessary and needed services, and, as a generative infrastructure, enables innovation in terms of new products or services and support for new business models. A successful platform needs to have a critical mass of users so as to bring positive network effects to all users. For this reason in their early phase in business, DBPs often subsidise some users in order to attract them to join the platform and help them to achieve scale.

More formally, drawing upon Gawer and Cusumano (2013, p. 418), we can define digital business platforms as organisational structures which combine digital technologies to offer products and services to individuals or organisations, which may also build their own business offerings when they become part of the business ecosystem offered by the platform. Starting from this definition, we might in some cases identify any particular platform with associated services and technologies, such as Microsoft Windows or the Linux operating system. We might also think about platforms as offering products and associated services and technologies, that enable a wide range of business functions, and with potential for innovation (generativity). For example, the Google platform includes the search engine, email, maps, browsers, mobile operating systems, cloud services, advertising, media, and videos. AWS offers databases, storage, computing power, web and mobile apps, and AI services, among many other services on demand.

From an economic perspective, DBPs create value by enabling transactions between different parties, some being suppliers of products and services, and others being customers/users. Both parties are able to interact productively because of the service offered by the DBP. Another way to see this is to say that a DBP is a marketplace; as markets, they benefit from network externalities and each party (buyers or sellers) gains more benefits the bigger the numbers of the other party. For instance, from a user perspective, the more developers of apps in a mobile platform, the better. From the developer's perspective, the more users on a mobile platform, the better. From the platform's perspective, the more users and developers, the better so that economies of scale can combine with network externalities. Because of network effects, there is a self-reinforcing mechanism encouraging platforms to pursue growth to establish their dominant position. See, for instance, the comfortable position of Facebook in the market of social networking, of Google in search and advertising, and of Android as a mobile operating system.

The emergence of DBPs has consequences for whole industries if and when a digital business platform becomes a key player, with other economic actors losing some of their relevance and market power. The more powerful a DBP becomes, and the more other businesses become dependent on it (locked in), the more likely are the chances that a bigger share of value produced is transferred to a platform's owners. We have seen this in recent decades with the increasing revenues of companies such as Apple, Amazon, Alibaba, Google, Microsoft, and Facebook, to name a few. The more economic agents become dependent on digital technologies, the more value these platforms are going to extract.

DBP leaders, as powerful intermediaries, need to balance competition and collaboration, not trying to squeeze the profit margins of their users too hard. Here the term ecosystem is a good metaphor: despite their powerful position, platform leaders need to keep fostering the businesses which run on their platforms. They thrive when their users thrive. This co-dependency between the platform and the businesses it supports means that the design evolution of a DBP needs to reflect this. For example, by supporting collaboration within the ecosystem as technology evolves, and recognising that changes in the platform are going to affect all businesses related to it. A successful DBP should not make such decisions alone without considering the impact on the ecosystem.

Enabling innovation through DBPs

DBPs can enable innovation in products and services by adopting a modular architecture which allows the creation and recombination of blocks. As we have seen in earlier chapters, this is a basic characteristic of digital infrastructures and favours innovation by allowing complex systems to be broken into manageable components, which interact with each other through standardised interfaces within a defined architecture. Innovation can come from the recombination of modules in different formats, sometimes guided by a new business model. Modularity also facilitates innovation insofar as developers do not need to know the whole system but can focus on specifics and limited areas of change and novelty.

By having a modular architecture, components of a DBP can be used and reused across many products, services, and technologies, bringing economies of scope for the platform itself and to all who participate in it. The economy of scope means that the cost of producing new combinations of components is reduced relative to producing the same product or service from scratch outside of the platform. For instance, a hotel owner can benefit from Google Maps service, on the hotel web page. Similarly, using Amazon as a platform for e-commerce is a cheaper solution for small and medium businesses than having their own website, providing proper security, privacy, and payment procedures.

The interfaces of a DBP – their API – are, in general, open to allow the creation of complements and innovative plug-ins. Indeed, the more innovation is created on top of a DBP (new layers, new apps, new business models), the greater the value of the platform for all economic agents who participate in the business ecosystem. The level of openness of DBPs to third parties varies, affecting the way these parties are going to be related to the platform. The openness depends on how much access to information is offered to the third party, as well as the rules of the interaction and the cost for participating in the platform. In this way different architectures and institutional arrangements foster more or less innovation.

The level of innovation probably should be curated by the platform owner to make sure the whole ecosystem keeps benefiting from it. Too many components may make the system too complex, creating a barrier to more innovation. Third parties might start to avoid creating new solutions for a platform that already has too many overlapping options. It may be necessary to select from potential innovations those that better contribute to the whole system. This happens, for instance, in open-source software platforms, when the community of developers decide which innovations are going to be incorporated into the system, rejecting innovations which are not contributing to the improvement of the whole. Thus, a platform leader needs to keep a level of control over the architecture of the whole system, avoiding the shortcomings of too much complexity.

On the other hand, as organisations and individuals aggregate around a few huge DBPs (because of the positive network effects), some DBPs have tried to centralise an increasing amount of power, enabling them to create barriers for other companies entering the market with competing solutions. This may reduce innovation in the long term, going against one of the key benefits of having platforms. The question thus is how to keep a balance between the interests of incumbent platforms vis-à-vis the market's needs for innovation and the interests of all suppliers and customers which operate on the platforms.

Connecting DBPs to digital infrastructures

In this section, we look at DBPs as specific layers of digital infrastructures and spell out some of the similarities between the two. The idea here is to understand the connections between DBPs and digital infrastructures, demonstrating how the first ones emerge from the second ones, and how key characteristics are inherited in this process.

The first similarity is related to the way DBPs gain scalability, evolving over time, drawing upon initial designs, but drifting in directions which have not been originally planned. Although usually owned by a company, which controls the design of a core part of a platform, the platforms we see emerge over time reflect the way core components, organised in modular structures, are assembled, used, and recombined by users (individuals and companies, suppliers and customers). In other words, they evolve by reflecting the environment in which they operate and the products, services, and technologies which are created there. Thus, there is co-creation and co-design of DBPs, in which the company which controls the platform adjusts its design and architecture to gain scale and scope, exploit linked innovations, and so as to become more attractive to more users.

The second similarity is about the development of layers. The development of new products, services, and technologies happens (in part) through adding new layers and new nodes to complex networks of technology, organisations, and people. The ability to add new layers depends on the degree of openness of a DBP, which requires clear interface standards and governance structures. DBPs usually are designed as modular architectures, with core components and the capacity to add more modules in accordance with the needs of users. In addition, users contribute to the creation of new elements, for example apps which run on top of Android or iOS platforms or games on Facebook.

The third similarity is that both are strongly affected by network effects: positive and negative externalities. On the one hand, the more participants a DBP has, the more benefits for the whole network. For instance, the fact that Facebook has a massive number of users is a benefit for those advertising on the platform, as this increases the chances of reaching potential customers. The network externality in this case benefits advertisers and Facebook itself and perhaps the users too (do you benefit from adverts?). On the other hand, the massive number of participants may also bring negative externalities. For instance, too many companies trying to sell social games on Facebook may make it harder to convince a particular user to try a new game or to accept an invitation from a friend to play a game. Excess of information can also become a shortcoming for a DBP when too many participants are connected.

The diffusion of DBPs

DBPs are everywhere around us. They have become pervasive enough to be part of our regular daily activities, even though some of us may have not yet paid attention to their actual business models and their relevance as enablers of new business models and new value propositions.

To illustrate the theoretical perspectives, we discuss now some examples of DBPs, summarising key ideas for motivating the reader to investigate more on the topics. The cases explore further links between DBPs and digital infrastructures, and reconnect the discussion with the concept of business models, not only because the platforms have business models themselves, but also because DBPs enable third parties to develop their own business models. At this stage, we can foresee that more DBPs are to emerge and more businesses will use DBPs to offer their value proposition to customer segments. The examples below are just signalling the relevance of DBPs.

Alphabet, Google, and Android

Alphabet (the parent company which owns Google and Android) has today one of the most pervasive DBPs, with a business model which allows the company successfully to offer a wide range of services to end users. A main service offered by the company is Google Search, which has the biggest market share in the search business. Since its earliest days, Google (now Alphabet) has aimed to become a major DBP, offering a collection of complementary products, services, and technologies which are all integrated into the same structure and aim to facilitate individuals and organisations to do business on Google's systems, and generate data for Google. For instance, the company offers email services (Gmail), Chrome Web Browser, office software for collaboration (packages with Docs, Sheets, Forms, Slides, and Sites), cloud storage (Google Drive), video platform (YouTube), blogs (Blogger), calendar, video conferencing (Hangouts), Google Maps (and Street View), Google Images, Google Books, Google Flights, Google Shopping, services for advertising such as Google AdWords and Google AdSense, and many other services, such as more recently Gemini (an artificial intelligence service). Individuals and companies may use these services in different ways in accordance with their needs. Some services are free (especially for personal users), and others are paid-for (especially for organisations).

Having realised the relevance of mobile infrastructures, Alphabet took a bold step to gain the biggest market share of mobile operating systems by launching Android, a free piece of software based on the Linux kernel (an open-source operating system). The Android operating system is targeted at touchscreen mobile devices such as smartphones and tablets. Android has been also adapted for televisions, cars, wristwatches (wearable technology), notebooks, game consoles, and digital cameras, among other devices. Android is a key part of Alphabet DBP and has in itself become a major platform. Android has an open API, allowing developers to produce a vast range of apps on top of it, and offer them through the Google Play Store. Although Android is free, Google Play Store has a business model based on commissions per sale of those apps Android has enabled. And the companies selling these apps have their business models enabled by the distribution channels offered by Google Play Store.

Apple and iOS

After struggling in the 1990s to redefine its identity in the PC market, Apple has reinvented itself to become one of the key DBPs, migrating from a more product-oriented strategy to a combination of products, services, and technology. Distinct from Google, Apple has as its core business the sale of hardware – computers (Mac), mobile phones (iPhone), tablets (iPad), television sets (Apple TV), wearables (Apple Watch), and wireless headphones (AirPods), among other products and accessories for these products. Apple creates its own software, supported by proprietary operating systems, OS X for Macs and iOS for Apple mobile devices. On top of these hardware and software layers, they offer services such as iTunes, App Store, Apple Pay, iCloud, Apple Mail, and Apple Remote Desktop.

Relying on the perceived quality of its products and a loyal customer base, Apple has been able to expand the sales of both hardware and services, changing its role in the digital industries. An important move in this direction was the creation of the service iTunes, associated at first with the iPod device (which was discontinued in May 2022, as mobile phones have become the channel of choice for music streaming). Despite the iPod being very innovative in its day as a carrier of digital music, the real value added by the device was the possibility of buying songs through the iTunes platform (available on Apple devices), which uses cloud services to store and manage music, videos, television shows, audiobooks, podcasts, and movie rentals. Interestingly, iTunes has opened the door to a new business perspective for Apple, i.e., a business model of intermediating the transactions between the final consumer and the recording companies, offering a platform to sell individual songs (instead of album CDs).

Apple develops operating systems and software which operate only on its hardware/platform, creating an environment in which the final user has a combination of hardware, software, and services sourced from the same company. In order to leverage the level of innovation in its platform, Apple has opened the APIs of the web browser Safari and of the iOS for mobile devices. In doing this, Apple has benefited from thousands of developers who have created software solutions (apps) to run on Apple devices and software. Apple launched the App Store for selling the apps created by these developers, thus on the one hand organising and managing the offer of apps on its platform, and on the other hand making viable a market to match users and developers, which would not be easy without Apple intermediation. In this business ecosystem, the App Store has a business model based on commissions upon sales, and the app developers have a business model which depends on Apple channels and digital infrastructures.

Microsoft

Microsoft has been a core player in digital industries for many decades. The company started offering operating systems and office packages for PCs. The Windows operating system is the most important system on desktop computers and smaller servers, and supports the larger Microsoft platform. In addition, the company is big in games consoles (Xbox). The company offers many software package services such as Word, Excel, PowerPoint, Edge, Outlook email, and associated services (such as calendar, contact lists, and management of tasks), and collaborative platforms such as Skype, SharePoint, and Teams. By virtue of these services that are widely used in business, Microsoft is a very significant DBP. There are few businesses or other organisations that do not use some of these products and services offered by Microsoft, although the company has competitors in all segments. Microsoft has also increased the range of services the platform offers to include significant industry-leading cloud services (Microsoft Azure). Microsoft embeds in its platform a family of artificial intelligence tools, which facilitate, for instance, writing. More recently, the launch of Copilot (a family of products which substituted Cortana and Bing Chat), powered by OpenAI technology, is an example of how Microsoft is integrating AI into their platform, including for their mainstream products (Word, Excel, PowerPoint, Outlook, and Teams).

Amazon

Amazon started as an e-commerce business: selling books on the Internet. Gradually, the company has become a synonym for e-commerce for most products a household may buy – and indeed many businesses also buy from Amazon. Our focus here, though, is on how Amazon has become a DBP, transforming the company from an online retail store to an online retail mall and service provider. The company changed its business model when it allowed small and medium-sized retailers to sell products on the Amazon e-commerce interface. In this way, millions of small and medium-sized businesses, which would find it hard to set up a platform from scratch to sell their products online, have entered the world of Internet sales. Amazon offers the platform for them to sell their products, with the advantage that they do not need to invest either in the interface (having a website) or in the security of payment (one of the biggest obstacles for any company to selling products online). Communication with the customer is also managed by Amazon as can be the logistics (Fulfilment by Amazon).

In addition, Amazon has become a cloud-service provider (Amazon Web Services, AWS). Relying on its knowledge of how to manage servers, communication, and security, it was a logical step for Amazon to start selling cloud services to third parties, a new business model for the conglomerate. The service supports online operations, thus the client does not need to have a server to run a business. A great advantage of this model is that the client does not invest money in a fixed infrastructure which may not be necessary for a small business, at the same time if or when the infrastructure becomes necessary, it is immediately available through the cloud (scalability). In addition, the system can be used for backup databases and big data analytics. And to make the platform even more attractive, Amazon has the Amazon API Gateway, which allows developers to create apps to access data and functionalities that a company runs on AWS.

WeChat

WeChat is a social media platform used mainly in China. Created by Tencent, one of the biggest Chinese digital business companies, WeChat could be better described as a super-app, which puts together a large set of functionalities and features, from social media tools (connecting friends) to instant messaging, purchasing and booking channels, and payment systems, among many other features and functionalities. WeChat provides an environment in which people can organise their digital activities fully. For instance, if a person wants to book a restaurant or a service, WeChat offers the features to have access to these services. The same app has social networks for organising a dinner, booking the restaurant, ordering the food, splitting the bill among friends to pay the restaurant, and requesting a cab to go back home. In this way, it can be described as an 'all in one' app. Mini programs – equivalent to apps – may be developed either by WeChat or by independent developers.

This centralisation of information in one service provider is a powerful resource in the hands of Tencent, which knows all that a person is doing in the day, from their emails and private messages to their photos and videos, conversations with friends, consumption of goods and services, savings in the bank, health records, entertainment preferences, etc. From the user's perspective, the convenience has been a reason for using the app, and many would be isolated if not adopting the same platform used by friends (remember that Facebook's and Google's tools are prohibited in China). However, the users become also vulnerable to the marketing strategies of a platform which has all sorts of information about them. Other companies and app developers have interests in joining the WeChat platform (creating mini-programs – sub-apps – inside WeChat), as this is the place people are all the time.

Digital business strategy

The business model concept can help us to better understand and design solutions in the field of information systems. As proposed by Osterwalder et al. (2005), it is necessary to have a good alignment between the business strategy and the information system infrastructure which supports this strategy, in order to improve business performance. The business model favours a better alignment between both the business and the information technology perspective, as business models bring more details on how a particular strategy is going to be delivered.

In this direction, the business model brings a common understanding of business strategies between the business and information system professionals, increasing the chances of success in creating a better strategic fit between both. In realising how this alignment could be done, the company is in a better position to define its requirements in terms of digital infrastructures. On a pragmatic level, the business model helps companies to make better decisions on their investments in information technology, as it is necessary to think about the long-term strategy of a company to build a robust infrastructure. Osterwalder et al. (2005) suggest that investments in information technology should take into consideration the nine building blocks of the Business Model Canvas, to explore how digital solutions could improve each of the blocks and the interaction between the blocks.

In reviewing the literature, we find other theories and frameworks which help digital business professionals to design strategies for organisations, aiming to reach a higher degree of competitiveness. Focusing on our interest in understanding digital business strategies in depth, the framework developed by Bharadwaj et al. (2013) is very promising. The authors propose to merge both ideas into a new paradigm for obtaining competitive advantages by adopting a digital business strategy. They argue that the traditional view, that the business strategy directs the information technology strategy, ignores the pervasiveness of digital technologies in businesses, and the speed at which changes are happening. Particularly, the authors propose to think about the scope, the scale, the speed, and the sources of value creation and capture as fundamental aspects when defining digital business strategies.

A few examples can help to visualise these strategic concepts. For instance, the digitalisation of goods (e.g., books and films) enables businesses to enlarge the scope of their offering. When selling physical goods, retail companies give preference to mainstream products, because of the costs of managing inventories. However, digital goods do not occupy large physical spaces, thus retail companies may have a broader scope of products attending the demand of parts of the long-tail markets (i.e., those market segments which individually buy low volumes, but that together may represent good business). The barriers to reaching new markets are lower when using digital distribution channels, thus fostering economies of scale. For instance, Netflix and many video game companies rely on AWS cloud services to have more capacity for offering services on demand for large markets. Additionally, digital platforms provide the necessary speed for product launching, leveraging the capacity to reach markets. Think about how fast an app can reach global markets using the App Store and Google Play. Finally, the exploitation of customer big data allows companies such as Netflix and Amazon to improve their value creation, through the right recommendations of products or even through a better provision of new products. Similarly, companies such as Google and Facebook use algorithms to improve the matching between advertisements and customers, increasing the value creation and capture for both sides.

From the perspective developed in this book, this conceptualisation of a strategy involving merging the digital technology and business elements is more coherent with the observed facts. Digital technology is changing so fast that established business strategies may become obsolete quickly in the face of new products, services, business models, and market expectations. The emergence of the AI infrastructure (see chapter 14) is an example of digital technologies bringing innovation into products (e.g., robots and drones), services (e.g., generative AI for customer services), business models (e.g., companies such as AWS, Microsoft, Google, IBM, and

OpenAI selling AI services in the cloud), and changing market expectations (e.g., from regular Google Search to prompt questions using OpenAI's ChatGPT, Microsoft's Copilot, Google's Gemini, to cite a few examples).

Another theory which can be integrated into this book's approach for extracting more value from investments in digital technologies is the Resource-Based View (RBV) (Barney, 1991; Teece and Pisano, 1994), which focuses on how companies use their resources for obtaining sustainable competitive advantage. Rather than following a managerial or leadership perspective (e.g., that leaders have visions and plan business success), the RBV theory proposes that a company must take into consideration the environment in their industry and markets, and focus on developing superior relevant capabilities and resources. These then become a solid basis for sustainable competitive advantage, which enables the business to obtain better profitability, and consequently to invest in more capabilities and resources for the next cycle. The key in this theory is developing and nurturing appropriate resources and capabilities, a perspective which fits with our understanding of digital infrastructures as layers, and collections of technologies and institutions, which develop over time in an integrated manner (as proposed in chapters 4, 6, and 7).

RBV suggests that competitive advantages come when resources are valuable and rare, and difficult to imitate or to substitute. Resources can be all sorts of assets (buildings, IPR, finance, partnerships, human capital) but also capabilities, processes, information, and knowledge that a company has to differentiate itself. Such valuable, inimitable, and rare resources may be in particular technologies, in their workforce and skills set, their partnerships, or in their branding. A distinctive combination of relevant resources with these characteristics can help a company to achieve competitive advantages in relation to other companies even if individual resources do not have all the characteristics. Again, considering the literature on digital infrastructures, we can see the similarity of this perception of how to manage resources with Ciborra's (2002) view on the cultivation of digital infrastructures (discussed in chapter 7).

The RBV strategy proposes that a firm must work on the means to reach sustainable competitive advantage. The development of the right mix of resources does not come by chance, or just by original design, but by attention over time to refining the resource portfolio. A firm must analyse its market and competitors, looking for the types of positioning (price, quality/differentiation, innovation, service, techniques, partners, etc.) which can help the company to reach the objective of competitive advantage. If the process of resource development is well established then the advantage is likely to be more sustainable. The RBV then is a good conceptual framework to understand better context and competitors in dynamic markets, thus overcoming some of the limitations discussed earlier.

From a digital infrastructure perspective, the RBV suggests to managers and strategists the best way of adopting digital technologies. If a company is adopting any digital resources in the same way as its competitors, the digital resources are unlikely to have the characteristics of being rare or difficult to imitate or substitute. Lots of investment in digital resources and infrastructures are lost because businesses copy others and follow buzzwords from experts, instead of deeply understanding their own industry, their own strengths and weaknesses, as well as those of their competitors. We learn from the RBV that investments in digital infrastructure, as with all other resources, do not pay off if they are not driven by a strategic perspective of building the right mix of resources and capabilities. A development of this perspective is the concept of dynamic capabilities (Teece and Pisano, 1994), when the firm creates processes for constantly improving their competencies in various areas. A process for building dynamic capabilities starts with a good capacity of sensing the environment to discover opportunities for change and for refining the resource base so as, in turn, to improve and innovate products, processes. or business models.

From a managerial perspective, the concepts of competitive advantages and digital business strategies complement the discussion on business models and DBPs. The current race for AI technologies is a good example of the relevance of having the right digital business strategy. The public launching of OpenAI's generative ChatGPT services triggered a fast response from Google's Gemini and Microsoft's Copilot. These services are promising integration with other services and products (scope), entering large markets (scale), providing fast technology development and update through cloud services (speed), and integration to the needs of business tasks and operations (value creation and capture). The fast response of these companies is only possible because of their long-standing commitment to developing resources and capabilities, as proposed by RBV. This allows them to respond quickly to dynamic changes in the market – in this case, the launching of ChatGPT. The richness and flexibility of their digital infrastructures and platforms allow these companies to respond to the new entrant OpenAI, with innovation in products, services, processes, and business models (not forgetting the strategic partnership between Microsoft and OpenAI in this domain). Together, the combination of theories of business models (view on blocks and relationships), digital business strategies (scope, scale, speed, and value creation and capture), and the RBV (resources and capabilities) allow businesses to respond quickly to the challenges of competitors.

References

Barney, J. (1991). 'Firm resources and sustained competitive advantage', *Journal of Management,* 17(1), pp. 99–120.

Bharadwaj, A., El Sawy, O.A., Pavlou, P.A., and Venkatraman, N. (2013). 'Digital business strategy: Toward a next generation of insights', *MIS Quarterly*, 37(2), pp. 471–482.

Ciborra, C.U. (2002). *The Labyrinths of Information – Challenging the Wisdom of Systems*. Oxford: Oxford University Press.

Gawer, A. and Cusumano, M.A. (2013). 'Industry platforms and ecosystem innovation', *Journal of Product Innovation Management*, 31(3), pp. 417–433.

Osterwalder, A. and Pigneur, Y. (2010). *Business Model Generation: A Handbook for Visionaries, Game Changers, and Challengers*. Hoboken, NJ: John Wiley & Sons.

Osterwalder, A., Pigneur, Y., and Tucci, C.L. (2005). 'Clarifying business models: Origins, present, and future of the concept', *Communications of the Association for Information Systems*, 15, pp. 1–25.

Perkmann, M. and Spicer, A. (2010). 'What are business models? Developing a theory of performative representations', *Research in the Sociology of Organizations*, 29, pp. 269–279.

Rayna, T. and Striukova, L. (2016). '360° business model innovation: Toward an integrated view of business model innovation', *Research-Technology Management*, 59(3), pp. 21–28.

Teece, D. and Pisano, G. (1994). 'The dynamic capabilities of firms: An introduction', *Industrial and Corporate Change*, 3(3), pp. 537–556.

9 The World Wide Web (WWW)

Introduction

The World Wide Web (WWW, or just the Web) is an information infrastructure that runs on the Internet in layers on top of TCP/IP. It in turn underpins many of the most important, widely used, and influential digital services in the world – for example, most e-commerce uses the Web, as well as all manner of reference sources, government services, online education, video sharing, social media, and many more.

The Web started out from a simpler ambition, to make the information in documents stored on computers available to people across the Internet. From the outset, the Web was intended to allow access to many kinds of digital objects in many formats (text files, PDF files, spreadsheets, audio and video files, pictures, etc.) and at many locations.

A web page is a kind of digital document that normally contains both information (e.g., text, images, or audio) and links to other web objects (hyperlinks). Indeed, the core innovation the Web brought when it was first developed in the late 1980s and early 1990s was to allow any given web page to contain hyperlinks that lead to other documents and pages. A hyperlink is a direct link in one document or web page that embodies an IP address in the form of a URL (Uniform Resource Locator). Click on or select that link, and you move on to the referenced web page. We are very familiar with these hyperlinks in web pages, seeing them as either explicit and clickable URLs, e.g., https://en.wikipedia.org, or as embedded in a clickable word, phrase, picture, or icon.

By using hyperlinks, there is no prescribed or hierarchical set of files, folders, or directories that need to be traversed to go from one page/object to another – the Web is not like a neatly and consistently organised filing cabinet where specific information is located in a pre-designated place. Rather, the links are created by people as they come to understand their particular needs. It is the user (author) of any given page who sets and revises the hyperlinks and who generally can update a page as and when they want. Information is more dynamic and able to be reconfigured as and when it seems appropriate.

The implications of this freedom for authors and publishers, and for how we access and present information have been profound. Now everybody can be an author, and (potentially) reach almost everybody else in the world. The digital economics of the written word, music, and visual materials has profoundly changed too. The amount of information in circulation in the world has exploded and much of this is now accessed 'for free' – for example, do you buy a newspaper, or do you now access news 'for free', leaving aside the adverts and the data extracted to track your interests?

The WWW is a digital infrastructure that supports a set of global information services. Well-known examples of such services are Wikipedia, YouTube, online newspapers, and social media sites like Facebook. It is an infrastructure, serving as a shared resource that underpins

DOI: 10.4324/9781003385578-9

the provision of all manner of information services to billions of individual users who provide (post) and request (browse for) information every day. In his early writing, Tim Berners Lee, the Web's founding father, describes it as a 'Global Information System' (Berners-Lee, 1996). But infrastructure is probably a better or more accurate word to describe it because of its emergence and development over time, and its role as a standardised service to support multiple different users and uses. In any case, from now on we will just call it the Web.

WWW architecture and protocols

Like any other infrastructure, the Web has its own architecture – described as a client-server architecture – and its own protocols. And, of course, this architecture is layered – layered on top of the Internet, and layered within the Web as extra functionality is added 'on top' of basic functionality – for example, as security is added on top of basic information transmission.

The Web's architecture is based on two types of hosts – clients and servers, linked together by the Internet, so of course using TCP and IP. Clients are computers that *request* information, and servers supply or *serve* it. Your computer is a client computer when you browse the Web, and depending on what you click on in a document or a web page, your computer then exchanges messages with the associated server to gather information from it. Both servers and clients run software that supports their role. Client computers run browser software, such as Edge, Safari, Chrome, or Firefox. Server computers, which hold web pages and other information resources, use server software. Indeed, the majority of web servers across the world use just one particular type of server software – the Apache HTTP server. This is an open-source product, freely available and maintained by volunteers in a collaborative effort.

The Web uses the Internet as its means of passing messages (data). Then, on top of TCP/IP, the Web has its own specific protocols and data structures to support its requirements. Two of these protocols that you are probably a bit familiar with are the protocols HTTP and HTTPS. HTTP stands for Hypertext Transfer Protocol and is the protocol that takes a URL (as typed in your browser or clicked on a page you are viewing) and sends a request message across the Internet to the indicated host server (a 'Get' message). In response, the server sends back the indicated web page which hopefully contains the information you want. The HTTPS is Hypertext Transfer Protocol Secure, and does the same connection, but with encryption.

So, if you click on www.ibm.com, a Get message is sent to IBM's web server (a host on the Internet), and the text of their home page is sent back to your client software (browser). You then see it on the screen. IBM's home page is full of text, images, and other hyperlinks/URLs so you can navigate onwards into the IBM website to find what you want by clicking on these hyperlinks. You could also use the 'search box' on the screen to find specific items on IBM's website (we discuss more general search engines like Google below).

In the familiar jargon, we 'surf' the Web – an ocean of information. Sticking with the IBM example, you might assume that you 'go to' their website, but it would be a bit more correct to say that it (or a bit of it) 'comes to you', as the text and the layout information, including pictures (i.e., a web page), is sent back over the Internet to your client computer and your client software. HTTP and HTTPS are the protocols that manage this request and send traffic.

So, what is the difference between HTTP and HTTPS protocols? HTTPS does in general the same job as HTTP but the added S indicates Secure – e.g., that the traffic the protocol passes to and from is encrypted. Some older sources describe the S as meaning 'Secure Socket Layer', a separate protocol for encryption, but this specific protocol is often not used today, being superseded by other better ones.

There is one last bit of this (rather simplified) model that we need to add. When the IBM home page is sent to you it is sent as some raw text and images *plus* some extra information to say how these should be displayed. So, to grossly simplify, when you click on www.ibm.com, and after HTTP has done its job of a Get, you see the home page with the words '*Fortify your data, systems and enterprise with security AI*' at the top of the screen (that was in August 2024). These words are in big black letters, but the text is sent separately from the instructions as to how large the letters should be and in what colour. The words and how they should be displayed – their size, colour, font, positioning, and perhaps associated hyperlink – are all coded separately in the HTTP message that arrives at your computer.

It is then your browser that puts it all together (renders it) on the screen. If you have a different browser on a different device (say a smartphone), then the way it looks may well be different. Remember too, if you 'go to' the IBM website in two years' time the website will still be there, but its content will be different. Indeed, the home page for IBM is probably updated more than once per day, which is central to the whole idea of the Web as a dynamic and constantly changing information infrastructure.

If you select the text on the IBM home page, right-click, and select 'Inspect' from the menu that pops up (for instance, using a Windows computer and Chrome browser) you see in a parallel window the actual text that IBM's server sent back to your browser. It is messy! And we are sure that most of you will not make much sense of what you see. However, all the codes are there to convey how the page should look and behave. They are written (coded) in HTML. Today any word processor you use can probably save a file in HTML format (e.g., with HTML codes), and that file can be opened and 'read' by any browser.

HTML is central to how the Web works, allowing an author freedom to show how a web page should look and then allowing the client software (browser) to make the best effort to achieve this look. As you may have noted, this has echoes of how the Internet also works on a 'best effort' basis, and it allows the two ends of a communication to 'negotiate' when things break down or become difficult – think of TCP.

The use of a client-server architecture for the Web, and the use of HTML, are both clever choices that distribute the work of getting and displaying information between the server that finds the page requested and sends it as a standard set of data including text and HTML mark-up, and the client who does the work of rendering the data for the screen of a specific device as best it can. HTML is a global standard, so if the server sticks to HTML then any client machine or software that knows HTML works. Again, we might see this as a return to the logic of the early era of the Internet when architecture was found that could support all kinds of machines and

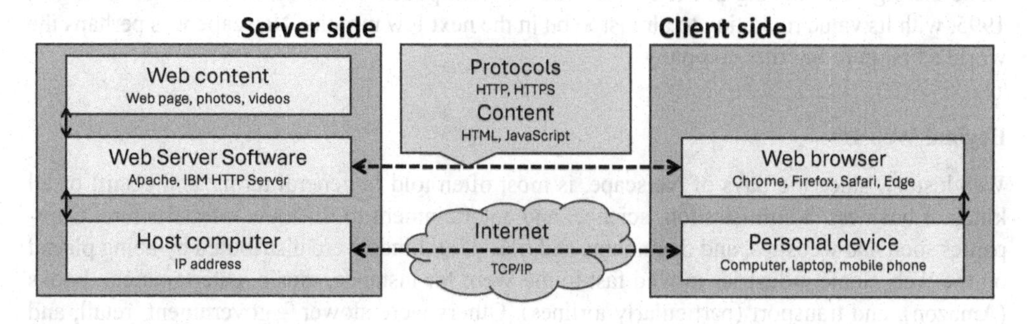

Figure 9.1 Client and server interface

adapt to them as they developed and grew. We should also note that HTML has gone through different versions over time, but these are generally 'backwards compatible' so using a new version does not make all websites using older versions inoperable.

Figure 9.1 shows a basic web architecture (its structure). It is, however, limited to the model of browser (with human user) and server (machine with web pages). But we could expand this figure in two ways. First to include the search engines that are a central part of the Web, and second to include the many machine-to-machine interactions that the Web supports (including the search engine web crawlers). More generally, when we think about the architecture of any infrastructure we need to look at the fundamental relations of the element involved and that usually means looking into the variety of exchanges, processes, and functionalities.

History of the WWW

The origins of the Web are associated with one person in particular, Tim Berners-Lee. In the 1980s he was a computer scientist working at CERN (European Organization for Nuclear Research) – the large European particle physics research laboratory on the border of Switzerland and France. He developed an early ancestor of the Web called Enquire to meet some local needs for documenting the extensive IT facilities of CERN. After some modest success, he developed his ideas further into the form of the Web we see today; that is, of documents (pages) that contain hyperlinks that lead to other documents (pages). It is as simple as that. Of course, choosing to make the URL hyperlinks a kind of IP address meant that any page could link to any other page anywhere on the Internet – anywhere with an IP address and an Internet connection.

Still, it was not an immediate success. In chapter 8 of Ryan (2010), you can read about the lack of interest that there was for the Web at CERN. Indeed, Berners-Lee continued on with the project despite his bosses shelving it on two occasions. The first 'browser' was written by an intern on a short posting at CERN. The major breakthrough came when CERN was persuaded to put their telephone directory on the new Web as an HTML document – not the most exciting project perhaps, but a foot in the door.

The Web really started to take off when more browsers were written, browsers that could run on common computers of that time. It was not until 1993 that browsers (client software) were available for most common desktop computers – an early one for the IBM PC was called Cello. But the big commercial success was a browser called Netscape which emerged from a US government research centre, The National Centre for Supercomputing Applications (NCSA), and their early browser Mosaic. The Netscape company was one of the first Internet start-ups that made the big time, raising about $1.4bn when it went public on the stock exchange in August 1995, with its value rocketing to almost $3bn in the next few months. Netscape was perhaps the world's first pure Internet company.

Beyond Web 1.0

Web history, since the days of Netscape, is most often told in general terms as the shift of all kinds of business, administration, science, and entertainment to this new infrastructure. Companies soon had websites, and documents and files of all kinds were distributed by being placed on the Web. Some industries moved fast to the Web: for instance, music, entertainment, books (Amazon), and transport (particularly airlines). Others were slower – government, retail, and financial services – often for good reasons (e.g., accessibility and security concerns). However, there is a more analytical perspective we should understand, which is the shift from the early web of static documents on organisations' websites linked by hyperlinks but with limited 'search' capacity, to today's Web.

The shifting and evolution of the Web are often summarised in the idea of an early, simpler, static Web 1.0, and a new, different, 'upgraded' Web 2.0 (also known as the social web). Ideas of Web 1.0 and 2.0 have been around since about 2004 (read O'Reilly, 2005, and 'Web 2.0', Wikipedia, 2024). As we moved from the initial Web 1.0, which focused on documents, to Web 2.0, individuals became empowered to express themselves and organise communities and social groupings. Of course, there is no one moment when it shifted, and it is not really about the Web changing in technical terms (though that does happen – infrastructures evolve), but rather our ideas of what we could do with it changed, as well as the speed of data transmission and the access to the Internet.

Focusing on these changes, in Web 2.0, for example, people interact more with each other, generating more of the content they consume online (user-generated content), e.g., in blogs, vlogs, or social media. Another powerful example of user-generated content is the online encyclopaedia we cite many times across the book, Wikipedia, where the content is the product of many enthusiastic volunteers. More generally, using Web 2.0 people can join in specific interest groups (digital communities) which may transcend traditional geographic boundaries and can include interests ranging from politics to stamp collecting to 1930s baseball statistics. People also expect to comment on others' efforts, contribute to them, or use them for their own purposes, for example on photo sharing sites like Instagram.

Some of the changes for Web 2.0 are in the services that the Web can offer. In Web 2.0 there are many more transactions, such as the kinds of transactions (and security) needed to have electronic commerce. These include, of course, financial services that let people pay online and help them trust websites they may have never heard of before. More generally, we can say that the Web 2.0 is a Web where different services (or servers) can interact together to deliver new kinds of service for Web users. E-commerce again demonstrates an example of how a website that sells clothes links to PayPal for secure payment services, and to a courier company to deliver the parcel. It may also ask its customers to comment on the goods it offers and give positive or negative reviews of specific products. All this happens on the Web, in careful interactions among the clothes retailer's separate companies and their clients, each providing separate parts of the service you want.

Linked to the Web, there also grew up a vibrant industry supporting web searches. At first these were sites (such as the original Yahoo) that kept lists of useful and relevant websites – a kind of directory (to some degree copying the logic of libraries, in which a catalogue would define the relevance of content). But this approach has given way to search engines, like Google or Bing, which perform dynamic searches and indexing on the Web, and on this basis allow people to do their own ad-hoc searches. The way that Google and other search engines work is complex and involves continuous Web 'crawling' to obtain information for a huge index of web content. One other key aspect of a search engine is not only to index web pages according to their content, but also to 'rank' them by how many other pages link to them. A page that contains content on topic x and is referenced by many other pages is judged to be more interesting and is thus shown towards the top of the list in a web search.

Most search engines are fairly literal, even a bit dim. They take words and phrases and index the Web on this basis. But there are many people, including Tim Berners-Lee, who are trying to create a different kind of Web – the Semantic Web, also known as Web 3.0 or the data web – and able to have a better sense of the meaning of Web content beyond text strings. For example, in the case of a video, or a picture, or a poem it is quite difficult for a web search engine to analyse 'what it is about', other than from the title. But in the case of a Semantic Web, with the associated infrastructures (e.g., standardised codes able to identify meaning), this might be possible and take us closer to the concept of the Web as a global 'brain'. The simplest approach has been by adding metadata to objects to allow search engines to understand the content, making the data more interpretable by the machine. For this to happen, content providers must add to their content the Web 3.0 standards, as approved by the W3C. These standards embed codes into Web content, allowing machines to uncover the meaning. In theory, the Semantic Web would allow a further level of automation in handling content. Important to say that although we call this Web 3.0, the concept of a semantic network was born in the 1960s (see 'Semantic Web', on Wikipedia, 2024), and later Tim Berners-Lee adapted the idea to the needs of the WWW, proposing the Semantic Web.

With AI, the capacity to understand Web content in a more intelligent way is changing by the day with the adoption of artificial intelligence solutions for managing the interpretation of digital content. AI can be used to analyse and interpret unstructured contents, enhancing the quality of the search not only through a better understanding of the meaning but also through a better understanding of the user's preferences and contexts, to find the right information for the specific user. With the development of AI for identifying meaning in texts, images, videos, tables, and graphs, and creating knowledge maps and clustering of ideas around meaning, Web searches will improve substantially, moving from lists of relevant links to summaries of relevant understanding and knowledge. Web 3.0 requires standards and coding of content, which are not necessary for the development of AI solutions with the aim of reaching similar goals (although we are still in the early days of this development too). It is important to say that we still have space for regular search, as the content provided by AI interfaces (e.g., ChatGPT, Gemini, and Copilot) aims to provide answers, summarised from a large dataset. We still may prefer to have access to the original content, and to interact with the content directly through links rather than through information mediated by machine learning algorithms (see further discussion in chapter 14).

Web engineering

The Web has become a rather complex infrastructure – at least in technical terms – and has gone far beyond simple HTTP protocol and the HTML-based pages of Web 1.0. Today's websites, full of videos, animations, secure financial transactions, encrypted data, and linked to sophisticated and intelligent services, require a high level of knowledge and skill to produce and to keep operational seven days a week and 24 hours a day for thousands or even millions of users. Thus, a discipline of Web engineering has emerged to embrace such skills and techniques.

Many organisations today are so reliant on their website that it is as important and central to their survival as the older 'internal' information systems. If the payroll program fails for a couple of days, it can be tolerated, but if the website is down for three hours it might cause chaos. How long could an airline, an e-commerce company like Amazon or Baidu, or a logistics company like DHL stay in business without a website? And how long could a country's government survive if its key websites were inoperative? So, Web engineering is not just about knowing how to build web services well, but also how to keep them running and respond to problems.

Problems, of course, come in many shapes and forms, but one class of problems are those associated with malicious attacks on web infrastructures. In chapter 5, we discussed an attack on the Internet in 2016 that disabled a part of the DNS. Reacting to such attacks (e.g., being prepared to move the DNS service to other services), or to maintain parallel websites on different servers, is part of the remit of Web engineering and a response to the Web being increasingly seen as a critical digital infrastructure.

References

Berners-Lee, T. (1996). *The World Wide Web: Past, Present and Future*. Available at: https://www.w3.org/People/Berners-Lee/1996/ppf.html (Accessed: 12 February 2024).

O'Reilly, T.P. (2005). *What is Web 2.0?* Available at: http://www.oreilly.com/pub/a/web2/archive/what-is-web-20.html (Accessed: 16 March 2024).

Ryan, J. (2010). *A History of the Internet and the Digital Future*. London: Reaktion Books.

'Semantic Web' (2024). *Wikipedia*. Available at: https://en.wikipedia.org/wiki/Semantic_Web (Accessed: 12 April 2024).

'Web 2.0' (2024). *Wikipedia*. Available at: https://en.wikipedia.org/wiki/Web_2.0 (Accessed: 16 March 2024).

10 The cloud and cloud services

Introduction

In the last 20 years, the cloud has become the basis for almost all computerised functions from core business systems of multinationals to the apps on our phones. The terms 'cloud' or 'cloud computing' (Wikipedia, 2024) are used to describe this dominant business computing architecture in which informational and computational resources are accessed as services via digital networks. From this book's perspective, the key idea behind the cloud is on-demand and pay-by-use services. We are less focused on the changed IT functions and responsibilities at the organisational level. For this reason, we mostly use the term 'cloud services' in the discussion here rather than cloud computing.

In this chapter we discuss the origins of the cloud and how it has evolved. We present a typification of cloud services and discuss their applications, advantages, and risks. The chapter focuses on aspects of cloud services relevant to business innovation. The cloud has many benefits for individuals too, such as access to software, storage, and backup for content, collaborative space, and access everywhere, but these topics as applied to the personal use of cloud services are mostly out of the scope of this chapter.

The network is the cloud

Businesses contract and purchase 'cloud services' from 'cloud providers', generally third-party companies. Providers offer their services to multiple customers drawing on their pool of sharable resources which may be physical, such as servers, data storage or networks, or be access to specific applications, data resources, or processing facilities. Examples could include email such as Gmail, storage such as Dropbox, core business software such as Salesforce or SAP enterprise resource planning (ERP), and access to AI resources.

The cloud approach is valid only because of the existence of a universal digital network that allows access to these cloud services, predominantly the Internet. The second fundamental element is an aggregated set of hardware, software, or data that can be dynamically shared (on-demand) by multiple users. Such services, as digital products, can then be combined together in accordance with individual needs and to serve specific functions. The focus is on resource pooling, an important step towards achieving economies of scale and scope (discussed in chapter 6).

The US National Institute of Standards and Technology (NIST) defined cloud computing in these terms:

> Cloud computing is a model for enabling ubiquitous, convenient, on-demand network access to a shared pool of configurable computing resources (e.g., networks, servers,

DOI: 10.4324/9781003385578-10

storage, applications, and services) that can be rapidly provisioned and released with minimal management effort or service provider interaction.

(NIST, 2011)

Cloud services are part of the applications layer as presented in the layered model discussed in chapter 4. As such, they follow communication standards and reflect all the other generic characteristics of digital infrastructures. The possibility of combining services from different cloud providers significantly increases the potential for innovation in line with ideas of generativity.

Cloud users determine the volume of services they need at any time. To achieve this, providers need to offer rapid and dynamic elasticity of supply, which is easier to achieve with resource pooling. Providers also need to be able to measure the amount of service used in order to bill the user. Providing cloud services is indeed big business with vast revenues. Statista Market Insights (Statista, 2023) estimated that in 2023 the global revenues in the public cloud segment were in the region of US$595 billion up from US$135 billion in 2016, led by Amazon Web Service (AWS), Microsoft, Google, and Salesforce (16%, 14%, 5%, and 5% of the market share, respectively) (Statista, 2023).

The emergence of the cloud

Although cloud computing and the cloud are relatively new terms, the concept is old. Campbell-Kelly (2009) argues that the first cloud service was offered in 1932, when IBM in America opened a service bureau offering the use of punched-card electric accounting machines (EAMs). Companies using this service would prepare the punch cards themselves and bring them to IBM and use IBM's EAMs to undertake their calculations. However, perhaps a more relevant starting point is when, in the mid-1960s, mainframe computers became more available and some companies who had acquired such machines started offering remote (by network) and 'walk-in' access to their computers. The business model was simple: companies with resources to buy and maintain mainframes could let out their 'spare' computing power to those who could not afford such an investment. It was not long before specialist companies, including the dominant computer manufacturers such as IBM, started offering such 'pay-by-use' services. Even large companies in this era preferred this approach and avoided the large capital cost and managerial overheads of purchasing and running their own machines.

By the 1980s the market for these first versions of what we today call the cloud came under pressure as more companies could afford new and powerful minicomputers and were moving rapidly to exploit the new personal desktop computers. The revolutionary IBM desktop PC was introduced in 1984. It was in the middle of the 1990s, that the idea of cloud computing and cloud services re-emerged in something like its current form. This was a time when communication costs were going down, in large part because of the Internet, and at the same time the management of computing infrastructure was becoming more complex and expensive, particularly given issues of rapid technical innovation, concerns over reliability, and increasing focus on security (Campbell-Kelly, 2009).

From the mid-1990s, contracting cloud services rapidly became an important form of outsourcing, i.e., the contracting of third parties for specific business processes and operations for a company. Cloud-service models (discussed later in the chapter) are often presented and evaluated in the context of outsourcing, although this is a broader concept and companies may outsource many other types of business operations. Taking a cloud route, as a form of outsourcing, means that instead of managing servers, storage, and software inside the organisation, third-party companies are contracted to provide these services through the cloud.

Cloud computing has since then become the dominant architecture for business computing. To achieve this dominance, it has had to evolve and reach new levels of service quality. One of the primary risks to service quality is the reliability of the network and basic computing resources. More robust hardware and software optimised to deliver on-demand services has helped cloud providers to reduce their downtime and increase their ability to respond as demand changes. At the same time, Internet backbones and ISPs (Internet Service Providers) have had to improve the quality and the resilience of their services, for example ability to cope with extreme weather, hardware accidents, software vulnerabilities, and network failure. The Internet has also become significantly faster (broadband, fibre, 5G), available via all manner of mobile devices, and cheaper.

In the core computing technology, there have been improvements in the efficiency of servers through new hardware architecture optimised for cloud operations and software virtualisation techniques, which allow arrays of servers to be split into virtual machines appropriate to the needs of individual users. It has also become easier and cheaper to duplicate and backup data, increasing the security of cloud services.

The end result of all these adaptations and improvements across the cloud is that economies of scale, scope, and positive externalities increase the demand for cloud services (as discussed in chapter 6). Another outcome is that the cloud-service market has come to be dominated by a few very large firms which have invested heavily in their infrastructures. Big cloud-service companies have built very efficient and large data centres and server farms, located where energy is cheaper and perhaps greener – normally remote places where land and building costs are also cheaper.

From a user's view, the basic arguments for adopting cloud services have been in terms of increasing operational efficiency, better quality of service, allowing management to focus on the main business, and reducing capital expenditure (CapEx). Cloud services are scalable and can meet peaks and troughs of demand thus shifting from CapEx to more flexible operational expenses (OpEx) which are matched to the business volume. But perhaps the most significant benefits of all are based around the concept of generativity: with cloud service, new ideas can be tried out and if appropriate rapidly scaled up. Such innovation may be in areas of new products and services, new business processes, or new business models.

Types of cloud computing

This section discusses the three types of cloud-service models generally recognised in the literature – Software as a Service (SaaS), Platform as a Service (PaaS), and Infrastructure as a Service (IaaS). The section also introduces the concept of cloud computing deployment models (private cloud, community cloud, public cloud, and hybrid cloud).

Software as a Service (SaaS)

In a SaaS contract, the customer has access to software (applications) running on a cloud infrastructure. Access is through client devices, typically web browsers, apps, or other dedicated programs. The consumer does not manage or control the underlying cloud infrastructure (network, servers, operating systems, storage, and applications), but they may get to define the configurations of user-specific applications. Google Gmail, Microsoft Office 365, and social media are good examples of SaaS as are most of the information and gaming apps on your phone. For instance, you can open your Microsoft Outlook email or Teams in a browser or in an app installed on your computer, but the content and the management of emails or videos are all in Microsoft's cloud. You can configure the interface a bit to meet your needs, but you cannot change the way the application is run by Microsoft.

SaaS has profoundly changed the way organisations manage their computing. Two decades ago or more, if a company needed a software package, it would need to buy a license, the cost of which would vary in accordance with the maximum number of users proposed. Most vendors would require a minimum number of licenses to be bought by a company. This business model was a barrier in particular for small and medium-sized enterprises (SMEs) without resources for the up-front investment or because the maintenance of the software and its integration with existing systems would be too expensive. Today SaaS is often offered in a freemium business model. This means that users can try out new services at minimal up-front cost. If their experience with the free service is good then they can move up to a version that costs money but offers more sophisticated or powerful functionality. In the consumer software market, free SaaS usually includes adverts while paid versions are ad-free.

An often-cited example of a successful business SaaS is Salesforce. This company offers a customer relationship management (CRM) product/service suitable for companies from the smallest to the largest (Salesforce, 2024). In the past, CRM software would be too expensive for SMEs to buy. With Salesforce as SaaS, an SME company can start using a professional CRM service from the beginning. As the company grows, the more features of Salesforce it may use, all on a pay-as-you-go basis. Salesforce also offers other associated cloud services, including APIs (application programming interfaces, as discussed in chapter 7) for developers to create plug-ins to extend or tailor the service, and, in the case of APIs, to manage interactions between companies and customers on social media. Salesforce also integrates AI in its platform: the Einstein service. They suggest that this can generate real-time insights based on the analysis of customer data, automate emails, and provide assistants (chatbots) to handle questions from customers and identify leads for new sales.

Platform as a Service (PaaS)

In a PaaS contract, the customer can create their own applications using programming languages, libraries, services, and tools provided by cloud services. The consumer does not manage or control the underlying cloud infrastructure, but does have control of the deployed applications and possibly configuration settings for the application-hosting environment (see IaaS below). PaaS is specifically for application developers, those who need software platforms to design new software and interfaces and thereby create new products and services. PaaS allows application developers large and small to create new software without the purchase and maintenance of hardware and software.

Microsoft Azure is a PaaS platform which provides programming languages, tools, and frameworks for developers (e.g., Microsoft Azure Pipelines) (Azure, 2024). Microsoft Azure also offers the infrastructure to host developed websites and apps and to manage the data necessary for a developed application to enter the market. Similarly, Google App Engine offers a PaaS platform for web applications which can be also hosted in its data centres. For small users, the Google service is provided for free (Google Cloud, 2024). Similarly Amazon Web Services offers the AWS Elastic Beanstalk, which is a service for automatically deploying and scaling web applications, freeing developers from building their own infrastructure (AWS, 2024b).

Start-ups can benefit from PaaS. Instead of using their capital to invest in a technical platform, they can use services in the cloud (pay-as-you-go) and save their money for other aspects of the businesses. With access to such resources, small and medium businesses may be able to enter markets and compete with more powerful and established providers. But it is not only small organisations that see benefits from shifting from CapEx to OpEx and many large businesses use PaaS as the basis for their development efforts.

Infrastructure as a Service (IaaS)

In an IaaS contract, the customer has access to processing, storage, networks, and other computing resources where they can deploy and run their own software and offer their own cloud services. The customer does not control the cloud physical infrastructure, but chooses which components of the service and service levels are required. Large companies such as AWS, Microsoft Azure, and GCP (Google Cloud Platform) are dominant providers of IaaS, though there are many other smaller or more specialised providers. Examples of IaaS include offering high-performance computing power to run software to solve complex problems or train AI models (see chapter 14). More simply, a customer may want the provider to host their website and increase its reliability and security. Other IaaS use cases might be to test new applications and websites in cloud environments before committing investments in a customer's own infrastructure.

An often-discussed example of IaaS is the partnership between AWS and Netflix (AWS, 2024a). As a video content creation and streaming service, Netflix needs very reliable digital infrastructures in order to create their product (films), and to guarantee a high-quality experience for their streaming customers. However, this poses a dilemma for Netflix in defining how big this digital infrastructure should be. There are moments at which not many people are streaming videos, and others at which the demand is very high. If Netflix invests in the infrastructure to cover the peaks of demand, this would be sub-optimum, as many resources would not be used for periods of time. On the other hand, if Netflix cannot cope with peak periods, customers will be disappointed and perhaps change streaming providers. Working with AWS as the supplier of IaaS solves Netflix's problem. It gets flexible access to computing capacity, storage, and network bandwidth on the basis of demand. Netflix does not need to concern itself with how much infrastructure is necessary. Rather, they just pay AWS to provide the needed resources, being relieved of the need to manage their own infrastructure.

Utilising IaaS from large cloud providers is the choice of many companies in digital industries and e-commerce when they either do not know when they might need more capacity, or they need more capacity but only in certain periods. An e-commerce service, for instance, may need much more server power close to holiday periods when people buy presents for each other.

Cloud deployment models

Most often when cloud computing is cited as a digital infrastructure, the concept refers to the public cloud provided for open shared use by any person or company through the Internet. This infrastructure is owned, managed, and operated around the world by businesses, academic organisations, and governments, but the overall intent is to be available to the general public.

There are, however, other cloud deployment models. In the case of private cloud, the cloud infrastructure is provided for exclusive use by a single organisation perhaps comprising multiple business units. A private cloud may be owned, managed, and operated by the organisation, a third party, or some combination of them. An example might be a private cloud run for the benefit of a large global banking group. Similarly, a community cloud is provided for exclusive use by a specific community from organisations that have shared interests (e.g., security requirements). Again, it may be owned, managed, and operated by one or more of the organisations in the community, a third party, or some combination of them. An example of a community cloud might be Weathercloud, (Weathercloud.net/en), a service for sharing meteorological data, models, etc. A hybrid cloud is then some composition of two or more distinct cloud infrastructures (private, community, or public) that are bound together by standardised or proprietary technology that enables data and application portability.

Cloud computing drivers

As stated at the start of this chapter, the cloud has become a fundamental part of the architecture of most business and consumer computing. So clearly there are advantages in cloud architectures which can explain why this digital infrastructure is so relevant for all sorts of organisations. Statista Market Insights points to three key drivers of growth in cloud services: technology adoption and innovation, the establishment of new services, and cybersecurity concerns. Their data suggest that companies do perceive the cloud from a business innovation perspective and go on to exploit it as an opportunity to reach the market quickly with better products. The fostering of innovation, together with an ability to ride new trends into new markets, is important and the cloud helps. Note that this is not a cost-based argument but one based on innovation and change.

The ten main providers of cloud computing (AWS, Microsoft Azure, Google Cloud Platform, Salesforce, IBM Cloud, Alibaba Cloud, SAP, Adobe Cloud, Oracle Cloud, and ServiceNow) (Statista, 2023) are in a strong competition to be providers of smart and creative digital services. As the interest in artificial intelligence applications has grown, most have brought to the market new AI offerings. AWS launched the Amazon SageMaker for developers to train their AI models, similar to the machine learning services provided by Microsoft's Azure and Google's Gemini. Through these cloud services (among many others), companies across a range of industries are entering the space of AI innovation even though they may not have resources for developing their own technical platforms.

Without cloud services, a small game development company, for instance, could not risk launching a new game in the market afraid either of not having enough users to pay for the investments in digital infrastructure, or having too many users but limited digital infrastructure capacity. This is a dilemma for the innovator: how much money to invest in digital infrastructure to accommodate potential customers? With cloud services though, the innovator can just launch the game using one or more cloud-service providers and wait to see what happens. The more paying users, the higher the revenue, thus more cash flow to pay the cloud providers. If users do not come, the game developer is not left with unrequired assets either.

The case of launching a game is also an example of scalability. Through cloud services, users have scalable computing resources on demand: the greater the demand, the greater the use of the system, and vice-versa (elasticity). Although no cloud provider has infinite capacity, from the individual user's perspective, cloud computing capacity is vast if not infinite and the limiting factor may be bandwidth. Knowing scalable resources are available, managers can spend less time estimating necessary computing resources, and instead focus on other aspects of the business, such as innovating and fostering sales – as in the example of Netflix using AWS cloud services.

At a more operational level, cloud computing often brings the promise of reducing costs, even if cutting costs is not the main objective. The economies of scale gained by the cloud-service providers are passed (at least in part) to the customers of these services. On top of cost saving for given levels of use, there is the element of speed in moving from the concept of an innovation to the working prototype to the product to markets. For some business cases, cloud computing may also reduce the carbon footprint of organisations if large server farms are more energy-efficient than other arrangements.

Moving business activities to the cloud can also reshape organisations' internal structures. For example, it makes it easier for staff to access resources and do their jobs from their homes and their mobile devices. This gives greater flexibility in the way work is done, staff are recruited and managed, and business conducted. At its best, this flexibility can promote better collaboration within and between companies, teams, and professional groups. Think, for instance, of the benefits of being able to collaborate with work colleagues using services such as Slack, Google Drive, or Microsoft Teams. However, it would be foolish to just assume that this kind of flexibility and related business benefits are a simple bonus for all organisations or all employees. We learned during the COVID pandemic and in the period after that there are many issues and problems associated with online working practices and 'working from home' (WFH). The technology works, but it is no panacea, and for some people the lack of face-to-face contact is a serious impediment to productive work and to mental health.

The adoption of cloud computing can be argued to support organisations in improving their capacity for managing complexity and change. In areas of technology management, cloud architectures can be a powerful way to reduce the need to understand digital infrastructures so managers can focus on the core business. The rapid rates of change across digital technologies, for example from AI, imply risks for the average user organisation. Cloud services from established providers can be seen as a kind of insurance against too much such risk – a way to keep in touch without over-committing. However, managing in the face of complexity and risk does require some understanding as discussed in the next section.

Cloud computing challenges

Despite the advantages and drivers set out in the previous section, there are challenges and risks for cloud-service users to consider. There are three main problems to think through when considering the business case for cloud services. The first is at the strategic level: does the use of cloud services align with the business objectives? This may not occur if there is a lack of understanding of the cloud options or of the business case, or both. The task of managers – often senior managers – is to build this strategic alignment. A second problem happens if there are no realistic estimates of the costs and benefits of cloud services, including alternative providers. This may occur due to the lack of information about the available services and their business models or the lack of understanding of one's own business and thereby inability to establish a credible return on investment (ROI). The third problem may be found in obstacles to getting the promised benefits (when failure happens in the 'benefits realisation' phase). A good strategic alignment, and a credible ROI, may be pointless if the benefits envisaged are not achieved.

Another set of challenges posed by cloud services relates to the compliance with regulations and laws, particularly in relation to data management. These laws vary in accordance with the country and international agreements. For instance, the Data Protection Act in the United Kingdom enforces data sovereignty for defined sets of data, and the European Union's General Data Protection Regulation (GDPR) defines how personal data must be managed across the EU. Thus, before deciding to use cloud services, an organisation needs to understand the relevant regulations and laws, in order to be sure that storing and managing data in the cloud is not breaching the legislation. One important aspect is the auditability of services. Can the service provider show that they respect legislation in different jurisdictions? It may be that specific kinds of data cannot be moved offshore, for instance, but does the cloud provider have servers inside the country and can they verify this? Cloud providers are responsible for the security of their own servers. However, if a data breach happens there is a risk of reputational damage to both the provider and the user.

Evaluating and choosing the right cloud provider is thus crucial. This will include considering the credibility and reputation of potential providers, and clarifying fundamental questions about the service level proposed, including the reliability of services (outages), the methods to measure usage (metering), the capacity of the supplier to maintain their investment in infrastructure, and the availability of customer support. An unclear pricing method is a potential area of conflict between users and providers of cloud services. Another key question when choosing cloud services is data portability. In other words, if a customer decides to change cloud provider a few years on, or move data to be managed internally, will the transfer be easy and in an open, standard format? The user certainly does not want the risk of lock-in – where the user cannot leave the service providers without losing their data, or cannot operate with multiple providers simultaneously.

References

AWS (2024a). 'Case studies', Amazon Web Services. Available at: https://aws.amazon.com/solutions/case-studies/innovators/netflix/ (Accessed: 24 March 2024).

AWS (2024b). 'AWS Elastic Beanstalk Documentation', Amazon Web Services. Available at: https://docs.aws.amazon.com/elastic-beanstalk/ (Accessed: 24 March 2024).

Azure (2024). 'Build in the cloud with an Azure free account', Microsoft Azure. Available at: https://azure.microsoft.com/en-gb/free/search/ (Accessed: 24 March 2024).

Campbell-Kelly, M. (2009). 'Historical reflections: The rise, fall and resurrection of Software as a Service', *Communications of ACM*, 52(5), pp. 28–30.

'Cloud computing' (2024). *Wikipedia*. Available at: https://en.wikipedia.org/wiki/Cloud_computing (Accessed: 16 March 2024).

Google Cloud (2024). 'App Engine', Google Cloud. Available at: https://cloud.google.com/appengine (Accessed: 24 March 2024).

Khan, F.A. and Anderson, J.M. (2021). *Digital Transformation Using Emerging Technologies: A CxO's Guide to Transform Your Organisation*. UK: Amazon.

NIST (2011). 'Final version of NIST cloud computing definition published', NIST (National Institute of Standards and Technology, US Department of Commerce). Available at: https://www.nist.gov/news-events/news/2011/10/final-version-nist-cloud-computing-definition-published (Accessed: 16 March 2024).

Salesforce (2024). 'What's new at Salesforce?', Salesforce. Available at: https://www.salesforce.com/uk/ (Accessed: 24 March 2024).

Statista (2023). 'Market insights: Technology, public cloud', Statista. Available at: https://www.statista.com/outlook/tmo/public-cloud/worldwide (Accessed: 24 March 2024).

11 Mobile technology

Introduction

One of the key characteristics of contemporary society is the presence of mobile technology in our hands. From very rich to very poor countries, the mobile phone is there, supporting communication and interaction. For some, it is the device of choice for doing business and working remotely. For others, it is the best way of keeping in contact with family and friends, and sharing nice memories. Some spend lots of time playing games and watching movies on these devices. Others see an opportunity for increasing engagement with customers and sales. All the many functionalities that are available through mobile technologies have become possible with the development of wireless networks, smart user interfaces, and compact computing for processing large volumes of data in small devices.

The more capacity the mobile device has to process data locally, and the more speed it has to transfer data, the more the operating system evolves to support more services, and the more developers are interested in providing apps to run on top of the operating system. Through this path, mobiles have evolved from being just phones and pagers (to send short texts only), to become devices with huge computing capacities, with GPS, Internet browsers, and broadband connections. Today mobile operating systems have evolved to become platforms for all sorts of apps – specialised software applications which run on mobile phones and tablets.

Thinking from the perspective of the Zittrain's (2008) layer model (chapter 4), there are many elements embedded in each layer of the current mobile infrastructure. The final result we have in our hands is a combination of hardware, software, and a collection of services, supported by corporate institutions and regulations. All parts of this complex infrastructure of layers upon layers rely on communication standards which connect each element to each other, allowing each part to develop with a degree of independence from the whole system, at the same time that the development of some elements enables other advancements in other parts of the infrastructure.

As discussed in previous chapters, digital infrastructures support each other to a great extent. There is a self-reinforcing feedback mechanism through the interaction of mobile technologies with other digital infrastructures (the Internet, the Web, the cloud and cloud services, social media, the metaverse, and artificial intelligence), which together attract more people to make mobile devices the main channel for access. The reason is simple: there is no value in a device without content, in the same way that the value of the content is lower when the access is difficult. The easier the access to the Internet services, the more people discover the value of these services in their daily lives.

DOI: 10.4324/9781003385578-11

This chapter focuses on mobile technology as digital infrastructures. The chapter does not provide a detailed account of the technology itself. Rather, the focus is on the impact of mobile technology on businesses and individuals, mainly mobile phones (although the same logic applies for laptops and tablets). We end the chapter by opening the discussion about another mobile technology which is gradually becoming more pervasive, the Internet of Things (IoT), which may be perceived in itself as an emergent digital infrastructure.

The pervasiveness of mobile technology

The innovation of mobile technologies in the last two decades has changed the perception of users about the benefits of these devices. On the one hand, there were many innovations in the technology itself. Mobile phones and personal computing have converged into one device (smartphones), gaining better interfaces (touch screens). Data transmission has become much faster (wireless broadband) and the spread of mobile cell towers has supported the expansion of the whole network. On the other hand, there was innovation in the services enabled by mobile technology. Operating systems (such as iOS and Android) have become more robust and flexible, offering open doors (via APIs – application programming interfaces, discussed in chapter 7) for other developers to create apps and plug their software into the mobile infrastructure. These apps have then been made available through mobile commerce services, such as Apple's App Store and Google Play. Payment systems have been added to the platforms through credit cards and electronic solutions such as PayPal, Apple Pay, Google Wallet, and Alipay. Public spaces and some businesses have added a layer offering free Wi-Fi to local users and customers.

Considering the flexibility and functionality of mobile technology, it is not a surprise that the sales of smartphones have passed the sales of computer desktops in many countries, and the number of smartphones is expected to increase from 6.4 billion to 7.7 billion people from 2022 to 2028 (Ericsson, 2023). As of 2023, in mature markets the penetration of smartphones was very high, such as in the United States (92%), the United Kingdom (97%), and Germany (97%) (Statista, 2022a, 2023a, 2023b). In China, the smartphone penetration rate was 71.8% (2022), with potential growth to 82% in 2027 (Statista, 2022b). In India, the smartphone penetration was 71% in 2023, estimated to reach 81% by 2027 (Statista, 2023c). This shows that developing countries are overcoming their disadvantages in terms of communication and computing infrastructures through advances in mobile technologies. The change is such that in Sub-Saharan Africa the penetration of mobile technology covered 46% of the population in 2021, a number expected to grow to 50% in 2025 (GSMA, 2022).

Availability of wireless broadband services is a fundamental reason for the increasing use of smartphones and other mobile devices. Access to communication infrastructure has been a significant obstacle for developing countries attempting to use more computing technologies. With wireless broadband, it has become easier to overcome some of the barriers to spreading computing and communication infrastructures among these countries. Consumers expect more innovation, with faster networks, more coverage, long-life batteries, and improvements to guarantee that mobile devices can deliver better services at any time and at any place.

Businesses have strongly benefited from mobile technology infrastructures in the last few decades, made possible by the reduction in communication costs and increase in the speed of access to data (BCG, 2015). This has happened in part because the new generation of mobile network technologies is much faster, with a massive migration of users from obsolete networks to new ones. To give an example, the 4G networks are at least 10,000 times faster than the 2G networks, and 5G networks are from 10 to 20 times faster than the 4G ones. Consumers accept paying more for getting more efficient access to content on their mobile devices. The trend of cost reduction for using mobile broadband continues around the world, although there are serious differences in costs between the high- and low-income countries, with the latter group paying more than others and having far less affordability for such services (ITU, 2023).

In a broad sense, mobile technology brings interactivity and access to information, enabling businesses to offer new products and services, and better customer engagement, thus reaching more customers, and changing operational processes to gain productivity. For instance, employees may have access to the customer relationship management system anywhere, and give better advice to clients, and work from their homes, saving commuting time. Customers may search for prices and product descriptions and pay for their purchase on their mobile devices (for instance, using NFC – near field communication). Collaborative technologies available through mobile devices give easy access to experts. Integration of calendars and contacts in the mobile makes it easier for professionals to manage their diaries and find the people they need at the correct moment. Localisation services help to provide better services when your customer is at the door, such as offering a free coffee to a regular customer and allowing your sales professionals to use GPS services to quickly find directions to the client.

Customers and employees go mobile

From the customer's perspective, mobile technologies have become a significant channel for purchase and payment. Worldwide, Statista (2024) estimates that in 2024, mobile commerce revenue represented 57% of total e-commerce. Statista expects that in 2028 this percentage may grow to 63% if the same trends are repeated. Although more people are adopting m-commerce (mobile-commerce) platforms, many users are still conservative in using the channel. For instance, Business Insider estimates that retail m-commerce sales in the United States will be around 44% of the total retail e-commerce sales in 2025 (Meola, 2022). This shows that there is plenty of opportunity for more users to adopt m-commerce, which is a market opportunity for some companies or a threat, for those businesses which decide to ignore the trend.

Emarketer's research estimates that 60% of US adults perceive mobile shopping as a necessity, also indicating the link between mobile shopping and the use of social networks (when consumers see the advertising on social media and buy through these channels), with customers giving preference to purchase through Facebook, YouTube, Instagram, and TikTok (King, 2024). PayPal's research (2022) in the United Kingdom confirmed similar results in relation to the relevance of social media platforms as channels for purchasing on mobile phones. These findings show the relevance of mobile technologies in supporting e-commerce, with implications for businesses which need to guarantee their presence on mobile platforms to reach customers, and understand the interplay between mobile technologies and social media.

From the employee perspective, the personal access to advanced mobile technology has changed their expectations about the technology companies should adopt. In some companies, there is a conflict between the expectations of employees and the investments made by the organisation. This situation is very different from the time in which people could expect to find the most up-to-date technology in the workplace, not in their own pockets. For overcoming the challenge, some companies have introduced a policy known as 'Bring Your Own Device' (BYOD), which allows employees to bring their own mobile devices for working in the business and for accessing the company's data and information from any place.

Instead of fighting with employees, companies have accepted the BYOD movement, seeing the opportunity to benefit from an investment which is made by employees. Advocates of the model argue that BYOD increases productivity, as employees invest their own time in learning how to use and maintain the device, being more motivated due to having chosen their own working tools. On the other hand, there are serious security risks: when not properly protected, these devices can be lost or hacked, giving criminals an entry point to the company's data. For this reason, companies which adopt the BYOD approach need to give employees support for the use of the technology and have special measures to protect the security of their assets. Encryption of devices and clear policies for accessing and storing data are among the measures which help the company to protect its information when employees use their own devices.

Changing communication patterns and behaviour

Mobile technology infrastructures have changed the way people communicate. For most of our history, we have either communicated in face-to-face encounters, or we have made ourselves available at a particular address for defined messages to reach us (see more on the history of communication in Standage, 2013). Consider the example of letters. Once upon a time, letters were the primary way to communicate with people across long distances when one could not meet the other in person. For one to receive a letter, it is necessary to have a defined address, a place either where a person lives or is expected to be present regularly to get messages. Even when the communication channels evolved to telegraphs, changing the speed of communication, still the receiver of a message had to be in a particular address. Thus, place has been very important for most of human history when we think about the way we communicate.

Computing has changed this pattern. The first change was brought about by emails. For the first time, a message could be available in a virtual space (a server), and people could access this email server using any computer. However, the computer at that time also would be at a fixed address. To access networks, computers would need to have access to a physical infrastructure which was available only in fixed addresses, such as offices and houses. One could access the email from different places, but in each of these places, there would have to be a prepared infrastructure of communication cables to allow the email to be read and answered. This was a huge step in terms of flexibility – one did not need to be in a defined place to receive a message – but still with limitations.

Mobile technology has liberated us from place to a large degree. We can now communicate from any location using our mobile devices. There are still limitations, as this mobile communication depends on the installed local infrastructure which supports the mobile devices. Many times your mobile device does not have a good connection as the mobile cell towers cannot serve al llocations. If you have a smartphone based on 5G networking, for instance, you can find yourself without communication in places where this network infrastructure has not advanced yet. You can travel to places where the local service infrastructure does not support communication with your device (poor roaming services). You can also opt out of using your device fully when travelling abroad for cost reasons, as roaming services are more expensive than the regular services, particularly for the transmission of data. Despite these limitations, we have never had such flexibility in our communication, and we can foresee that most of the current limitations to mobile technologies are going to be sorted out in the future.

Implications of new communication patterns

Changes in communication patterns have implications. For instance, because we are now available independently of place, we can also observe changes in the expectations about when employees should be available for work. This is not a trivial issue. In the past, people would go to the office for work, and would then go home and live their own lives. There was a clearer separation between working and personal life. Nowadays, people are potentially available 24/7 on their mobile devices. Should a professional be available to answer emails at the weekend? And during vacations? In spite of legislation on these matters, which mostly protect workers from overworking or working without payment, there are social norms which in practice override the legislation. The change in communication patterns has thus also changed working patterns, with more people not being able to differentiate their working time from their personal lives. The boundaries between work and personal life have become even more blurred after people were forced to work from home during the COVID-19 pandemic.

On the other hand, we also need to define when the moment for communication related to our personal life is. Today more people use part of their work time to manage their personal communication using their mobile devices, but some companies stipulate that employees should not use working time for managing their private businesses. However, in practice, it is impossible to control what people do (at least in democratic countries, which have legislation protecting citizens and employees). A solution for companies is to change the focus of measurement from behaviour to outputs: as it is not possible (or legal) to ensure a particular behaviour is adopted, checking the quality and quantity of outputs becomes a better way of managing people. This means other forms of management are emerging, with a smaller number of managers (fewer hierarchical layers) and more digital control of outputs (for instance, how many customers have their problems sorted out in less than five minutes in a call centre). To be clear, this phenomenon does not happen only because of mobile technology; rather, it is a result of the increasing use of information technology in general. However, mobile technology has reinforced this trend.

Changes in communication patterns have also affected other aspects of our behaviour in society. It does not take much effort to see this in public spaces. You enter any public transport system, or any coffee shop or restaurant, and observe how many people are interacting with their mobiles at any given moment, even when they are in face-to-face conversations with other people. Indeed, one can see this at home too or in the classroom. We know that a reasonable number of students are checking their social media during any given lecture. The use of mobile devices is not perceived to be offensive or distracting. Or is it?

These are areas in which new social norms are to be discussed and agreed. The myth of multitasking has already been challenged by research (see the debate by Meyer, 2016). If we are using our mobiles at the same time as we are sorting out other problems, chances are that we are not doing any of the tasks properly. Some authors argue that at the cognitive level we are losing our attention span and concentration because of the excessive exposure to fragmented flows of information (Carr, 2010). These studies are generic about Internet use as a whole, but mobile devices are the culprit that makes the Internet and social media available at any time, even in our bathrooms and bedrooms (see more on this in chapter 12).

Once people form an opinion on the combined benefits of mobile technology, and start using this technology everywhere, it becomes more difficult to imagine one's life without this interface. Boston Consulting Group's research (BCG, 2015) found that more than 50% of mobile users would give up going out for dinner, having a pet, or going on vacation if necessary to keep their mobile devices. More than 50% would accept cutting out one day per week of their income in exchange for a mobile connection. Happily, we can keep it all. However, this research shows that mobile technology has become a fundamental part of our lives, information which is confirmed by many other research reports. One can question, however, whether this happens because of real benefits or because of perceived benefits, or even because of social norms. As everyone is online 24/7, and most people are communicating through social media, no one wants to be left behind (see 'Fear of missing out', or FOMO, on Wikipedia, 2024).

Privacy and surveillance

Our understanding of privacy and etiquette is also affected by the changes in communication patterns brought about by mobile devices. As we can talk to people at any place, the boundaries of what can be said in public has become blurred, as have the boundaries of where we can use our mobile devices. In any big city around the world one can stop on a busy street and listen to others' private conversations. People act as if they were talking inside a transparent bubble when they are using their mobiles. But there is no bubble. Very interesting, and very private, topics may be listened to in public places.

Mobile technology brings the risk of more surveillance (some would say the opportunity of having more information about individuals; see more on the topic of surveillance in Morozov, 2011). Having a mobile with us all the time means that it is always possible to know where we are. At least the mobile service provider knows, and many other app developers also ask for our location. More specifically, companies may install apps on the mobiles of employees to track their localisation. Unfortunately, this has also happened in the private sphere, when partners try to track each other.

Indeed, mobile technologies have become a point for collecting and storing data about people, which can be useful in supporting other digital applications and tools. Our mobile devices have the technology and data to know what our key interests are, who our friends are, which places we go regularly, when and by which transportation means, what time we wake up and go to sleep, how many steps we take in a day, and even your heart rate. In some cases, you need to set up your mobile device to collect such data, downloading the specialised apps and allowing the data to be stored for further analysis, but not always. Your basic location, for example, is known by default through the phone network.

Mobile technology is the perfect host for all sorts of localisation services. The basic one is offering a map, with GPS features (for finding directions). It is a fundamental feature to help people find their way to destinations, leaving paper maps behind. It is also a way of getting a better customisation of advertisements: a mobile provider knows you are interested in buying a new bag and informs you of a promotion by your preferred store, which incidentally is just around the corner. Location services help track the delivery of products, such as when e-commerce services estimate the time for a delivery. Location services can be used to track physical activity, to monitor the route used by sales professionals, and to check alternative routes when there is traffic. One can also find friends who are close to a particular place so you can spend time together using location services such as Foursquare.

There is currently a particular interest in collecting data with the help of wearables, such as digital watches, wristbands, and glasses. These devices can help collect data from your movements and activities, for instance, measuring the number of steps you have walked, the time you have spent running, the total calories you have burnt in the day, how many hours you have slept, etc. In addition, mobile phones have apps for you to add other data, feeding a larger database that can be used by your doctors. Indeed, these databases are powerful tools for us to learn more about ourselves and make informed decisions about changes which may be useful in our lives. Based on the collected data, fitness apps may, for instance, recommend new activities and exercises, gradually helping you to become fitter. In a less positive scenario, an insurance company could increase your premiums if you are not active enough.

App services

One key change brought about by smartphone interfaces is the emergence of app services. Part of the software layer of mobile technology infrastructures, apps are the interface to a myriad of specialised services, from social networking and calendars to gaming, weather forecasts, e-commerce, and e-banking. Apps help us to book restaurants and services, to get the latest news, to read books and watch films, to purchase from our preferred stores, to make payments, to manage our finances, and to collect data on our health and activities, to cite just a few examples.

All mobile phones and tablets come with some pre-installed basic apps, such as email clients, calendars, web browsers, maps, and the interface to download other apps (the app stores). Apps today also offer the more traditional desktop application software packages, such as Word, Excel, and PowerPoint (or similar solutions). These apps have increased productivity and allowed people to work when commuting to different places. For instance, the interval between meeting two clients may be used to answer emails, prepare documents, and collect information on the interests of the next contact to be visited.

There are specialised apps for organising tasks and priorities, integrating communication channels, making conference calls, organising passwords, taking quick notes, designing ideas, integrating calendars with maps, checking bus and train timetables, planning journeys, controlling expenses, managing customer relationships, among many others. There are apps to capture how you are spending your time online, for you to analyse later to see if you are perhaps wasting too much time with useless tasks and hopefully then go on to improve the quality of your time. In addition, coaching apps can help you to achieve your goals, showing how well you are sticking with new habits and progressing towards your objectives. Apps have also changed the way we understand entertainment time, making games, music, and films available everywhere (as long as the broadband connection is good enough).

It is difficult to estimate with precision the number of apps around the world. Based on numbers from Appfigures (2022), Statista estimates that there were 3.5 million apps on Google Play, 1.6 million apps on Apple App Store, and 483,000 apps on Amazon Appstore in 2022. The data for running the apps are partly in the mobile device and partly in the cloud services, thus the quality of the broadband connection is an important aspect to ensure the high-quality experience the final user is expecting. Research from Insider Intelligence (Dolan, 2023) found that in the United States, people would spend on average more than three hours per day on their mobile apps, which is more than three times the amount of time spent on browsing the Internet through traditional web browsers such as Firefox or Safari. Apps tied to specific platforms or services are the preferred way users access content on mobile phones, as they offer a better user experience for defined tasks.

The app services have multiplied the value of mobile technologies. Users customise their mobile devices through the choice of apps and through the way the apps are arranged to achieve a particular configuration and deliver aimed outputs. This capacity of combining apps from a choice of thousands of options, and of deciding how each app is going to work on one's mobile, mean that each mobile device is different from one another. This is the most flexible computing technology we have ever had. The app layer has brought to the hands of users the capacity for innovating: in choosing apps to fit individual needs, each user has the potential to create their own solution to a particular problem or objective.

The apps enable other innovations such as the personalisation of services. The more the mobile operating system knows about the chosen apps, the easier it is to recommend other apps or to understand the profile of the user, and to use this information on other interfaces. For instance, if a user has lots of games on their mobile phone, it may be a good idea to add more advertisement on games next time the user is browsing apps. Going beyond, as the key mobile operating systems (Android and iOS) integrate the mobile experience with other devices used by the individual, so if you have downloaded a mobile phone app on learning to cook, you may see advertisements for kitchen utensils and devices when using Chrome or Safari on your computer.

Apps may support businesses to create more customer loyalty. A coffee shop chain, for instance, may create an app to make the lives of its loyal customers easier by using mobile GPS and integrated map facilities to find their closest shop and give directions on how to get there. It may even incorporate extra information such as queueing time and allow online purchases, so the customer can get their order straightforwardly when arriving at the shop. The same app can integrate information about the customer purchases, being able to quickly communicate repeated orders to the store. The app can also give reward points to regular clients, as the store will have an easy interface to manage the relationship with customers. Even a small catering provider – like an independent coffee shop or family restaurant – could benefit from such an app.

The Internet of Things (IoT)

The Internet of Things (IoT) is one of the current developments of mobile technology, becoming a digital infrastructure in itself. The IoT means that digital connectivity is associated with any physical device – from machines and domestic devices to buildings, clothes, or biological beings – through digital sensors, which can communicate with digital sensors of other physical devices. Any object can be connected to others, creating a network of communication among objects which send and receive data automatically. The digital sensors in each device are able to collect and distribute relevant data and to respond to the information that they receive through the network. This allows remote control of objects, but also the pooling of data from multiple objects for an understanding of how they work and how they can work better.

These digital sensors associated with things are able to collect data (e.g., temperature, pressure, motion, acceleration, light, proximity, humidity, vibration, energy consumption, performance, vision, sound, biomedical parameters, etc.), which are used in the management of processes or for informing decision-making. For instance, adding biochips to farm animals may allow a farmer to manage each animal's specific diet, gaining a level of information which could not be captured otherwise. Digital devices associated with machines, such as cars and airplanes, may measure the performance of distinct parts of the technology, collecting enough data to provide preventive maintenance before they fail, reducing costs, and improving productivity and safety. You can see the immediate advantage of being able to collect earlier warning indicators from machines, reducing the negative impact of having failures in critical moments. The data collected by IoT contributes to the formation of large datasets about the behaviour of materials, equipment, and living beings. These big datasets are used then to investigate patterns of behaviour, which feed artificial intelligence models (e.g., machine learning) (see more in chapter 14).

In manufacturing companies, IoT has many applications. It can monitor production lines and detect issues in real-time, including information on possible problems with equipment which may need maintenance to avoid downtime. IoT may be used to identify levels of stock of products and manage the transport of products automatically, reducing the need for human labour to be involved in the decision-making and in the transportation. Goods and assets can be tracked in supply chains, including the vehicles used for the transportation (e.g., tracking cars and trucks). IoT may be used for quality control, management of energy consumption (e.g., controlling lighting and heating systems), for safety management, and for providing data to enhance analytics for process improvement. An advanced example is the use of automated robots to manage the transportation of goods in Amazon and Alibaba warehouses. The automated robots have defined tasks to be done (for instance, bringing shelves with a particular product for humans to pick up and add to packs). However, the robots themselves manage the order of their movements on the floor, considering all the other robots which are operating at the same time, using IoT to sense each other and to coordinate with each other their collective actions to collect goods without accidents and with high efficiency and speed.

The IoT is already very close to many of us, through mobile wearables. When you have a digital watch tracking your activities, this means you have a digital interface to transform your activity into data. The data are transferred to an online database, for you (or your healthcare provider) to analyse, so you can make decisions on your health and physical activities. You become a 'thing' in this Internet of Things when you use a wearable to measure your health or sleep performance. Also, smart homes use sensors for managing a variety of devices, from TVs, ovens, refrigerators and pet feeders, to heating, electricity, and security systems, and even smoke and water leak detectors. On a larger scale, we are applying the IoT to manage entire cities: the smart city approach.

An important application of IoT is in autonomous cars. For the car to be autonomous, it needs to measure all relevant aspects of the physical context in which the car is moving to decide on the right movements. Autonomous cars depend on IoT for collecting data on how to drive a car correctly (big data), to feed the AI models which are then used to drive the cars autonomously. IoT (cameras, sensors) capture the data from the context, and these data are processed by the car computers, using the AI models to decide what the car should do next to reach a particular objective (e.g., drive to an address, or park the car). Similarly, IoT is used for training and flying drones automatically.

In healthcare there are many IoT applications evolving quickly, such as remote patient monitoring. Through wearables, IoT devices measure biological indicators, passing information on in real-time on the conditions of patients. In this way, more patients can go home earlier because the monitors will check whether the patient needs to stay in the hospital for further observation. This saves resources from hospitals at the same time that it increases the well-being of patients, who can be treated at home with reduced risk of hospital infections. The same logic of equipment maintenance applies to hospitals, with predictive maintenance reducing costs and improving efficiency. Smart glucose monitoring helps patients to manage diabetes. Smart clothes and wearables may measure vital signals to monitor the pulse, heartbeat, level of stress, quality of sleep, and level of activity, among others.

The more interoperability between devices, the better the exchange of information and the capacity for integrating decision-making which manages groups of devices. On this matter, there are two competing forces influencing manufacturers of smart devices. On the one hand, there is interest in the idea that devices become interconnected independently of producers, allowing faster growth of usage through network effects. For instance, Google, Amazon, Apple, and hundreds of other companies are collaborating to develop open-source IoT standards for smart-home devices, named the Matter standard. The more households, companies, and governments use IoT solutions, the more benefit for all through network effects, and, most importantly, it will become cheaper for all (economies of scale). The network effect has the benefit of connecting devices, making their management easier, and collecting more data, which can improve the performance of all devices. This is one of the positive impacts of learning from big data: once we learn something, the marginal cost of reproducing that knowledge across the whole network is negligible (see discussion on marginal costs in chapter 6).

Cybersecurity is a major issue for the IoT however, as the weakest link in a network may compromise the whole network. The more integration a house or a company has, the more vulnerable it can become to cyber attacks. On the one hand, companies have not been able to build more security into the machines; on the other hand, individuals do not know the level of risk and how to prevent it. IoT is literally invisible. If users do not have a deep understanding of the way it works, they may make the wrong assumptions, including the belief that the manufacturers have embedded all the necessary protections. One can imagine the damage if hackers gain access to the control of security systems, self-driving cars, or drones.

In the worst-case scenario, the vulnerability may be built by design. For instance, in 2020 there was an infamous case in which photographs of people inside their homes, taken by automated vacuum cleaners (Roombas), reached social networks. Guo (2022) reported that this robot was trained in the houses of families who were not aware their photos were being collected at all times. The manufacturer sent the photos to a company, which was responsible for labelling the image content for generating the data for training the robot (machine learning). First of all, the users did not know their photos were seen by other people in this way. Second, the company outsourced the labelling work, and someone in the company they outsourced to decided to breach the privacy of individuals and distribute their very private photos through social media. Indeed, individuals had given the authorisation for the Roomba robots to monitor them, although it is very likely that these people did not know their photos would be seen by people labelling the photographs, let alone distributed via social media (see more on discussion on privacy and security in chapter 15).

References

Appfigures (2022). 'Number of apps available in leading app stores as of 3rd quarter 2022', *Statista*. Available at: https://www.statista.com/statistics/276623/number-of-apps-available-in-leading-app-stores/ (Accessed: 12 February 2024).

BCG (2015). 'The mobile revolution: How mobile technologies drive a trillion-dollar impact', *Boston Consulting Group (BCG)*. Available at: https://www.bcg.com/publications/2015/telecommunications-technology-industries-the-mobile-revolution (Accessed: 16 March 2024).

Carr, N. (2010). *The Shallows: What the Internet is Doing to Our Brains*. New York: W.W. Norton & Company.

Dolan, S. (2023). 'How mobile users spend their time on their smartphones in 2023', *eMarketer*. Available at: https://www.insiderintelligence.com/insights/mobile-users-smartphone-usage (Accessed: 12 February 2024).

Ericsson (2023). 'Number of smartphone mobile network subscriptions worldwide from 2016 to 2022, with forecasts from 2023 to 2028 (in millions)', *Statista*. Available at: https://www.statista.com/statistics/330695/number-of-smartphone-users-worldwide/ (Accessed: 12 February 2024).

'Fear of missing out' (2024). *Wikipedia*. Available at: https://en.wikipedia.org/wiki/Fear_of_missing_out (Accessed: 24 March 2024).

GSMA (2022). 'Mobile penetration rate in Sub-Saharan Africa from 2021 to 2025', *Statista*. Available at: https://www.statista.com/statistics/1133365/mobile-penetration-sub-saharan-africa/ (Accessed: 12 February 2024).

Guo, E. (2022). 'A Roomba recorded a woman on the toilet. How did screenshots end up on Facebook? *MIT Technology Review*. Available at: https://www.technologyreview.com/2022/12/19/1065306/roomba-irobot-robot-vacuums-artificial-intelligence-training-data-privacy/ (Accessed: 17 March 2024).

ITU (2023). 'The affordability of ICT services 2022.' Policy Brief. International Telecommunication Union. Available at: https://www.itu.int/en/ITU-D/Statistics/Documents/publications/prices2022/ITU_Price_Brief_2022.pdf (Accessed: 24 March 2024).

King, J. (2024). 'Guide to mobile commerce and its business applications', *Emarketer*. Available at: https://www.emarketer.com/insights/mobile-commerce-shopping-trends-stats/ (Accessed: 24 March 2024).

Meola, A. (2022). 'Rise of m-commerce: Mobile e-commerce shopping stats & trends', *Business Insider*. Available at: https://www.businessinsider.com/mobile-commerce-shopping-trends-stats?r=US&IR=T (Accessed: 17 March 2024).

Meyer, K. (2016). 'Millennials as digital natives: Myths and realities', *Nielsen Norman Group*. Available at: https://www.nngroup.com/articles/millennials-digital-natives/ (Accessed: 16 March 2024).

Morozov, E. (2011). *The Net Delusion: How Not to Liberate the World*. London: Penguin Books.

PayPal (2022). 'PayPal research reveals consumer shopping habits and attitudes to emerging commerce trends', *PayPal Newsroom*. Available at: https://newsroom.uk.paypal-corp.com/e-CommerceIndex2022 (Accessed: 24 March 2024).

Standage, T. (2013). *Writing on the Wall*. London: Bloomsbury Publishing.

Statista (2022a). 'Number of smartphone users in the United States from 2009 to 2040 (in millions)', *Statista*. Available at: https://www.statista.com/statistics/201182/forecast-of-smartphone-users-in-the-us/ (Accessed: 12 February 2024).

Statista (2022b). 'Smartphone penetration rate in China from 2018 to 2022 with forecasts until 2027', *Statista*. Available at: https://www.statista.com/statistics/321482/smartphone-user-penetration-in-china/ (Accessed: 12 February 2024).

Statista (2023a). 'Smartphone penetration rate in the UK 2020–2029', *Statista*. Available at: https://www.statista.com/statistics/553707/predicted-smartphone-user-penetration-rate-in-the-united-kingdom-uk/ (Accessed: 12 February 2024).

Statista (2023b). 'Smartphone penetration rate in Germany 2020–2029', *Statista*. Available at: https://www.statista.com/statistics/568095/predicted-smartphone-user-penetration-rate-in-germany/ (Accessed: 12 February 2024).

Statista (2023c). 'Smartphone penetration rate in India from 2009 to 2023, with estimates until 2040', *Statista*. Available at: https://www.statista.com/statistics/1229799/india-smartphone-penetration-rate/ (Accessed: 12 February 2024).

Statista (2024). Mobile commerce revenue and share of total retail e-commerce worldwide from 2017 to 2028. Statista. Available at: https://www.statista.com/statistics/1449284/retail-mobile-commerce-revenue-worldwide/ (Accessed; 24 March 2024).

Zittrain, J.L. (2008). *The Future of the Internet – and How to Stop It*. New Haven and London: Yale University Press.

12 Social media

Introduction

The term *social media* is a generic name used to conceptualise a category of digital tools which allow individuals and organisations to create and share information and knowledge, to communicate and to collaborate with each other through computing infrastructures. These communication and collaboration efforts may be in closed groups (such as on Facebook and LinkedIn), or they may be in public online spaces (such as X and blog services). Some experts prefer to use the term 'social technologies' to refer to these tools, including in this case the proprietary tools offered to companies to foster collaboration among employees and contributors (such as Microsoft's SharePoint and Teams). In this book, we adopt this broader conceptualisation of social media as social technologies, including proprietary tools.

The fundamental aspect of this definition is the capacity to interact through social media platforms, using Web 2.0 applications (which allow people to publish their own content, and interact online with others, as discussed in chapter 9). The value of social media infrastructures emerges from the interplay of an enabling tool (which allows people to create profiles, write content, publish photos and videos, and connect to and communicate with others) and billions of individuals who believe there is value in interacting online with others through these channels. There would not be social media if the user was not interested in generating content for sharing on these interfaces, and in giving a great amount of time to interacting with the content of others too.

Social media started, nonetheless, before the facilities of Web 2.0 (see Rheingold, 2000 [1993], for a good account of the emergence of virtual communities). The first interfaces of social media were computers connected to private networks, which would allow users to access discussion lists (similar to online forums). These discussion lists would be hosted by organisations, which would have dedicated servers to keep track of email conversations. The idea behind the creation of discussion lists was that computing technology would enable people to form communities mediated by digital channels. These communities would be able to share information, but would also allow people to give emotional support to each other. At that time though, cloud services were not fully developed, and organisations would need to build their own digital infrastructure to host discussion lists on their servers. Today, companies such as Facebook, LinkedIn, and WeChat offer services in the cloud, thus nobody needs to worry about investing in their own digital infrastructure, although in some circles the use of discussion lists is still pervasive.

From this account, we learn that the idea of building communities was present at the very beginning of the first conceptions of social media, although at that time nobody called these tools social media. Thus, this chapter focuses on the community roots of social media, and how this

DOI: 10.4324/9781003385578-12

affects the use of these tools for collaboration, innovation, and marketing. Again, we focus here on the aspects more important for organisations, with a few insights beyond these boundaries.

The relevance of social media

Never before in human history have so many people been able to communicate with each other using shared channels. This is the biggest change brought about by social media. Think about more than 3 billion people connected to the same communication interface, Facebook (Meta Platforms, 2024). Then factor in the millions (or even billions) of users of other social media such as X, LinkedIn, Instagram, Pinterest, WordPress, Tumblr, WhatsApp, TikTok, and YouTube. For instance, YouTube has more than 2.7 billion unique visitors per month. Within the segment of office social technologies, Microsoft Teams leads with monthly active users of around 320 million people (Redmond, 2023). The Chinese government blocks many of these social media in China, where we can find other social media tools with similar functionalities, such as Sina Weibo and Tencent Weibo (microblogs), WeChat (social network, named Weixin in China), QQ (instant message services), Youku (video sharing), and Douyin (the Chinese TikTok). WeChat alone has around 1.3 billion users (Tencent, 2023). These numbers demonstrate the relevance of social media as digital infrastructures.

In the case of social media, size matters. The fact that people are using the same social media service to communicate with each other speeds up the process of transmitting information and of getting new connections (with economies of scale and positive network externalities, as discussed in chapter 6). Think about your own experience. You meet a person and would like to keep in touch with them. Immediately, you connect through social media tools, such as Facebook, LinkedIn, or WhatsApp. If you like the opinions of a person, you might just follow them on X. In this way, you preserve this valuable connection for the future, either a mutual connection in which both agree to share a link confirming the relationship, or a unilateral connection in which one follows another. The fact that we are using similar communication channels leverages the capacity we have for building and maintaining connections in the long term. You can also get to know people through digital interactions, in discussion groups or through friends. You choose who you would like to connect to (and vice versa, others may connect or not to you), and the terms of the interaction are to be agreed between both, considering the limitations of the tools and the level of privacy defined by the parties.

There is a great variety of social media tools. A comprehensive classification of social media as social technologies has been proposed by McKinsey Global Institute (Chui et al., 2012): *social networks* (enable connections through profiles), *blogs/microblogs* (focus on publishing content, although they also allow connections), *ratings and reviews* (evaluation of products, services, and opinions), *social commerce* (group purchasing and sharing opinions on products and services), *wikis* (creation and storage of knowledge), *discussion forums* (spaces for debate and access to expertise), *shared workspaces* (co-creation of content and projects), *crowdsourcing* (harnesses collective knowledge or pool of resources), *social gaming* (game interfaces for playing with others), and *media and file sharing* (sharing of content). There are many tools which would be classified in more than one of these categories.

In their research, McKinsey Global Institute concludes that companies use social technologies for a variety of applications (Chui et al., 2012). For product development, social media are channels for getting insights from customers and engaging customers in product co-creation. For operations, social media help with forecasting the context and distributing work. For marketing and sales, social media are principal channels for advertising and branding, in addition to bringing customers' insights, generating sales leads, and supporting social commerce.

Related to marketing, social media allows a better customer service. For business support, social media improves collaboration and communication, facilitating the matching of expertise to tasks. The report concludes that a large majority of companies benefit from using social media as channels for getting quicker access to knowledge; reducing communication, travel, and operational costs; and increasing productivity (e.g., spending less time searching for information).

Focusing on this aspect of connections, McAfee (2009) has defined a useful concept about social media, which he coined *emergent social software platforms* (ESSPs) (observe that McAfee uses the word platform in a different way from how we define this concept in chapter 8). First, *social software* refers to the fact that these tools allow people to connect and collaborate online, forming digital communities. Second, these tools are *platforms* because they offer a variety of features to be combined, and the results of the collective contributions are visible and durable over time. Third, they are *emergent* because the tools do not define the way people are going to interact; rather, the social structures of interaction are enacted by the people using the tools (in combination with the flexibility of choosing tools). These social arrangements are collaborative and foster innovation, topics which are discussed in the next section.

The emergence of collaborative interfaces

There are many arguments as to why companies should foster more collaboration through social media. One perspective is that through social networks a company can get access to people and data that they could not access without these digital tools. McAfee (2009) develops the concept of 'Enterprise 2.0' upon the idea that social media could reinforce our weak and strong ties with people we already know and facilitate the connection with people who we do not know yet. Access to people is thus a key benefit of social media: a company may get easier access to experts and customers. Instead of seeing companies as silos of expertise which do not communicate with each other, this perspective fosters the visibility of knowledgeable people (experts), and the interaction as a way of creating and sharing knowledge. McAfee proposes that companies which use social technologies to foster new forms of organising are more collaborative, in contrast with more traditional, hierarchical forms of organising.

An alternative view focuses on knowledge, emphasising that knowledge emerges from the interaction among people. Taking this perspective, we could see the benefit of using social media to enable the formation of communities of experts. The pool of knowledge which emerges from such a community is bigger than the knowledge in the heads of each individual: knowledge is recombined through conversations, and experts can rely on each other's strengths to reach new levels of understanding. As explained by McAfee and Brynjolfsson (2017), organising crowds through virtual interactions is likely to foster knowledge creation and diffusion. In this direction, the concept of communities of practice may be helpful here (see more details in Brown and Duguid, 1998). These communities are organised groups of people who share common concerns and passions in a particular area of knowledge and are willing to share their knowledge with others within these groups (which may be restricted to the boundaries of an organisation or be broader communities organised by digital interfaces). From this perspective, social media facilitates communication in communities of practice.

A third view of the relevance of social media collaboration comes from authors who study innovation processes. Doing a historical analysis of innovations over the last centuries, Johnson (2010) argues that what matters for innovation is not only the number of nodes in a network (individuals or organisations), but the way these nodes are connected and the quality of their interaction (relationships). In order to have more innovation, people should be inside environments in which all are exploring new boundaries. In this direction, the Internet and social media are infrastructures which favour innovation through improving the connections and the quality of the interactions among experts. This view complements the idea that digital infrastructures themselves foster innovation through their generative characteristics (as discussed in chapter 4), adding the human layer (people and relationships) to the model presented by Zittrain (2008).

In a further analysis, we can also discuss how social media may enable humans to create new social structures for knowledge creation and innovation. The idea behind this thought is that we can create spaces for collective superintelligence through new forms of organising and linking individual human minds and artefacts (see more in Bolstrom, 2014). In other words, a superintelligence could emerge from the positive network effect of connecting people and content in particular ways, breaking complex problems into manageable smaller ones. Digital infrastructures, in general, provide means for large amounts of content to be available and reachable – think about the Internet and the Web. In particular, social media provides the means to connect people, enabling new ways of organising collaboration. As communication costs are reduced and social media provides details on the profile of individuals, it is not difficult to foresee the emergence of algorithms to foster collaboration and innovation. The more people are educated and connected through social media infrastructures, the more we can expect developments in the direction of fostering collective superintelligence.

Using an economic perspective to interpret the benefits of using social media, digital collaborative technologies allow more direct interaction between participants. This makes part of the coordination efforts redundant, allowing companies to reduce the managerial levels in a hierarchy (i.e., companies need a lower number of managers to coordinate work). The speed of processes also could be increased, again reducing costs and improving competitiveness. An example of the efficiency of digital collaborative technologies is the production of open-source software. This production is supported by the voluntary work of thousands of programmers around the world, who can develop sophisticated and competitive operating systems and specialised applications (see more on decentralised open-source structures and their efficiency in Benkler, 2006). The open-source community shows that individuals may collaborate with minimum coordination from others (the coordination is done by rules and tools).

When discussing collaborative technologies, we need to recall the concept of positive network effects: the idea that the more people are connected to a network, the more benefits for all in the network (see discussion in chapter 6). In social networks, the more people are connected to the same infrastructure, the lower the cost of communication between any two points in the network, and the lower the cost of searching for interesting ideas and connections in the same network. Let's think about collaborative technologies such as Microsoft's SharePoint and Teams. Although these tools are proprietary, they use the very same logic of social technologies such as LinkedIn and Facebook. These proprietary tools allow thousands of employees and associated professionals to interact, within and beyond the boundaries of an organisation. Each person adds their profile with details of their past experience, their current projects and interests, their expertise, their availability, and their professional connections. In addition, the tools allow the creation of discussion groups, which can come together to share opinions and information on particular topics; and working groups, which are temporary organisations for solving a specific problem or executing a project. They also facilitate collaboration in producing documents together.

Collaborative technologies like these examples from Microsoft have changed the way people work together. They smooth the hierarchical structures, creating channels for people to contact each other directly, based on their expertise, instead of their department or localisation. They facilitate the clarification of questions through discussion groups, the distribution of work through working groups, and the production of common documents. They also make who is contributing to different projects more visible and enable innovation in the organisation. Microsoft Teams is also a good tool for organising communities of practice, fostering communication, creating common repositories of documents, and facilitating access to experts.

The use of collaborative technologies is going to move to another level with the inclusion of artificial intelligence assistants (read more on the AI infrastructure in chapter 14). Using the example of the Microsoft platform, the company has embedded Copilot (an AI tool operated by prompts in natural language) into Teams, to assist co-workers during or after an online meeting. Based on real-time conversation transcripts, users may ask Copilot to summarise the meeting or the opinion of anyone in the meeting at any moment. Copilot is going to provide answers in accordance with the prompts. For instance, you can request a summary of the conversation (simple output) or you can request a table with the key points discussed in the meeting, separating the pros and the cons for each key item and the names of people who have presented these ideas (a more elaborate output).

Adding AI layers into social technologies changes the traditional understanding of the process of knowledge creation and codification. In a Teams meeting, without AI assistance, individuals would work together to interpret arguments, and reach a consensus which would be documented. Following the knowledge management framework developed by Nonaka and Konno (1998), when professionals collaborate to generate this agreement, we can say that they are *socialising* to transfer tacit knowledge (the knowledge in one's head) to each other, and they are working together to codify that knowledge (which becomes explicit in text, images, graphs, mathematical models, and so on) through *externalisation* processes. With Copilot, Teams can summarise the consensus based on the discussion, thus complementing or substituting humans in the process of knowledge externalisation. AI tools will change the way we use social technologies for knowledge creation and sharing, and for all sorts of collaborative activities which require the exchange of information and knowledge for decision-making.

From this discussion on how social technologies help the creation of knowledge, it is easier to understand that in order to protect their intellectual property and competitive advantage, in addition to the privacy of customers and employees, companies prefer to use proprietary tools. In this way, they have more control over what is produced and who has access to the content. However, we can see many similarities in outcomes if one decides to combine free social media. Indeed, people form informal groups on LinkedIn and Facebook to discuss topics of mutual interest. They find new contacts through searching the profiles of people in these services. And they share the content they produce individually or collectively through these services and beyond. Thus, knowledge professionals are more likely to use a combination of open and proprietary social media channels to manage their access to knowledge and their contribution to interest-based communities and groups.

Social media marketing

Organisations have increasingly been using social media for marketing. For instance, companies use social media to improve brand awareness, have more conversations with customers and potential customers, or publish content these audiences would appreciate. Through these interactions, the company may come to know more about customers' needs, using their ideas to create new products and services. Companies also use social media for advertising, aiming to improve their ability to reach the right customer at the right time.

Considering the overall spending in marketing, there is an estimation that 62% of money now goes to digital marketing, with the second most important channel being TV with 23% (Zenith, 2022). In accordance with Gartner (2022), social advertising represents 10.1% of total digital marketing, closely followed by search advertising (9.8%), digital display advertising (9.3%), digital video advertising (8.8%), and SEO (search engine optimisation) (8.5%). Among the main social media channels used globally, Facebook (89%), Instagram (80%), LinkedIn (64%), YouTube (54%), X (44%), and TikTok (26%) are cited as the most preferred by marketers (Frankwatching, 2023).

By having better information on individual profiles and interests, social media provides a better fit between the advertisement and the customer, increasing the chances of converting the viewing of an advertisement into sales. More technically, social media uses the information gathered from users to build powerful algorithms based on profiles, behaviours, interests, and beliefs. Even emotions can be added to the algorithm to improve the fit of a particular advertisement with a particular customer in each interaction. The better the algorithm, the better the result for the same investment in advertising, thus reducing transaction costs (as discussed in chapter 6).

To understand the way companies use social media for marketing, Tuten and Solomon (2014) propose a framework focusing on the nature of the interaction with customers. They divide social media into four zones of activity. The first is the *social community* channel, in which the company interacts with customers through sharing, socialising, and conversing. The second is the *social publishing* channel, in which the company focuses on the content to be published, either produced by the corporation or generated by customers. The third is the *social entertainment* channel, in which the company engages with customers through games, music, and art. The fourth is the *social commerce* channel, in which the company participates in spaces in which customers share ideas and opinions on products, in order to cultivate the relationship with the customer.

Particularly concerned with the consistency of customer experience through social media (for marketing, branding, customer service, and customer interaction), Smith et al. (2011) propose a framework to guarantee the quality of content creation, the capacity to analyse the data generated on social media through analytics, and the provision of clear rules of governance for guiding employees when using social media. The authors say there are six critical success factors for companies to succeed when using social media: context, culture, process, metrics, people, and policies. This framework offers a more strategic view on social media adoption for marketing and beyond, emphasising that companies should have a strategic view rather than a fragmented approach when planning for the adoption of social media.

The *context* should take into consideration the business environment and objectives, and the regulatory environment. The *culture* should focus on understanding habits and behaviours, ways of working, and the subcultures of different parts of the organisation or segments of the audience. The *processes* should be aligned with the objectives of the organisation, having the leadership to guide the development of the strategy. The *metrics* would require the organisation to have enough technical and human resources to measure the performance on social media (such as sentiment analysis). *People* should be trained to use social media as defined by the company, with clear roles and responsibilities and best practices. Finally, the *policy* means the company makes clear to employees what is expected from them when using social media, empowering people to better use the tools within limits. The best results, as concluded by the authors, would be achieved by companies which design social media strategies taking into consideration these six factors (Smith et al., 2011).

An alternative approach to discussing the best strategy for using social media in customer engagement and marketing is to focus on the social media functional building blocks (Kietzmann et al., 2011). The authors suggest that social media tools have seven key features, i.e., the functional building blocks. The *identity* feature measures how much the users reveal of their identity, allowing companies to better understand users. *Conversations* measure the speed and frequency of communication, and how ideas diffuse in the network. The *sharing* feature measures the type and frequency of the exchange of content, and the social graph of content production and distribution. The *presence* informs whether users know when others are available for real-time interaction. *Relationships* show how users are related to others in their social networks; for instance, who the influencers are. The *reputation* measures how much a user can know about the opinions of others, which reveals sentiments and reactions. *Groups* mean users can form communities, which create their rules and protocols. This framework of building blocks understands that companies should combine these features in accordance with their strategies in order to get more benefits. The end goal is the same as per Smith et al. (2011), but with a different approach towards the functional blocks of the tools themselves. Indeed, we see that both frameworks are complementary, as they allow us to critically analyse the phenomenon from different angles.

Mapping social media tools helps organisations to find where relevant communication and interaction is happening, and who the influencers are in these interactions. In the social media landscape, the company is not controlling the conversation. At any moment, in any node, a new piece of information may be generated and become relevant, depending on how it spreads. The company thus needs to be prepared for using the available analytical tools to get more insights (such as X Pro, Google Alerts, Google Analytics, and Facebook Analytics). These insights may also be about competitors, when the information is public. Finally, the curation of content is also important: the company needs to know what sort of content is of interest to the audience, and when that content is welcome.

Knowing the customer is a critical factor in business success. Companies have always relied on surveys and demographics to know about customers and potential customers, to better target advertisements, and to develop products and services. Social media offers a shortcut to the process of better knowing your customer. For instance, Facebook has crucial demographic data of more than 3 billion people, knowing with a high level of precision what people like, what their interests are, what they are talking about, who their friends are, and even how they feel today. Facebook's algorithm collects individual data and adjusts the offering of ads in accordance with individual profiles.

In addition to offering services to better target potential customers, Facebook also offers advertisers the tools for obtaining the data analytics of their advertisements. With these tools, companies can check whether a campaign is doing well and decide which campaign they are going to invest in more. Data analytics allow companies to see how people are reacting to the advertisement, with emoticons, sharing, or commentaries on top of the number of viewers. Based on the feedback, the company can adjust their target audience by country, region, age, and even by interests (through keywords). Other social media offers similar services based on demographics and 'psychographics' (which uncover the psychological characteristics of individuals, for fine-tuning the efficiency of an advertisement) (see 'Psychographics', on Wikipedia, 2023). With proper analytics and customisation tools, advertisers may reach their target audiences with more precision, improving the return on investment of their marketing campaigns on social media.

Risks and challenges of social media

Social media has brought many risks and challenges to individuals, companies, and societies, and we need to address these concerns with great attention in order not to jeopardise the benefits of using these tools. We list here some of these risks and challenges from the perspective of organisations, with some recommendations. Considering the limitations of this book, we need to summarise the topics. Much more could be said in terms of risks and challenges of social media for individuals, organisations, and societies.

The roots of these challenges and risks are many, and most of the time they come from a combination of factors. Some of these roots are: the design of the tools (the technical features); the contractual agreement between the service provider and the user (policy agreements); the way individuals use the tool, following or not the norms defined by a social group; the legal and regulatory framework (or the lack of those); and the unexpected outcomes from the interaction of all factors together. Added to this complexity, there are billions of users around the world, each one with their own interests and views, and we can imagine that new concerns will emerge over time.

Security and privacy

As with any other digital infrastructure, social media are open to cybercrime. Hackers may either take control of social media channels or may use social media channels to spread harmful content, such as viruses, Trojans, and spyware. Companies are aware of these risks, and in general they have security systems in place to try to impede such attacks. However, there is a particular weak link on social media: the people. Cybercriminals are specialised in socially engineering their attacks by using psychology and what they effectively know about people to get access to more information on social media, and from there to prepare further attacks. Companies have a special concern in protecting the privacy of customers and employees. In addition, in order to add more security layers, companies may also invest in training employees to avoid socially engineered attacks.

However, not only hackers jeopardise security and privacy. Check the 'Facebook-Cambridge Analytica data scandal', on Wikipedia (2024), for instance. Millions of Facebook users had their personal data and interactions shared without their explicit consent. This case is particularly controversial considering the arguments that the data collected could have been used to influence voters in the United States and the United Kingdom. This case called attention to techniques of psychographics. The combination of demographics with psychological profiling has strong power in influencing individuals, as it targets each one in exactly the way they may be more vulnerable to manipulation in one direction or another. Depending on the degree of vulnerability of individuals, this approach may not only be an invasion of privacy but also a threat to our understanding of free will and even a threat to our democratic institutions. Organisations must be accountable for the way data are used.

Damage to reputation

There are many ways in which reputation can be damaged on social media. We focus here on situations in which customers have made public their complaints about products and services, gaining attention from other customers. In a matter of hours, a company may have serious reputation damage if action is not taken quickly to sort out the problem (an example of negative network effects, discussed in chapter 6). Sometimes the damage lasts longer, particularly when the complaint is not addressed or when the criticism attracts many other people with similar feelings. One interesting case is the viral criticism known as 'United Breaks Guitars'. A group of Canadian musicians, Sons of Maxwell, made a song to express their disappointment with United Airlines, gaining viral attention for their complaint. Although the case was in 2008, the protest song is still available on YouTube (search for the video 'United Breaks Guitar').

Damage to reputation may also be caused by the spread of fake news, or twisted misunderstandings which go viral and out of control. We often discuss fake news in the sphere of individuals and societies, and the damage it can cause to all of us. The old type of fake news was mainly about writing text with incorrect information, aiming to trigger behaviours. With the introduction of AI tools which can generate fake images (photos and videos), the risks have become much bigger, as fake news can appear more realistic. Considering individuals' aim to make rational decisions based on the right information, the spread of fake news through social media is a big risk for societies. From time to time, social media channels are infested with a wave of fake news, and this may be about your company, or about a professional in your company.

A video or sentence out of context can be enough to generate a chain reaction of online mobs. As one cannot guess from where such an event will come, the best organisations can do is to have an expert team at hand (either working within the company or contracted as consultants) which can help by interrupting the process (the viral spread of fake news), clarifying the truth, spreading the right information as quickly as possible, clearing the Internet and social media channels of the wrong information (for instance, contacting those responsible for reproducing the fake news or the social media platforms and requesting removal of content), and finally prosecuting those involved, even if they are just individuals who have distributed the fake news in good faith. We as a society will not get rid of fake news while individuals are not liable for their communication with others. Fake news becomes irrelevant if well-intentioned individuals do not distribute it. The enforcement of libel laws may be necessary to defend one's reputation online (see, for instance, 'McAlpine v Bercow', on Wikipedia, 2023; a libel case in the United Kingdom based on the distribution of defamatory material through X, then Twitter).

Waste of time and resources

Many companies are concerned that the excessive use of social media is reducing corporate productivity. The obvious argument here is about the distraction. People are checking their social media interfaces many times in the day, and thus not concentrating on the work to be done. The more people spend time in these social media conversations, the higher the risk of reducing productivity. Naturally, within limits, the conversations are supposed to increase productivity. However, nobody has a clear rule about how much use of social media is adequate for not losing productivity. The information overload produced by social media brings another element which favours the reduction of productivity in companies as it increases the level of complexity when individuals need to make decisions (as discussed in chapter 6).

A further question is the impact of social media tools on our cognitive capabilities. This is a more serious concern. Some authors argue that the excessive use of social media has a lasting impact on our brains, reconfiguring our synapses in such a way that we lose the capacity of concentration, learning, and reflection. As social media spreads very fragmented pieces of information, our brains learn how to jump from one topic to another very quickly. However, in exchange, the brain loses the capacity to concentrate on the same topic for long periods, and to develop deeper analysis. This would be the result of having our attention span reduced because of the excessive use of social media. This is an open discussion, but we need to keep in mind both questions: whether social media is affecting our productivity, and whether social media are changing our capacity for concentration and thinking. To find out more about this discussion, see Carr (2010).

Lack of strategy and leadership

Many companies start using social media by following others, without carefully thinking about how social media could help the organisation to get closer to its strategic objectives. Without aligning social media with the business strategy, the organisation runs the risk of not choosing the right tools and the right level of support in the use of tools. Companies need to think in advance how to coordinate efforts across departments, also fostering consistency in the content which is made available on different channels. Companies should have a plan on how to collect and analyse data generated by social media, and how to make policies for using social media clear with both rules for reward and accountability. Similarly, professionals should have a clear strategy for their individual use of social media. You can see more on this matter of the relevance of having a strategy for social media in Smith et al. (2011), which is aligned with our discussion about having a digital business strategy for gaining sustainable competitive advantages (as discussed in chapter 8).

Employees may be interested in participating in social media, but are perhaps not sure of the benefits and risks. In corporate environments, organisations may work to enable such leadership to emerge. These leaders should first keep social media activity in alignment with the corporate strategy, designing proper social media architectures (a combination of tools and features). Second, they should use analytics to drive their actions, recommendations, and capacity for coordinating the efforts of others. Third, they should guarantee that the content produced is relevant, that the correct people are reached by the communication, and that users have the means to filter the content in accordance with their needs. (See more on social media leadership in Deiser and Newton, 2013).

Enshittification or platform decay

The term 'enshittification' was coined by Cory Doctorow in 2022, meaning a pattern of decreasing quality of online platforms which connect two-sided markets, such as social media which are monetised by advertisements. The author also uses the term 'platform decay' (see 'Enshittification', on Wikipedia, 2024). The key idea behind the term is based on the concept of value creation (a topic discussed in chapter 8, alongside business models). For a platform to succeed, it needs to create value for all parties involved, including for the company itself. For instance, Facebook needs to create value for users, advertisers, and Meta's stakeholders. There is thus a fine-tuning exercise so as all parties receive enough value.

Platform decay happens, however, when the platform starts reducing the value to users and advertisers (or any agent in the two-sided markets), in order to get higher share of value for itself (through higher monetisation), thus aiming to benefit more the shareholders. In a more extreme situation, the two sides of the market would leave the platform and look for another option. This would certainly be bad news for the platform and its shareholders, but also for all stakeholders who have created value in the platform. For instance, if a social media platform closes, how would users feel about losing their content and connections?

However, we do not need to reach this extreme situation to already be affected by the platform decay. For instance, if a social media platform decides to extract more value through selling more advertising, it may bombard users with more and more ads, thus reducing the value these users perceive in staying on the platform, as instead of getting more interactions and relevant content, they are instead seeing too many ads. On the other hand, the advertisers are paying more to get the attention of more individuals, but this does not mean that these individuals are buying more (which means transaction costs are increasing instead of being reduced). Perhaps they are even buying less, overwhelmed by too much information. In this case, the return on investment from advertisers also goes down. In sum, for the platform to increase revenues and profits to shareholders, the other parties (users and advertisers) have lost value (either measured in terms of time spent on the platform, or content, or advertising cost, or conversion to sales, etc.). This may also happen in an aggregated fashion: each individual social media platform finds the right balance of advertisement exposure; however, collectively the users are exposed to an overload of ads, resulting in the reduction of return of investment to all advertisers on any platform.

The implications for advertisers are obvious. Efforts to add more content or ads to social media platforms may not bring about the expected results. There is a loss of efficiency and profitability if the platform is in a process of decay. For companies, the best way of measuring the phenomenon is to keep gathering data for analysis and verifying the marketing efficiency of different channels. It is also important to measure whether changes in efficiency are coming from the way platforms work, or from the changes in the profile of one's customers. There are lots of variables moving around, from algorithms to overload of information and changes in customer preferences. Because the return on investment depends on campaign by campaign, channel by channel, it is not possible to come up with standardised expected numbers. Advertisers need thus to define their targets, measure those targets systematically, compare the targets from one platform to another, and make the fine-tuning to escape the negative impact of platform decay. Users will do the same, allocating time to social media channels which bring them more value.

References

Benkler, Y. (2006). *The Wealth of Networks: How Social Production Transforms Markets and Freedom*. New Haven and London: Yale University Press.

Bolstrom, N. (2014). *Superintelligence: Path, Dangers and Strategies*. Oxford: Oxford University Press.

Brown, J.S. and Duguid, P. (1998). 'Organizing knowledge', *California Management Review*, 40(3), pp. 90–111.

Carr, N. (2010). *The Shallows: What the Internet is Doing to Our Brains*. New York: W.W. Norton & Company.

Chui, M., Manyika, J., Bughin, J., Dobbs, R., Roxburgh, C., Sarrazin, H., Sands, G., and Westergren, M. (2012). 'The social economy: unlocking value and productivity through social technologies', *McKinsey Global Institute*. Available at: https://www.mckinsey.com/industries/technology-media-and-telecommunications/our-insights/the-social-economy (Accessed: 16 March 2024).

Deiser, R. and Newton, S. (2013). 'Six social-media skills', *McKinsey Global Institute*. Available at: http://www.mckinsey.com/industries/high-tech/our-insights/six-social-media-skills-every-leader-needs (Accessed: 16 March 2024).

'Enshittification' (2024). *Wikipedia*. Available at: https://en.wikipedia.org/wiki/Enshittification (Accessed: 16 March 2024).

'Facebook-Cambridge Analytica data scandal' (2024). *Wikipedia*. Available at: https://en.wikipedia.org/wiki/Facebook%E2%80%93Cambridge_Analytica_data_scandal (Accessed: 17 March 2024).

Frankwatching (2023). 'Leading social media platforms used by marketers worldwide as of January 2023', *Statista*. Available at: https://www.statista.com/statistics/259379/social-media-platforms-used-by-marketers-worldwide/ (Accessed: 12 February 2024).

Gartner (2022). 'Share of budgets allocated to online marketing according to CMOs worldwide as of March 2022, by channel', *Statista*. Available at: https://www.statista.com/statistics/1222784/marketing-budget-share-channel/ (Accessed: 12 February 2024).

Johnson, S. (2010). *Where Good Ideas Come From: The Natural History of Innovation*. New York: Riverhead.

Kietzmann, J.H., Hermkens, K., McCarthy, I.P., and Silvestre, B.S. (2011). 'Social media? Get serious! Understanding the functional building blocks of social media', *Business Horizons*, 54(3), pp. 241–251.

McAfee, A. (2009). *Enterprise 2.0: New Collaborative Tools for Your Organization's Toughest Challenges*. Boston, MA: Harvard Business Press.

McAfee, A. and Brynjolfsson, E. (2017). *Machine, Platform, Crowd: Harnessing the Digital Revolution: Harnessing Our Digital Future*. New York, London: W. W. Norton & Company.

'McAlpine v Bercow' (2023). *Wikipedia*. Available at: https://en.wikipedia.org/wiki/McAlpine_v_Bercow (Accessed: 17 March 2024).

Meta Platforms (2024). 'Number of monthly active Facebook users worldwide as of 4th quarter 2023 (in millions)', *Statista*. Available at: https://www.statista.com/statistics/264810/number-of-monthly-active-facebook-users-worldwide/ (Accessed: 17 March 2024).

Nonaka, I. and Konno, N. (1998). 'The concept of "ba": Building a foundation for knowledge creation', *California Management Review*, 40(3), pp. 40–54.

'Psychographics' (2023). *Wikipedia*. Available at: https://en.wikipedia.org/wiki/Psychographics (Accessed: 17 March 2024).

Redmond, T. (2023). 'Teams grows to 320 million monthly active users', *Microsoft Blog*. Available at: https://office365itpros.com/2023/10/26/teams-number-of-users-320-million/ (Accessed: 12 February 2024).

Rheingold, H. (2000 [1993]). *The Virtual Community: Homesteading on the Electronic Frontier* (revised edition). Cambridge, MA: MIT Press.

Smith, N., Wollan, R., and Zhou, C. (2011). *The Social Media Management Handbook: Everything You Need to Know to Get Social Media Working*. Hoboken, NJ: John Wiley & Sons.

Tencent (2023). 'Number of monthly active WeChat users from 3rd quarter 2013 to 3rd quarter 2023 (in millions)', *Statista*. Available at: https://www.statista.com/statistics/255778/number-of-active-wechat-messenger-accounts/ (Accessed: 12 February 2024).

Tuten, T. and Solomon, M. (2014). *Social Media Marketing*. Harlow: Pearson.

Zenith (2022). 'Distribution of advertising spending worldwide in 2022, by medium', *Statista*. Available at: https://www.statista.com/statistics/376260/global-ad-spend-distribution-by-medium/ (Accessed: 12 February 2024).

Zittrain, J.L. (2008). *The Future of the Internet – and How to Stop It*. London and New Haven: Yale University Press.

13 Metaverse
The 3D Internet

Introduction

The metaverse can be thought of as the 3D Internet; a way to experience new worlds through immersive Virtual Reality (VR) or through a hybrid mix of the real and the virtual worlds we call augmented reality (AR) – consider Pokémon GO. Today, there are examples of the metaverse in many applications across many fields as ideas are tried out. It probably does not merit being described as an infrastructure today in the same way as the WWW, but it may be on the way to such a status. It is an interesting and very contemporary example of how digital innovation is cultivated, but we have not reached a mature and widely used metaverse. Thus, this chapter is somewhat speculative and often discusses potential and smaller-scale innovations that could diffuse and scale up. This potential is intriguing and could become of great significance over time and if or when the metaverse establishes at scale its own core enabling infrastructures. If or when this happens, this potential metaverse infrastructure could deeply affect the way we socialise (social media), purchase products and services (e-commerce), enjoy entertainment (gaming, shows, movies, experiences), work together (manage projects, virtual offices, manufacturing), deliver education (virtual classrooms), and train people in new skills (simulators).

Humans have a long history of enjoying immersive experiences and alternative realities. Think, for example, of young readers entering the world of Harry Potter when reading the books, the 'muse of fire' Shakespeare offered the audience of *Henry V* in the Globe Theatre in London in the 1600s, or returning to a distant past in a galaxy far, far away when watching the *Star Wars* films. Today there is potential for digital technologies to extend and expand our access to such worlds – offering us an extended reality (XR) that we might use for all manner of purposes (Accenture, 2024).

Metaverse means a reality beyond or outside of our physical universe (see 'Metaverse', on Wikipedia, 2024). The term was first used in this sense by Neal Stephenson in the science fiction novel *Snow Crash* (1992). We all share a common understanding of the physical reality around us and our senses such as sight, hearing, touch, and smell keep us informed of what is going on in this reality. To take people to an immersive other reality, we need to link up with at least some of these senses. Digital technology can do this, for example creating 3D landscapes for people to move around in, digital personas (avatars) to interact with, and all supported by relevant stimulation in the form of sights, sounds, touch, or even (one day) smell.

When this extension of reality is overlapping with physical reality, we call it augmented reality (AR). A good example of AR was Google Glass, which allowed the person wearing them to view simulations as they moved around the world. AR can also be based on the cameras in our mobiles, as in Pokémon GO. Another simple example of AR is the IKEA app that lets you check how a new piece of IKEA furniture fits in your room. You point the phone camera at the place you

DOI: 10.4324/9781003385578-13

might want the furniture to be, and the app will 'add' the furniture to the image. Certainly, the furniture is not there, but it is as if it were.

When the extension of reality requires a more immersive experience, we call it virtual reality (VR). For this, we need to leave our reality behind and isolate the user from it to some degree. This can be done through a headset which blocks the vision and sound from the physical reality and feeds only the virtual reality. This will be only a partial VR, of course. Your body and sensations are still mostly attuned to the physical world. You can still feel the pull of gravity, space, and smell scents of the physical world even if sound and sight are taken over. Still, as humans we seem to give more relevance to the visual and audio aspects of immersion so we are able to 'suspend disbelief', just as we would reading *Harry Potter*.

Metaverse infrastructure is what potentially underpins and enables the creation of extended realities. In its simplest forms, we can experience a kind of metaverse through 3D virtual reality represented on the computer screen, for example in many computer games. In more advanced forms, metaverse infrastructures can create the illusion of a user being inside a 3D virtual space and moving around within it, interacting with what is there. This is usually achieved using headsets such as Meta Quest or Apple Vision Pro.

Using a headset, users isolate themselves from their normal visual reality and experience another world which is generated and animated by mathematical models and techniques of image rendering. In the future, researchers may want to go further and create a direct brain-computer interface to transmit information directly to the brain – the ultimate API. In such a futuristic metaverse the experience might be richer and more seamless, including perhaps smells, tastes, and other sensory and emotional experiences. You have seen this already at the movies in films like *Ready Player One* or *The Matrix*.

But we will leave such speculation about the future here. Our goal is to focus on what is already at hand, how a foundational infrastructure might emerge, and how this may affect businesses and societies in the near future.

A few basic ideas can be established. The first is that any kind of digitally extended reality or metaverse will depend on the Internet and on cloud-computing services accessed via high-quality broadband (speed, bandwidth, and reliability). The second is that the cultivations of the metaverse are closely bound up with other digital infrastructures and technologies such as artificial intelligence (AI) (see more in chapter 14) and the Internet of Things (IoT) (see more in chapter 11). The third is that the user technology for the VR experience is complex and not cheap. Gamers may choose to pay for many versions of rapidly evolving headsets – but will the average business user rush into this world?

The metaverse as business

Where are we today in achieving a metaverse? With a degree of certainty, we can say that the metaverse is more than a fad or a dream. There are many examples of digitally created virtual realities in the world around us. Think, for example, of the flight simulators that pilots use to learn and refine their skills, or the many training roles that are fulfilled using these technologies ranging from engineers learning to weld to surgeons practising performing appendectomies. These targeted uses are here because they have proven their value. But that does not make a metaverse a new space for interaction among large numbers of people – moving us from a 2D (graphics) to a 3D (spatial) experience. Because of costs and current technical limitations, we will be using regular Web and app interfaces and e-commerce platforms for some time. Looking to the future, however, we may one day be happy to shift some of our online activities to the 3D metaverse.

There is certainly a growing interest in the metaverse by the large digital services businesses. Meta – the owners of Facebook and one of the largest tech companies – has spent a few years and many billions trying to create a metaverse product to seduce us. Other large digital companies are working on metaverse-related systems and services too. This suggests that the metaverse may become a new and important layer of the digital infrastructure even if what we see today is limited and expensive. Meanwhile, the AI boom has diverted some attention and investment elsewhere.

Infrastructure, however, as we know, evolves and adapts, drawing on an installed base and powered by innovation and generativity as has been observed many times in the short history of the Internet and digital infrastructures. A new layer grows and develops as users are found, ideas are tested, and demand is cultivated (chapter 3). As discussed in chapters 1 and 7, there are some identifiable characteristics that make some infrastructures more potent and likely to generate the critical mass to take them forward.

We have been here before. About 20 years ago a start-up called Second Life developed the first significant platform to offer a 3D experience with immersive avatars. The graphics were on flat screens, thus headsets were not necessary, and the immersion was not what we might expect today. Second Life tried to establish a large and diverse user community where users could customise their avatars and create their own environment for interactions – for example, setting up a shop and transacting in the Second Life currency. At its peak, Second Life had more than one million users and is still operational today. However, it failed to thrive or scale up its use base. The idea was well thought out and the software works, but users just were not impressed.

Today's new generation of metaverse platforms draw upon similar ideas of being a virtual space for interaction, serving a large user community, but with more functionalities and a better sense of immersion. The most discussed large-scale metaverse platform today (2024) is from Meta, the owner of Facebook. The company even changed its name to Meta in 2021. Their intention was to send a message to the market that Meta would focus on this new 3D layer of the Internet, creating the infrastructure needed, attracting users to their platform, and supplying the hardware such as headsets (e.g., Meta Quest). Meta gained a great deal of publicity with their large investment in the metaverse through their Reality Labs division. This has included marketing campaigns showing how the metaverse might affect the way we live and work, with emphasis on entertainment, social networking, e-commerce, education, and working together. However, while they do offer many development tools for third parties, there are no substantial user products so far.

Microsoft, as you might expect, is more focused on business use of the metaverse through their Mesh interface. Their platform is integrated with their established software, such as Teams, and allows users to create customised avatars (as does Meta's Horizon), and meet in virtual environments. Their idea seems to be that people collaborate better in these spaces, achieving more engagement. Microsoft's headset, HoloLens, opens a door to other kinds of interaction, for example by creating augmented realities to support employees in tasks such as maintenance of machines, and construction work, where workers might visualise their tasks on site before undertaking them.

The idea of togetherness, highlighted by Meta and Microsoft, is also seen in Google's Starline project, a flatscreen which enables a 3D image of a person. The project uses AI to create the image on screen as if there was a real (3D) person in front of you. This is an interesting technology because it does not depend on a headset to create an immersive experience. Rather it is a technology which reproduces people as a digital version of themselves, the image based on a model instead of by real-time transmission of pixels, as in other video conference tools. People are not represented by an avatar but by a 'digital twin'. Meta is also investing in similar technology, although their approach requires the use of the headset to have a similar experience of seeing a person in 3D.

Game and entertainment industry companies are also investing in metaverse spaces. During the COVID-19 pandemic, Epic Games, the developer of the popular game *Fortnite*, organised Travis Scott's online concert (in 2020), attracting millions of fans to their virtual environment. This event gained headlines around the world, showing that people are interested in new digital experiences in the metaverse style, even when the interface of the interaction is the flat screen. In China, WeChat's owner Tencent is using XR for games, while other Chinese firms including Baidu and ByteDance are vying to create their own metaverses for games and entertainment.

How many metaverses?

Observing this multitude of companies and platforms, a natural question to ask is: 'Do we need one metaverse or many metaverses?' This question may appear to be trivial or at best premature, but it has generated lots of expert debate. If we interpret the metaverse in a broad way as an infrastructure similar to the WWW, then there is or will be pressure to end up with one metaverse. After all, resource pooling, openness, and standards as well as positive network externalities, would seem to lead in this direction. However, across the digital landscape, there are many spaces to which one cannot go – either because there is a paywall or login, or because there is a firewall which censors content for some users or countries. So, although there is one Internet and one WWW, the user often experiences them as multiple spaces. In the same way, there can perhaps be many different platforms presenting the concept of a metaverse, and these platforms do not need to even be interoperable. If you pay for Microsoft Mesh, you do not get access to Meta Horizon. Even moving personal digital assets from one platform to another is not facilitated today. Thus, although we may talk about *the* metaverse as one virtual space, we do not, and perhaps will never, experience this space as one, but as a variety of spaces. In this sense, we might talk about metaverses in the same way we understand our present multiple social media platforms.

The perception of separated spaces brings us to the discussion of interoperability. In the metaverse, if you buy a house on platform X, this house is not going to be identified on any other platform. The metaverse platforms are using different protocols and standards in their development, and no one company has a strong motivation (so far) to adopt a standardised protocol to facilitate interoperability. As discussed before in this book, this is not a problem in principle as the various multiverse platforms may become (inter-)connected through APIs (application programming interfaces) (see chapter 7). There may be a good business in providing logistics and moving services between various metaverses. But it is likely that the big companies will keep investing in their own standards for their own metaverse platforms. The best to expect is perhaps interconnection via APIs, and only when there is a business case for doing so – for example, if it allows a dominant metaverse to recruit from other, smaller, ones. However, perhaps the pressure will not be on to provide migration and users will prefer to distribute their VR and AR experiences among different platforms.

Meanwhile, each company operating in the metaverse will try to get the network effects working in their favour. Meta has experience with Facebook, Instagram, and WhatsApp, and we must assume wants to have a similarly strong market share in its Horizon Worlds. Creating an attractive environment, albeit closed, appears to be the strategy, and it is not a new one. As users of social media know, when we share content online, this content mostly stays on the platform. We can delete content, but we cannot easily move content to another platform. This favours incumbents. Facebook has benefited from network effects – people prefer to be in the place others are – and has contributed to the downfall of other social networks such as Google+, a case of winner-takes-all (or almost all). We can conclude that Meta has strong incentives to keep the gates of interoperability closed for now, especially if they expect the current users of their social media platforms to migrate to Horizon Worlds.

The question of timing was fundamental for the fate of Second Life: a good idea that was too far ahead of its time and faced other substitute products such as social media. The same question is asked about this new generation of metaverse platforms. For gaming, the terrain is very solid, with users adopting the technology and happy to pay the price. Gamers playing massively multiplayer online games (MMOs) value the more immersive experience. The same may be true for other entertainment genres such as music or drama. But in business use cases it is still hard to make a strong case. Immersive virtual reality requires headsets which are still expensive for the majority and which may not have the quality of sound or image that meets expectations. How long will office teams be interested in meeting in virtual spaces with their avatars? This is the kind of questions investors ask companies like Meta and Microsoft. A related question for potential business users of VR and AR is when (if ever) will it be the right moment to migrate their operations or their digital products to metaverse platforms?

The challenges and risks of the metaverse

The key question for the tech giants in relation to the metaverse is how quickly and broadly this technology will diffuse among customers and companies. Although the metaverse offers promising use cases, it requires massive investments in technologies that are moving fast themselves. A too-early investment may be lost if the state-of-the-art technology changes too quickly.

From the user's perspective, three main variables need to be taken into consideration. First, users will ask about the actual added value of the metaverse experience. Does it take more time to buy a pair of shoes in the metaverse than the regular website interface? If a person could try clothes, shoes, and bags together in AR, this may have stronger appeal and one does not need a full immersive VR experience to do this. Cheaper AR approaches, using mobile phones, may prevail. Second, potential users will think about the costs. The XR technologies, e.g., headsets, are expensive and may be uncomfortable to use for long periods. Some users feel motion sick after using VR headsets. The speed of the broadband and processing power of headsets is a limitation: the latency in the transmission of information and poor images diminish the user experience. Third, platforms do not offer interoperability (as discussed earlier in this chapter). Business users will want the facility of moving assets around, not being locked into one particular metaverse.

In terms of risks, the same problems affecting all digital products and services are repeated: privacy of personal data, security and cybercrime in terms of facing new tools for phishing and hacking, as well as for harassment and bullying. There are also issues of accessibility and equity: how to make it accessible to all people in society including those with physical and cognitive impairments. As with all digital infrastructures, there are important issues of sustainability too: metaverses require high levels of energy consumption to process the needed data. Any metaverse will evolve and use more and more AI and machine learning tools, which may bring more risks of applying biased algorithms if the training datasets themselves have biases. There are also concerns related to users' health since we do not know to what degree the use of VR headsets may trigger physical or mental health problems, including social isolation and addiction to virtual realities.

Metaverse use cases

Research from McKinsey (Aiello et al., 2022) shows a growing interest in using the metaverse for activities such as shopping, medical appointments, education, travelling, socialising, attending events, collaborating, and meeting new people, in addition to traditional gaming. The list is long and the potential is evident. In the sub-sections below, we explore a set of use cases for the metaverse. All the ideas discussed below are already under discussion or implemented in one shape or form. However, most of the ideas are not pervasive and may fail to develop. These use cases demonstrate both the opportunities companies, institutions, and governments have of exploiting the metaverse for business innovation and the inherent barriers to diffusion that this technology faces.

All of these use cases are opportunities, but all require significant investments and knowledge, and a capacity for putting together complementary technologies. All are ultimately at the mercy of their putative users, who may be pleased with their experience, but may also be unimpressed or even hostile. Thus, although the use cases exist and some users and customers might benefit from them, companies must verify whether there is a business case for any investment. Being a first mover is very expensive, and requires deep pockets for investment as well as a willingness to innovate business models. When reading through the use case examples below, it is interesting to ask which ones have the potential to create a breakthrough for the metaverse – what might be the metaverse's 'killer app'? The application that will turn it from a minority and marginal digital phenomenon to a significant and perhaps vastly profitable layer in the global digital realm?

Social media

The metaverse changes the quality of interaction on social media, moving from flat 2D dimensions to a 3D one. This allows individuals to create their own spaces, expressing themselves more broadly. Compare, for instance, the experience of building an identity on Facebook, using your profile and cover photos, with the possibility of interacting with friends at a party in your 'house' in a virtual 3D space, or going together to an online live concert. The more realistic or playful the experience, the more likely users are to prefer this metaverse over the 2D social networks.

The space for creativity, even generativity, is improved with all the possibilities of creating 3D spaces and digital objects, but this also requires a user to put in more time, effort, and (perhaps) money into the iteration. Some may prefer to keep it simple as it is today. More likely, users are going to choose moments of intense and synchronous interaction, such as a party or an online event, and moments involving more quiet, incremental, and asynchronous interactions. We can make a parallel with the way we interact on WhatsApp, sometimes with video calls or voice notes, and sometimes with emojis for a quick response.

Network effects will play a strong role in the potential use of the metaverse for social media interactions. Migration will happen only if and when we see a good number of people to choose the new channel. The preference will be, as ever, to be where others are. We can also relate this movement with the idea of opportunity cost: if the costs in terms of money and time are too high, people may prefer to keep it simple.

Advertising

The expectation of companies like Meta is that there will be a migration of advertisers from the flat screen and search engines to the 3D virtual spaces, in which advertisers will be more able to match the customer by accessing information about their virtual life. More information may be available in the metaverse if trusting users take the time to build virtual spaces close to their identities and aspirations. If the interaction is more emotional and genuine then advertisers will be better able to target their messages. Such a psychological profile may be more important than the search history that is the basis for online advertising today.

The right moment to show an advertisement can be predicted better, as happens today with dynamic advertising in games at the moment the gamer is most satisfied with their performance. Advertising may be more smoothly integrated into the action. Today on social media channels, the advertisements interrupt users. In the virtual world, the advertisements may be blended into the action. For instance, instead of being shown a picture of a fashion bag in a news feed, users may come across a digital catwalk model carrying the bag just in front of their avatar.

Companies will explore the best way of integrating advertisement into the action in virtual spaces – perhaps using a personal assistant to give information about objects. This sort of interaction between the seller and the potential buyer may improve conversion rates of those who show interest in a product or service, reducing transaction costs for sellers and buyers (as discussed in chapter 6).

It may be that the experience will become closer to the in-game advertising (see 'Advergames', on Wikipedia, 2024), in which the platform chooses the best emotional moment to add the advertisement. Another potential use of the metaverse is for brands to create their own games. For instance, Louis Vuitton created *Louis the Game*, in which the main character Vivienne explores locations to find 200 candles to celebrate the 200th birthday of the founder Louis Vuitton. This is an example of the gamification of advertising, when techniques of gaming are used in marketing strategies in order to increase the engagement with customers (see 'Gamification', on Wikipedia, 2024).

The concept of social media influencers may change too. Over time, digital humans (also called virtual humans) are more likely to be adopted by brands as social media influencers, as they are cheaper and easier to manage. Digital humans are software agents that present themselves in human-like bodies, communicating like humans, with language, facial, and body-language expressions, and having a sort of constructed personality powered by AI platforms that generate conversational content in natural language. We already see a movement towards digital humans in marketing campaigns (for instance, see the case of Miquela (also known as 'Lil Miquela', on Wikipedia, 2024), a trend that is easily transferable to the metaverse. Businesses may also use digital humans for customer service, training, and education. See, for instance, the services offered by companies such as Synthesia and Digital Humans Lab.

Entertainment

New forms of content may become viable in the metaverse. Virtual concerts will gain larger audiences, which cannot be accommodated in physical spaces. There are already successful examples, such as *Fortnite* organising the concerts with Travis Scott (mentioned above), Ariana Grande, and Marshmello, with many millions of people simultaneously attending the events. These experiences will help companies to reach economies of scale (audience size) and scope (variety of products) (as discussed in chapter 6). The audience may interact as well, creating new social connections as would happen in a physical environment (with positive social network effects).

Additionally, imagine the difference between watching a movie or a theatre play and being in the movie scene or on the theatre stage with the actors. The audience may also be able to tailor their experience, adjusting, for instance, the sound volume and the lighting of the environment, or the language being used. In a more sophisticated experience, the audience may choose the direction of the plot, through interactive storytelling – each member of the audience getting a different plot and outcome perhaps? This approach would bring a new understanding of how cultural experiences are created, decentralising creativity to a new level, and fostering high levels of customisation and personalisation in cultural experiences. Does that sound good to you, or does it seem to challenge the shared basis of most cultural experiences?

E-commerce

The metaverse might change the shopping experience. The more realistic the virtual reality, the more it could become a substitute for high street stores and for other forms of web-based e-commerce. Customers would have the opportunity to interact with objects in three dimensions, having a more complete view of the objects and a better understanding of dimensions and materials. The level of information increases if customers can ask bots – digital assistants – for extra information, using natural language instead of searching for keywords. This experience may be closer to talking to a sales assistant who is an expert in the product, making all information available at the time of request, thus reducing transaction costs for customers.

For some products, the metaverse platforms may offer facilities such as checking the fit of clothes and shoes. If the person has entered their information (height, weight, vital measurements, or even a body scan) into the platform, it is possible to find the perfect fit for clothes and shoes, with the advantage of being able to see one's avatar or digital twin wearing products. The customer has a customised experience which is to some degree more complete in terms of information than the regular experience in physical stores.

Companies such as Nike (Nikeland) and Gucci (Gucci Garden) are leading the way to make their presence felt in the metaverse, buying digital land in platforms to guarantee buyers can find their brands there. Chanel offers the app Chanel Try On for customers to try a virtual makeover before deciding which products to buy. Amazon has started the AR mobile app View in Your Room, which is used to show how some decorative and design pieces, such as furniture, would fit your room, similar to services offered by IKEA (furniture manufacturer) and Houzz (home design company), using the smartphone camera integrated with information about the furniture. Amazon also has the AR mobile app Virtual Try-On Eyewear and Shoes. In clothing, there are examples of XR in all price ranges. Walmart bought the company Zeekit to launch their mobile app Be Your Own Model, allowing customers to see how clothes fit on their bodies. At the other end of the spectrum, Farfetch, an e-commerce company specialising in luxury clothes, offers the Virtual Try-On app, with similar features.

These examples demonstrate the advantage of enhancing the customer experience and reducing information asymmetry, with customers being more confident to make decisions. With these apps, companies are reducing customer dissatisfaction and their costs for managing the return of products too.

E-products

As and when people move their interactions to metaverse platforms, a category of e-products may emerge. These e-products are already common in games, when players buy outfits, tools, weapons, and vehicles to better perform in the game, or to better represent their identities through avatars. As the metaverse expands to other sorts of interaction, other e-products may become available. For instance, Gucci and Balenciaga selling digital bags in the metaverse, and art galleries offering paintings for virtual spaces. These e-products become possible as individuals build their identities around their avatars, and they want to present themselves as associated with these e-products and brands. A new space for the co-creation of products emerges, as companies allow all sorts of customisation of digital products that would not be viable in the physical world (economies of scope).

In this environment, two questions arise. First, what is the value of a digital creation that may be reproduced with a marginal cost of zero? The value is in the eyes of the beholder, and if an object is perceived as a way of representing social status, attracting attention, or making an opinion known, people may pay for it in the same way they pay for bumper stickers or expensive watches that tell the time as well as cheap ones. The sense of scarcity does play some role; although the marginal cost of reproducing digital goods is close to zero (as discussed in chapter 6), companies might restrict access to goods through pricing and limiting the number of copies. Second, how does the buyer sell the digital product later? The metaverse platforms have the perfect match through blockchains. When you buy the e-product, there is registered evidence that the product is yours, and then you can later sell the same product and transfer ownership (see discussion of NFTs, non-fungible tokens, in chapter 6; see also 'non-fungible token', on Wikipedia, 2024).

Workplace

There are many possible applications of the metaverse in workplaces. The most obvious is to facilitate the interaction of remote teams, helping people to work together, reducing the time of commuting, and enabling collaboration between different locations. During the COVID-19 pandemic, many companies and professionals learned the advantages of virtual collaboration, using tools such as Microsoft Teams or Zoom. The metaverse could be an extension of this, in which a more relevant and interesting environment can be created to promote interaction.

The metaverse might offer better room for testing ideas out. New products may be able to have their virtual prototype tested among professionals and customers, who can make suggestions for product improvements. One example is BMW which ran a virtual factory on NVIDIA Omniverse to test the design of facilities before building the actual factory. This experiment tested processes to be implemented in the factory and allowed important design improvements. The metaverse can also be useful in providing all sorts of training, not least because virtual classrooms can be more convenient and flexible than physical ones. Motive.io, for instance, developed a virtual reality environment for training in the mining industry, allowing professionals to become familiarised with equipment and spaces before going to sites. Similarly, surgeons can train on operations in virtual environments. The company Flaim trains emergency services to face highly hazardous situations using immersive VR and simulations, and Walmart uses VR to train managers on how to manage the challenges of Black Friday sales.

The maintenance of equipment and machines can be facilitated by the use of augmented reality (see Internet of Things, IoT, in chapter 11). Sensors can capture information from equipment and machines – for example, an airplane jet engine – and a digital twin can then be built in the metaverse, representing the physical object. This digital twin can allow engineers to find problems in the physical world. GE Renewable Energy uses AR to support employees as they assemble wind turbines on-site, passing the right information at the right time. Overall, these approaches have been described as the 'industrial metaverse' representing an innovative combination of digital technologies that potentially deliver a new and more effective style of engineering and manufacturing (MIT Technology Review, 2024).

Education

The idea of the metaverse supporting collaboration in the workplace carries over to education. The same platforms for delivering interactive training are being trialled in all levels of education. The goal is to improve collaboration and engagement, deliver better education with better educational outcomes, and span geographical boundaries. At its best, this kind of education can benefit from both economies of scale and of scope. The sorts of content to be shared in educational virtual realities can have different qualities. For some disciplines, traditional learning approaches through books and small co-located groups may be perfect. For others, the richness of the learning experience in a virtual interactive environment might be transformational, not least because the experience can be tailored for the individual.

These experiences might allow students to ask more questions, receive more individual assistance, and absorb materials at their own pace. In addition to the quality and depth of the content and the interaction, the metaverse may facilitate access to education and amplify the options for students with special educational needs or disabilities. Even teachers may benefit from these new developments perhaps freeing up their time for more in-depth or one-on-one discussions. But we must not get too carried away with dreams of a 'technical fix' to be applied to what are essentially social domains. Technologies always embody different interests and need to get worked out in use – that is be cultivated in fertile soil (chapter 7). They seldom bring unalloyed benefits, and often they imply more problems. Just think of the messy and unclear outcomes for education that the mobile phone has brought.

Tourism

Perhaps what we can call tourism will be changed by the metaverse. There are many reasons why a virtual experience may be preferable to real travel: virtual tours for those who prefer to experience other places at lower costs, lower carbon footprints, and lower risks. The COVID-19 pandemic and the impossibility of travelling did open our imagination for travelling at home. For instance, Thomas Cook created a virtual reality holiday, 'Try Before You Fly', through which customers could choose to go to a selection of places virtually using the immersive 360 Samsung Gear VR. Could such virtual travel open a new market for virtual tourism in its own right, or could it motivate more people to explore more challenging physical travels after having lived the virtual experience? Time travel may also get a boost if virtual worlds can take us back to the past with very realistic representations of historical facts and places, or even travel forward to an imaginary future. Such a use case for tourism could be easily associated with social networks, as people may want to share the experiences synchronously.

References

Accenture (2024). 'Extended reality.' Available at: https://www.accenture.com/gb-en/services/technology/extended-reality (Accessed: 17 March 2024).

'Advergames' (2024). *Wikipedia*. Available at: https://en.wikipedia.org/wiki/Advergame (Accessed: 17 March 2024).

Aiello, C. et al. (2022). 'Probing reality and myth in the metaverse', *McKinsey*. Available at : https://www.mckinsey.com/industries/retail/our-insights/probing-reality-and-myth-in-the-metaverse (Accessed: 12 February 2024).

'Gamification' (2024). *Wikipedia*. Available at: https://en.wikipedia.org/wiki/Gamification (Accessed: 17 March 2024).

'Metaverse' (2024). *Wikipedia*. Available at: https://en.wikipedia.org/wiki/Metaverse (Accessed: 17 March 2024).

'Miquela' (Lil Miquela) (2024). *Wikipedia*. Available at: https://en.wikipedia.org/wiki/Miquela (Accessed: 6 August 2024).
MIT Technology Review (2024). 'The emergent industrial metaverse.' Available at: the-emergent-industrial-metaverse-update-2024.pdf (Accessed: 29 April 2024).
'Non-fungible token' (2024). *Wikipedia*. Available at: https://en.wikipedia.org/wiki/Non-fungible_token (Accessed: 17 March 2024).
Richter, F. (2023). 'Meta's money pit: Metaverse bet bleeds billions', *Statista*. Available at: https://www.statista.com/chart/29236/operating-loss-of-metas-reality-labs-division/ (Accessed: 17 March 2024).
Stephenson, N. (1992). *Snow Crash*. New York: Bantam Spectra Books.

14 Artificial intelligence

From algorithm to infrastructure

Introduction

It is always dangerous to make bold statements about a technology that is evolving quickly. However, many experts do seem confident that in the 2020s we are in a revolutionary moment, when the applications of artificial intelligence (AI) across all human activities are becoming clearer. AI technology is emerging from decades of over prediction and under performance. It does so by harnessing the computational power available in cloud infrastructures and applying it to machine learning (ML) algorithms. On this basis, AI is becoming a digital infrastructure in its own right, with platforms providing 'artificial intelligence as a service' (AIaaS) and potentially fostering generativity across the economy and society. This new AI is being integrated into many existing activities, powering office tools, e-commerce, social media, gaming, data analytics, self-driving cars, healthcare, and legal systems. The list is long and demonstrates strong evidence for the pervasive potential of AI, even if some of these areas will be more transformed than others.

The generic term AI encompasses any software that executes complex tasks considered to require human-level intelligence (or beyond). It has been applied to a number of technologies over the years since Alan Turing wrote about the 'Turing Test' in 1950, addressing the then very new computer's potential for intelligence. Over the years, progress in this direction has been slow, with each iteration developed to address a particular application. These have included tasks such as image and voice recognition, natural language processing (NLP), translation, conversation, medical diagnosis, creation of texts and images, and sophisticated decision-making. All these types of tasks have been targets for AI research, some for many decades.

But we are living through a breakthrough era in AI based on a group of AI techniques called machine learning (ML): mathematical algorithms which use statistical methods to learn from existing data and to apply the learning to analysis of new data or to create new outputs that draw on the learning (see 'Machine learning', on Wikipedia, 2024).

The earlier approach to developing intelligent software has been for programmers (humans) to write rules to be executed by the software. For this to work, we need rules to express the output we expect from the software given a certain input. For instance, if you are using a spreadsheet, you expect that the input '=2+2' is always going to result in the same value '4'. This method of coding rules into software has allowed us to digitalise most of the activities computers undertake today. First, there is a rule, second, someone encodes the rule into the software, and third, the software responds to inputs following the rule.

Coding rules into software works if you know the rules. When rules are too complex to be defined by humans or when humans do not know the rules, we hit a wall. Humans have the capacity for identifying images and faces, differentiating cats from dogs, and understanding that a voice has a tone of sadness or excitement. But can we explain the rules used for executing

DOI: 10.4324/9781003385578-14

these tasks? The answer is probably 'no'. So how can machines do these tasks if we humans do not understand the rules we use? Attempts to create rules for such 'tacit knowledge' have often failed and this rule-based approach for creating intelligent software that can mimic small bits of human intelligence has made slow progress, finding applications in more formally structured environments. So an autopilot can safely land a plane based on the rules of physics and some rules that experienced pilots can explain.

A new generation of AI researchers, with vast computing power available to them, moved on from the idea of programming rules made by humans. The new paradigm is for the software to learn the rules from its own statistical analysis of available data, and create a mathematical model which represents the rules. The software adjusts the model to become more accurate or efficient through calibration of the weight given to variables in accordance with their relevance in predicting a desired result. Instead of informing the machine of the rules for identifying cats, just supply millions of photos of cats and ask the machine to create an algorithm (model) good enough to identify cats in images. In the AI world, a model is a trained set of algorithms ready to exhibit 'intelligence' when providing outputs (observe that the word model here is used as a synonym of the algorithm, which is different from other parts of the book when a model may mean a conceptual framework, as in chapters 4 and 8).

Given enough cases to consider, some sort of rule for identifying cats can be discovered by the ML algorithm without human intervention. From the photos, the machine learning algorithm chooses the variables to use. Is it about the colour, the position of the eyes, the type of fur, the size of the nose, the type of ears, or something else? Indeed, it is about all those things and many more. The machine learning algorithm calculates all sorts of mathematical and statistical relationships and tests whether the evolving algorithm is good enough. A measure of 'good enough' can be established by applying the model to other datasets: if the model identifies cats with a high level of precision, it is working well.

There are four implications from the use of this type of ML. The first one is that the optimisation of the algorithm takes into consideration the training dataset available. If you need to improve the model, you may need more or different data, or you may need to remove poor or misleading data from the dataset. If the dataset has no Siamese cats in it, the model may deny them their cathood – a biased model.

The second is that the model trained to identify cats is useless at playing chess or identifying birds. It does only what it has been trained for. However, the same algorithm may be able to be retrained, expanded, or adapted for other similar functions, e.g., identifying small mammals.

The third implication is that the environment is stable – the training data represents the world as it is documented in datasets. The cat model will remain effective over time – cats do not change their appearance much from decade to decade. In areas that do change, the retraining of algorithms must be done often. Cybercriminals are always innovating in the way they work. An AI model trained to identify and block cybercrime must be regularly updated to the state of the art in the domain.

The fourth implication is that the model is probabilistic, rather than deterministic. When you use a spreadsheet for calculating '=2+2', the answer must always be the same deterministic one, '4'. When you ask the AI algorithm to identify cats in a photo, the answer will be right most of the time, but not always. It is important to understand the limitation of probabilistic models and not expect from them what they cannot deliver. AI for medical diagnosis can work with probabilistic image analysis – but can it work in the same way for robotic surgery?

The second implication illustrates the gap between AI models, which are trained to solve one problem or a family of related problems, and the dream of artificial general intelligence (AGI), similar to humans (see 'Artificial general intelligence', on Wikipedia, 2024). We are not yet close to AGI – as of today our ML AI models are for defined domains. However, there is movement in this direction. In November 2022, the company OpenAI made available the application ChatGPT (Chat Generative Pre-trained Transformer). ChatGPT belongs to the family of generative AI able to create (generate) text output following prompts by users. These prompts are made in natural language in the form of questions or statements to trigger a conversation. The generative capability of ChatGPT and other similar technologies is based on their statistical models. Given what the model has learned from previous patterns, the application is able to generate new content, considering the probability of one word following another during the creation of the text, based on the prompt. ChatGPT does not meet most experts' tests for AGI, but it is nonetheless impressive in the scope of knowledge and tasks it can do – even if it makes many mistakes.

ChatGPT's outputs are based on the vast corpus of knowledge (files found on the Internet) used to train the model. You can ask ChatGPT to write a text about the history of AI, the architecture of Spain, or the working of a steam engine. The tool will then start with this objective, looking within the body of knowledge it was trained with for the statistically most relevant sources. It will then use a generative model to add words one after the other, considering the probability of these words coming together in the right sequence. In this way, it will reach the objective defined in the prompt, following as closely as possible past patterns of expressing similar ideas and contents.

A similar learning and generative strategy is used by ChatGPT to write computer software. It has been trained with open-source code libraries found on the Internet, and is able to reuse and adapt this code to new requirements, generating 'new' code from natural language requests for functionalities, or improvement of a provided code, or translating the code from one software language to another. OpenAI, the developer of ChatGPT, has trained other generative AI models to create images (DALL-E) or videos (Sora) following text-based prompts provided by users. These OpenAI resources are available to all through the Web and Internet, providing the first experience of AIaaS to many people. There are equivalent services for business users and embedded uses accessible by APIs (application programming interfaces), particularly for organisations which want to create new products on top of ChatGPT. Other cloud providers have similar services, such as Amazon, Microsoft, and Google, and the Chinese Tencent, Baidu, and Alibaba.

Types of Machine Learning and other AI methods

There are three common machine learning categories. Understanding these helps to understand if AI might provide a solution or not to a given problem, and which type of AI might be most appropriate for a defined objective. The discussion here is at a conceptual level only, avoiding statistical models or technical language.

Supervised learning

In supervised learning, the ML uses labelled training data for creating a model able to identify a defined category of 'things'. Labelled means that the thing of interest is clearly identified. The ML algorithm then learns which characteristics and patterns are likely to indicate the categories of interest: 'cats', 'dogs', or 'people', for instance. The trained model can then be tested in its ability to identify cats, dogs, or people by using other unlabelled datasets (in this example, simulating 'computer vision', i.e., the identification of images). In this approach, a human agent has to label the 'things' to focus on: cats, dogs, or people, and score the test results. In such training, there is no concern about elephants or birds. Supervised learning is useful for identification and classification tasks. It is also useful for categories of problem, when the inputs and outputs are numerical or can be interpreted in numerical ways, and where there is an expected relationship between variables (e.g., credit scoring is related to incomes and previous behaviours in paying back loans).

Unsupervised learning

In unsupervised learning, the ML learns from unlabelled data, thus patterns are identified independently of human inputs. ML clusters observations into groups, defining its own relevant patterns, although the machine does not *know* what has been clustered. This approach is useful for defining tasks that revolve around similarities and differences. Because the training set is not labelled and there is no input from humans on variables to be used, the final model after training may be large. If so, it may be possible to apply a technique of dimensionality reduction to find a smaller set of variables which allows a good if not excellent clustering (the more variables in a model, the more processing power is necessary to run it). Some examples of business applications for unsupervised learning are: image classification, spam detection, predictions for customer behaviour, and cleaning datasets.

There are also hybrids of these first two methods. For example, in semi-supervised learning, the model learns mainly from unlabelled data, with a few inputs of labelled data. This approach may be appropriate if a dataset is available but not fully labelled, or if a dataset could be labelled for better results, but labelling the full dataset would be too time-consuming or expensive. The results of the hybrid mode may be more accurate than unsupervised learning alone, and tend to be faster too. There are other learning strategies, such as deep learning and generative adversarial networks (GANs), but they are beyond the scope of this book.

Reinforcement learning

In reinforcement learning, the ML learns through rewards. When the output is better, it is told so. The more the ML goes in the right direction, the more rewards and the more reinforcement. In games, the model needs to have the objective of winning, and to develop strategies to deliver this objective. This may be achieved independently of humans defining strategies for the game. A good approach to speed up the learning may be to put two ML algorithms into play against each other. Very quickly, they can play the game millions of times. In this way Google DeepMind's AlphaGo Zero learned how to play the game Go without receiving input from humans other than the basic rules of Go. The same rationale has business applications. For instance, reinforcement learning is used for creating algorithms for self-driving cars and drones, training robots to move objects around in warehouses, or dynamic pricing strategies. In environments of dynamic change, reinforcement learning models can adapt, using new data and new feedback for learning new strategies.

AI foundation models and infrastructures

Whatever learning model is used, locating and preparing relevant data, and providing the powerful computing resources needed for training represent significant challenges. Supplying these services is the business of the AI infrastructure. The architecture emerging has a layered structure (as discussed in chapter 4), where fundamental sharable and reusable components/services needed to train a model are offered to a broad base of customers. Like any other infrastructure, the aim is to share resources and bring economies of scale and scope while serving a wider set of users and diverse usage (as discussed in chapter 6). The potential generativity that AI platforms and infrastructures will foster is one reason why so many commentators are convinced of the economic and social impact we should expect from them. It is also the reason so many large tech companies are investing so much in the area.

At the heart of the AI infrastructure as it emerges today are foundation models (FMs). These are large machine learning models (enabled by neural networks) that are trained with vast data resources which can then be reused and tailored for developing multiple new applications. Basing an application on FMs saves time and money for users who need AI for new uses, bypassing the need to start training the ML from scratch (economies of scale). FMs are able to perform generic tasks such as generating texts, images, and videos from natural language prompts. FMs are bigger and more expensive to initially develop than the traditional ML models developed for specific tasks. Training FMs is very resource heavy – it can take months and millions of dollars of electricity to power the highly specialised computing resources. Thus, only big or well-funded companies have such resources to draw on. It is not surprising that the driving forces in supplying AI services for business are the world's biggest and richest tech companies. FMs do not emerge out of small start-ups unless they have very substantial backing.

The FM approach to implementable and useful AI for businesses speeds up the development of targeted AI applications. The industry structure seems to be emerging with big tech companies creating FMs and offering them on their platforms as well as via APIs. Other organisations, big and small, can create apps or services to run on top of these AI infrastructures (as we have discussed before in the case of digital business platforms, in chapter 8). Some examples of FMs already offered in this way are Google's BERT (Bidirectional Encoder Representations), OpenAI's GPT (Generative Pre-trained Transformer) and DALL-E, Amazon Titan, AI21 Jurassic, Anthropic's Claude 2, and NVIDIA's NV-Dinov2.

AI adoption

AI is thus not a one-size-fits-all technology, or one-service-fits-all either. As discussed, ML models need to be specific for the task, and trained with relevant data. There is almost certainly a need to collect, clean, and label data before training. A model then needs to be tested and optimised using separate test data, and then put into action with new 'live' data. As things change and time passes, models will need retraining – both the foundational models and the apps built on top of them. Some applications may require continuous retraining cycles in turbulent environments – think of stock trading, for example.

For most organisations, AI is or will be based on the reuse and adaptation of foundation models or on simpler generic models, for example, a chatbot. Even quite large companies cannot easily justify the investment to train their own models from scratch. It seems more likely that the majority of the commercial use of the new AI will be based on foundation models and their adaptation delivered as a service. As more companies use these services, the costs for all will be reduced (economies of scale, discussed in chapter 6), at the same time that the potential variety of uses from the same models will allow economies of scope (same resources generating a larger variety of outputs, also discussed in chapter 6). The full architecture that will evolve is not clear at this stage, but will probably have parts of the models in the cloud, and other more local edge applications that manage clients' data and address their specific needs.

In the process of creating AI applications, one concern is about having a business strategy which enables the organisation to develop better-integrated solutions. A fragmented approach may later generate problems of interoperability and management of legacy systems. This is not to say that it is impossible to design such a new digital infrastructure (we discussed this design limitation in chapter 1), considering that tools and solutions in this domain are changing so fast. Any architecture must be flexible enough to accommodate the growth in terms of new applications and solutions (following the layer strategy discussed in chapter 4). In addition, decision-makers need to focus on the right timing for such investments. Rogers (2003 [1962]), discussing the process of diffusion of innovation, saw that the first adopters are innovators who have more resources to accept the risk of innovation (as discussed in chapter 2). As AI technology matures and is better understood, other more risk averse agents may embrace it. The timing of their investment is important. Gartner's concept of the hype cycle is helpful here (check Gartner, 2024) for assessing to what degree the technology is perceived positively or negatively, and to what degree there is maturity around the technology and a good understanding of pros and cons for different use cases.

As emphasised throughout this book, digital infrastructures are not designed from scratch, but are cultivated. From what we know about infrastructures we can predict that AI platforms are likely to evolve as other cloud-service infrastructures have, following a modular architecture (allowing different combinations of blocks), delivered via APIs and charged on a per-use basis. Their architecture will be driven by their economy of scale and of scope, and by their generativity capacity, based on their ability to exploit standards and open APIs. How open these standards and APIs will be is not clear. The size of investments required to develop the infrastructure clearly implies that the platforms will expect a solid revenue model – but how do you monetise intelligence on tap? Is it the Google search model where the data processed is the payment, is payment by results, is payment based on resource consumption, or is payment by subscription?

From the user perspective, ways for businesses to embed AI tools in their activities may take different routes. One is to use platforms and services that have embedded AI. For instance, Microsoft Copilot is embedded in many Microsoft products. A company can benefit just by exploring the availability of such tools and training employees to use them. The second and harder way is to revise processes within the organisation in a way that they can exploit new AI tools, and perhaps restructure the organisation itself. Again, this approach to new technologies has been seen before, for example, in the 1990s fad for 'business process reengineering' (BPR). AI models have limitations and pose risks – remember, the model makes up its own rules, and may be too complex to be understood. Perhaps for this reason applications that 'enhance' decision-making and support professionals, but keep humans in the loop, will be preferred – perhaps as a sort of reimagining of the older idea of decision support systems.

Where does AI find its role?

There are plenty of unknowns when considering the future of AI as a service. What is far clearer is the areas where AI tools and services are already working across many businesses. In this section we briefly identify some of these key use cases. From the examples below, we can foresee that companies may benefit from AI with economies of scale (AI accessible for a lower cost), economies of scope (a higher variety of outputs can be reached with the same technology), and with opportunities for improving or innovating business models (e.g., with new value propositions).

- *Data analytics*. The essential idea of data analytics has evolved over many decades as statistics, operational research, business intelligence, big data, and expert systems. Behind these concepts, the enduring concern has been how to obtain high quality data which can be analysed by models and algorithms in support of better and faster decision-making. Doing data analytics with AI tools is another step forward. IBM Watson Content Analytics, for instance, is a trained model able to process structured and unstructured data from many repositories, preparing data for analysis or training other models as well as discovering relationships and anomalies in data. Google used DeepMind to recalculate the use of energy in their data centres, being able to optimise the energy consumption for cooling facilities, with savings in the order of 40%. Social media platforms benefit from AI-powered data analytics for better understanding the preferences of users.

- *Customer support*. AI applications for customer support are often in the form of chatbots answering customer questions (voice or text), including understanding sentiment and mood during a conversation, classifying reasons for the contact, making recommendations and giving information, analysing contact data, and predicting customer behaviour. Generative AI models can create virtual fitting rooms and other immersive customer experiences. Amazon and Netflix both use AI for making recommendations to customers, with better targeting and better conversion (sales or retention). Clients of Salesforce use Einstein, a CRM (customer relationship management) tool powered by AI, for managing customers and social media interactions. Retail and banking services and platforms particularly benefit from the application of AI for customer support.
- *Cybersecurity*. AI applications are used for identifying and stopping threats, identifying weaknesses, and suggesting areas for improvement. AI tools may identify anomalies in behaviour that could indicate a potential risk or an actual attack using the identification of individuals by biometrics and deciding their permitted level of access. Mastercard, for instance, has been using AI for more than a decade to identify patterns of fraud. The key to stopping financial fraud is to be able to detect anomalies in real-time and act promptly, as well as recognising that there will be false positives (legitimate operations identified as frauds). Email systems such as Outlook are using AI to identify potential phishing attacks. All sorts of online services benefit from the use of AI for cybersecurity, including governmental operations.
- *Content creation*. Generative AI can create content in forms such as text, images, and videos. Content creation can offer levels of personalisation for services and goods, relevant across areas such as education, entertainment, gaming, and social media. Meta provides AI tools for advertisers to automatically create different backgrounds and texts, taking into consideration the preferences of different audiences. Broad questions about creation and authenticity arise. For example, what are the rights of owners of the content used to train the generative AI models? There is also a serious concern among creative professionals. In 2023, the Writers Guild of America (WGA) organised a strike to force a discussion on the risks of generative AI substituting humans when producing scripts for films and TV shows. The strike happened in parallel with one organised by the Screen Actors Guild – American Federation of Television and Radio Artists (SAG-AFTRA), to protest against studios using their digitalised faces to digitally produce performances. More broadly, across all the creative industries we can predict a significant impact on the way people perceive culture and interact with cultural products and experiences. AI tools are already enabling individuals with no skills in content creation to 'create' visual and written material through prompts (ideas expressed in natural language).
- *Product development*. Advancing one step from content creation, AI tools can support the development of new products, working in collaboration with (or in place of) designers, engineers, and product developers. AI models can improve the understanding of customers' needs, and are able to propose innovations. AI can inspire new ideas and help to visualise, design, or experiment with them, for instance generating images of prototypes or even prototypes themselves (for software products). For example, BMW uses machine learning to

simulate the impact of crashes in cars, helping to improve the design of vehicles for more safety. In an environment in which AI is a co-developer of products, professionals will at the very least need to adapt their roles more towards bringing insights to trigger AI responses. AI tools may inspire new ideas and challenge assumptions, which is likely to have positive impact on the innovation of products and services.

- *Process automation.* One of the biggest promises of AI is related to process automation. From the birth of business computing in the 1950s, computers have been seen as the tool for undertaking routine tasks, such as data entry, order processing, invoicing, reporting, and quality control – key operational activities which absorb resources. AI tools may be able to learn about current practice and generate more efficient or effective processes. For instance, IBM Instana uses AI to automate the monitoring of the information technology infrastructure, identifying when any part of the system has problems (poor performance, bugs, dysfunctionality), thus avoiding or reducing the downtime of operations. During the development of the COVID-19 vaccine, Moderna used an AI tool for automating work related to testing the design sequence of the messenger RNA (mRNA), moving their capacity for producing and testing from 30 mRNA sequences per month to a thousand, mainly using the same resources (Ransbotham et al., 2021).
- *AI assistants.* These AI tools aim to provide support to professionals and individuals as they perform their tasks, undertaking tasks such as answering questions (e.g., Alexa, Google Assistant, Microsoft Copilot, Siri), managing calendars, selecting documents for analysis, organising paperwork in the right order for a process or in order of importance, and generating transcripts and translations in real-time. For instance, IBM watsonx offers a mix of tools to help individuals and teams, and Google Maps and Baidu Maps use AI for tailoring and contextualising recommendations to drivers in real-time based on current information on traffic. There is an expectation that AI assistants will increase human productivity across many functions and industries.
- *Generation of synthetic data.* ML models depend on large datasets with quality data. However, sometimes the ideal datasets are not available, or they would take too much time to be constructed, or they are too expensive, or they are incomplete or biased. To overcome this limitation, computer and data scientists are generating 'synthetic data' to train AI models. The assumption is that if the synthetic training dataset has the same characteristics as the actual data, the machine will learn. For instance, synthetic data on insurance frauds could be added to the dataset, in order to have more 'instances' to be analysed and learnt from, speeding up the training of the model. Also, if the actual dataset has biases (e.g., gender, ethnicity, socioeconomic status, etc.), a synthetic dataset could be created by randomly distributing attributes in such a way that the model would 'learn' that these attributes are not important (avoiding biases).

AI risks and challenges

Discussions on the risks of AI have taken many directions, some of them very concrete and obvious, and others informed more by the unknowns around these applications and the way the technology may evolve. Two main aspects can be identified and are briefly discussed here. The first is about how the current generation of AI operates through ML. The second is about the expectation that it is only a matter of time before AGI, or something that looks quite like it, will be developed – technology that takes us beyond human intelligence, and may be much more autonomous and potentially uncontrollable.

First, let's focus on the current limitations of ML. As explained in this chapter, ML is a technique based on statistics and probabilities rather than deterministic programming. Thus, although the solution presented by any ML tool may be good enough the majority of times, occasionally the response will be wrong; you cannot trust the answers 100%. We also cannot be 100% confident about human answers. If machines are better than humans, should we be happy using machines? There is a crucial difference we need to think about though: we can ask people to explain how they justify their decisions or hold them responsible; we cannot do this to the same degree with ML tools. The methodology which makes ML so powerful in defined environments makes the code very difficult to explain (low explainability) and there is low transparency on how AI models make decisions (low interpretability). When the model fails, it can be difficult (if not impossible) to understand why and then how to fix it, and in any case the identification of problems after failure is not very comforting. This adds an obstacle to the broad adoption of such technologies and makes many people deeply uneasy at every step along the way.

For instance, a human resource management tool trained with a database of cases which have favoured appointing men instead of women may well generate an algorithm which is biased against women. The ML does not directly discriminate. The model does not know the difference between women and men beyond a simple categorisation in the data. If in the past the category 1 has performed systematically better than the category 2 in a job, the ML is going to recommend mainly individuals in category 1. If in the past recruitment officers have been biased and given more and better jobs to men, and if managers have been biased in promoting mainly men, the machine is going to 'learn' that the category 'men' has better attributes to do the job and to progress in the job. Is it possible to eliminate such biases? One could remove the information on gender, but the algorithm may find other data points which are proxies for the same information. For instance, women and men in a society may have cultural preferences for some sports, or they may use different words to express the same meaning in a cover letter. For these reasons, it has proved difficult to remove all forms of biases from training datasets, even when all protected characteristics are removed. The model still reflects the world as it is represented in the datasets.

The probabilistic nature of the models means that 'mistakes' will happen. Check, for instance, the risk of 'hallucinations' in generative AI. If you use generative AI tools such as ChatGPT by asking questions you are going to see, for example, that the tool may create references which do not exist, or may confuse facts related to one entity with another, or may just invent facts to make a good story. Where is this bad behaviour coming from? ChatGPT produces text based on large language models (LLM), driven by calculating the probability that one word follows another word. The output then depends on how the sequence of words starts. Occasionally, the model will present a very well-formulated but still totally wrong answer. A person who is an expert in the domain may immediately recognise the mistake, e.g., attributing the development of Google Maps to IBM (a result obtained in one of our prompts). But the non-expert may not see the error. Obviously, if the dataset has errors, the chances of having errors in the model increase. The old management saying applies to AI: garbage in, garbage out.

Second, let's focus on the increasing capabilities of AI models and the scope of their application. As they become more pervasive, it becomes more difficult for humans to differentiate between true facts and AI-generated facts, including texts, photos, and videos. Deepfakes can be used to blackmail people, destabilise democracies, or trigger other cybercrimes. In 2023, a deepfake video of BBC journalists announcing a new investment scheme offered by Elon Musk to British residents had broadly circulated on Facebook. The post on Facebook was linked to a fake BBC page, 'confirming' the news and providing links for potential investors to apply (see research by Full Fact, an organisation which checks the veracity of potential fake news or deepfakes) (see https://fullfact.org/). Although most people would ignore such an offer on the basis of common sense (following the rule of 'too good to be true'), we all will be taken in sometimes.

There are some entrepreneurs, academics, scientists, philosophers, and futurists who are very pessimistic about the existential risks AI poses to human beings. At the core of their concern is the understanding that AI algorithms will become increasingly complex, thus difficult to understand and control, and that AI companies will inevitably pursue the aim of artificial general intelligence (AGI), combining a better-than-human intelligence with infinitely more capacity and speed for processing data and taking action; a scenario with great potential for bad consequences. In a situation in which AI solutions are pervasive, very integrated across processes, and dependent on a few providers, a critical incident with AI may quickly spread damage across organisations, societies, and countries (an example of a negative network effect, as explained in chapter 6).

These experts defined the concept of AI 'singularity' to refer to the moment intelligent machines became more intelligent than humans, thus achieving the level of AGI. So far, the AI tools are domain-specific, very good and better than humans in many aspects, but always within a narrow domain. The singularity would mean that AI tools are better than humans in all domains and perhaps beyond domains humans can manage. This scenario for some is not only possible, but a source of deep concern as humans could lose control of the technology itself. For others, this scenario is hypothetical and may never happen. And for the most optimistic among us, this scenario would bring about the opportunities of a new era for humans, who would use the tools very wisely.

The Future of Life Institute published an open letter in March 2023 with thousands of signatures from experts asking for a pause on all large AI experiments, for a period of six months. The time was proposed in order to understand the risks and mitigations before something uncontrollable happens. Their main concerns were how to avoid the negative impact of flows of fake news misleading people and organisations, and the problem of intelligent machines substituting humans in jobs and decision-making – there is evidence for both issues and concrete actions that could be taken. We can observe that there is a battle between institutional interpretations of the level of risks and acceptance of AI technologies, which will affect the way AI services will diffuse across societies. This tension is also present in the discussions on whether AI tools and services must be regulated (see more in chapter 15).

But for AI developers and the big tech companies, the time is now. They are racing against each other to create more precise and powerful AI tools and to stake out their presence on (possibly) the most important digital infrastructure in our future. The genie is out of the bottle and even if some countries try to control the development of AI through robust governance, other countries or non-state actors will not.

References

'Artificial general intelligence' (2024). *Wikipedia.* Available at: https://en.wikipedia.org/wiki/Artificial_general_intelligence (Accessed: 17 March 2024).

Gartner (2024). 'Hype cycle.' Available at: https://www.gartner.co.uk/en/methodologies/gartner-hype-cycle (Accessed: 18 February 2024).

'Machine learning' (2024). *Wikipedia.* Available at: https://en.wikipedia.org/wiki/Machine_learning (Accessed: 17 March 2024).

Ransbotham, S., Candelon, F., Kiron, D., LaFountain, B., and Khodabandeh, S. (2021). 'The cultural benefits of artificial intelligence in the enterprise', *MIT Sloan Management Review.* Big Ideas Research Report, in collaboration with BCG. Available at: https://sloanreview.mit.edu/projects/the-cultural-benefits-of-artificial-intelligence-in-the-enterprise/ (Accessed: 17 March 2024).

Rogers, E.M. (2003 [1962]). *Diffusion of Innovations* (5th ed.). New York: Free Press.

15 Issues of governance and regulation

Introduction

The layered model has been used in this book to explain how digital infrastructures evolve from fragmented pieces to products and services which support economies and businesses (see chapter 4). We can use this idea of layers also to better understand the governance and regulatory aspects of digital infrastructures by taking two perspectives. The first is that governance and regulations are themselves layers of digital infrastructures, as they affect the way the other layers are going to interoperate and the way people and organisations are going to use the other layers. The second is that governance structures of digital infrastructures evolve over time as new uses and new users occur. In the same way that digital infrastructures evolve through the addition and change of their associated elements within layers, governance rules and regulations evolve with shifting technologies and altered practices of use. Nobody could have decided from the beginning how to guarantee the governance of the Internet because the network was always going to evolve in ways nobody could foresee. And today, nobody really knows how current digital infrastructures are going to evolve from now, or the governance and regulations that will be necessary.

There is a fundamental reason why we should care about the governance and regulation of digital infrastructures. It is that they have become a fundamental part of our lives. The more businesses and society are dependent on digital infrastructures, the more we need to be sure that these digital infrastructures do not get out of control. The fact is that digital infrastructures have become critical for the wellbeing of societies, and for producing wealth. We cannot run the risk of having such resources being misused or abused. For instance, if governance rules are not in place, a country may use the Internet to attack the digital infrastructure of another country in a cyberwar. Indeed, we are already in a poorly disguised cyberwar: daily, companies and governments suffer systematic attacks from criminals, some sponsored by governments, trying to steal research, commercial data, and security and defence information. What would happen if a country could not use Internet resources for one week or one month? What would happen if a country had its mobile communication system stopped by another government?

This chapter develops topics that can help our understanding of why it is necessary to have governance and regulations of digital infrastructures, to protect critical services in our economies and societies. However, it is also necessary to be critical of how governance and regulations are going to be used, in order not to destroy the benefits of having open digital infrastructures which can be used by all. Any sort of governance means that some international and national bodies have more power than others. Thus, this discussion is also about which international bodies and systems are to be trusted to protect the interests of people. We do not have an answer to these questions, but we want to share interesting questions on the matter.

DOI: 10.4324/9781003385578-15

Conceptualising governance and regulation

Governance and regulations are terms related to the establishment of principles, norms, rules, and procedures which allow organisations and institutions to better manage a particular process or a particular asset. The aim of having governance and regulations is to get better efficiency and reliability in relation to expected outcomes, and to reduce the risks involved in the management of processes and assets. Corporations, for instance, have governance mechanisms and processes in order to control and direct the way things are done and ensure that decision-making is legitimate in its environment. The governance rules should define the corporate policies and inform who is involved in decision-making, and how the organisation monitors and controls the actions and practices of its employees, directors, and service providers. The corporate policies should be based on laws and regulations to be sure the organisation is doing as good a job as possible to protect the interests of stakeholders and society.

There is, however, a big difference between defining the governance of a corporation – which is already a complex task – and defining the governance of a digital infrastructure which operates around the globe. Trying to control the development of digital infrastructures centrally is almost impossible; businesses, governments, and individuals will find ways to not follow imposed central rules, thus bringing unexpected outcomes for the whole infrastructure. Therefore, a bottom-up approach may be more effective in bringing social actors together to build a public good which is in the common interest of all (see more in Constantinides and Barrett, 2015).

Think again about the layered architecture (discussed in chapter 4). We have argued in this book that digital infrastructures are not designed from scratch. Rather, they evolve over time through the interaction of many layers. In such a model, any digital infrastructure is not coordinated centrally by any institution. Each part of the big assembly which results in a digital infrastructure has its own history, with legacy systems (installed base) not only in terms of hardware and software, but also in terms of the institutional and regulatory bodies which support different elements of these layers. This is the task behind discussing governance and regulation structures for digital infrastructures which have become critical to our societies.

Internet governance and regulation

The Internet is a globally distributed network which is not owned by any one person, organisation, or government. It is a collection of individual networks which voluntarily connect themselves to the whole through communication standards. However, in order for each network to be able to join the Internet, and in order for the Internet to be operational, it is necessary to create norms of governance and regulations, which are adhered to by each of the networks on a voluntary basis, to have in exchange for the benefit of being connected to the whole. For communication to flow from any point of the Internet to the other, the governance rules and regulations should be respected by all parts involved in this communication, at least in the fundamental levels of communication standards and protocols.

Imagine a government which decides that a country is not following the established governance and regulations of the Internet in terms of protocols (software layer). The first outcome would be that the network in this country would not be able to connect to the other networks. However, even if the hypothetical country was able to connect to the Internet, the other nodes of the network would not be interested in connecting back, depending on the sort of damage that this particular network would bring to the whole. In other words, the other nodes could decide to isolate a specific country if the governance rules were not respected. Thus, although adherence to governance rules is voluntary, in the case of the Internet, the decision not to follow the rules may have a cost of not being allowed on the Internet.

In order to work as an integrated system, although it is indeed a collection of parts which are interoperable, a lot of institutionalised structures need to give support to a particular form of governing a digital infrastructure. In the case of the Internet, civil society bodies, corporations, government, and academic and research institutions come together to cooperate and agree on the governance model. For instance, if you decide to open a new company and want to have an Internet address for this business, you need to have a domain (an online address). You cannot go online, for instance, and publish content in the name of www.wikipedia.org or claim the property of this domain, because Wikimedia Foundation is already using this domain (and pays for it), and owns the trademark.

If the Internet is free and people can do much of what they want, how is this sort of abuse avoided and controlled? This is possible only because there is a global institution called ICANN (Internet Corporation for Assigned Names and Numbers), which registers domains and controls who has the legitimate right to a domain. The domain is a unique identifier of particular content. If many people could use the same domain, the Internet would be useless, as nobody would be able to find the expected content. It would be impossible to reach particular content with security, and search engines would not work properly.

ICANN is a global organisation directed by professionals who represent corporations, government, and civil society. However, ICANN's Affirmation of Commitment is defined by the US Department of Commerce, and the American governmental body. This situation has its roots in the way the Internet has evolved historically: the Internet has been developed in the United States, and since the beginning has been regulated by the American government. The United States was the first country to create the domain rules. Once other networks decided to join the American model, they also accepted the rule of ICANN, which in addition to domains regulates Internet Protocol addresses, application port numbers in the transport protocols, and other technical matters. There is a path dependency in this process, as the original governance bodies are still working in a much more extended network.

From this situation, there is plenty of debate as to whether ICANN should be a truly independent institution controlled by all countries. However, there are many issues within this discussion. For some, the United States is doing a very good job of providing the rules of governance for the Internet, with a very democratic body of institutions influencing ICANN. Why should we bother to change? Others would say this arrangement gives too much power to one country, and that today we should have a collaborative attitude, but tomorrow we may decide to change the rules of the game. On the other hand, the American government may not have any incentive to change the rules. The global Internet depends on ICANN, which empowers the position of the United States in the whole game. A government may decide to isolate itself from the Internet to define its own rules on its own network (see the North Korean model). However, collectively, most people and organisations want to be in the place others are (positive externalities), thus they play the game following ICANN rules.

The technical aspects of the Internet and the standardisation of the Internet core protocols (such as the IPV4 and IPV6) are defined by another institution, the Internet Engineering Task Force (IETF). This is a non-profit organisation which gathers professionals from all around the world to work on relevant topics and define by consensus (or the closest to a consensus possible) what the new Internet standards should be. The objective of the IETF is to have technical professionals who can contribute to the definition of Internet standards, including activities such as testing the proposed technical developments. This organisation works as an open community of voluntary professionals, who are, however, mainly sponsored by corporations and governments.

Although the IETF was also created by the American government, since 1993 it has been managed by the Internet Society, which is an international non-profit organisation focused on providing leadership on Internet-related topics, such as standards, education, access, and policies.

Also, the World Wide Web Consortium (W3C) defines the standards of an Open Web Platform that supports the development of applications for the Internet. The idea is to have a collection of standards for different types of data and applications that allow developers to create rich interactive experiences for the final users in any sort of device – from computers and mobile devices to printers, televisions, and cars. In addition, the W3C aims to provide an environment in which access to the Internet resources is universal, meaning that anyone who wishes to publish on the Internet should have the means, independently of the sort of device and software they use, and the sort of Internet access they have. These W3C standards define, for instance, the use of HTML5 language, the Semantic Web Stack, XML (Extensible Markup Language), and many APIs (application programming interfaces). The W3C works through consensus building to make technical recommendations on software development for the Internet, providing governance and regulations through the definition of standards.

In addition, there is the Internet Governance Forum (IGF), created in 2005 by the United Nations, with the objective of having a multi-stakeholder body – organising the collaboration of governments, corporations, civil society, academics, and researchers – which focuses on defining Internet public policies. The IGF can propose topics of interest and make recommendations, but it cannot impose a decision on any party. The organisation discusses topics such as openness (human rights and freedom of expression), security (hacking and cybercrime), privacy, diversity, and Internet accessibility. It also discusses further issues, such as the role of the Internet in fostering development, how to improve digital trust, and how to understand the relevance of the Internet economy.

Governance layers

Yochai Benkler (2000) argues that Internet governance has three layers: the physical infrastructure layer (hardware), the code and logical layer (the software and the architecture, which control the Internet as a digital infrastructure), and the content layer (which refers to the information which is available on the Internet). The content layer is the most obviously controversial one, as there is a wide range of interpretations about how much and what kind of information should be freely accessible on the Internet and other digital infrastructures. But governance is by no means limited to the content layer (see, for example, the discussion on net neutrality later in this chapter).

Some authors have argued that Internet governance needs to go beyond its technical aspects, entering the levels of the outcomes one may have for using (or not using) the network. From this perspective, it is necessary to consider the legal, economic, and sociocultural aspects of the network, exactly because of its relevance as a critical infrastructure of economies and societies (see more in DeNardis, 2010). Some would like Internet governance to include discussions of the content of the network, which has become a place also for cybercrimes and copyright infringements. However, any attempt to control the content of the Internet may lead to censorship and surveillance, which are against the ideals of the Internet being a place of freedom.

In terms of content, there are plenty of disagreements on how to regulate the Internet. Lawrence Lessig (2004), for instance, has advocated the reduction of copyright protection for content that can be distributed through the Internet. As discussed earlier in this book, digital goods can be copied at a marginal cost close to zero. Although the cost of producing the first copy of a digital good may be high – for instance, producing a film – it is very cheap to produce copies of the same product. Copyrights thus creates an obstacle for the copying and distribution of protected content. By restricting reproduction, copyrights protect the right of producers to sell their products. But how much protection is fair from the perspective of consumers and society as a whole? When people remix copyright content, for instance, to create a different thing, should this be protected by copyright? We can see that this discussion is not straightforward: there are many stakeholders with divergent interests in this debate.

Access to content can also be filtered by governments, which may disagree with the overall governance of the Internet on this matter. For instance, the Chinese government prohibits some sorts of content and some services, such as Gmail, Facebook, X, and YouTube. European governments have strong rules regarding hate speech. The Iranian government prohibits the search of keywords which can allow a citizen to reach the content of opposition movements. The Saudi Arabian government controls content it considers improper for the country's culture and religious beliefs. Governments may use Internet service providers (ISPs) to filter or control what people can access online.

At the same time, governments around the world have made efforts to stop illegal content being accessed in their countries, many times relying on the goodwill of search tools and service providers to filter the content or to inform authorities on suspicious use of the Internet. Many citizens would expect governments to be able to investigate the Internet communication to restrain and avoid cybercrimes. They also would expect governments to be able to investigate the Internet to find criminals and terrorists who use the network for communication and organisation. However, in order to deliver these expectations, governments need to increase the surveillance of all, meaning reduction of privacy. There are trade-offs in whatever regulation a society chooses.

Sometimes the regulation of the Internet comes from the content or service provider. For instance, Facebook defines in its policy what users can publish on the network. When the policy is not respected, Facebook deletes the content independently of the will of the user. Facebook may also punish the user by suspending their account. Is this acceptable? Some would say Facebook is a proprietary service, thus the company can decide what content is acceptable. If a user is not happy, just change to another social network. However, others would say that Facebook has become too dominant to be allowed to make decisions alone, without further regulation. Facebook policy is imposed top-down, not necessarily taking into consideration that national laws may protect freedom of expression and speech of citizens.

Self-regulation and industry regulation

Governance rules and regulations are not neutral. There are always interests behind the technical choices, which influence the way we behave online and how the content we publish can be, to a greater or lesser extent, controlled by others – companies and governments. Lessig (2006) argues that code is law: the code which supports the Internet is also an instrument of controlling society. We can see this idea of code as law in a broad way: even when not used for surveillance and controlling of society, a technical device is going to influence behaviour. The point is thus to guarantee that the governance of the Internet is done in the most democratic and transparent way. At least in the code layer, it has been more viable to have self-regulation of the Internet through the participation of a diverse range of stakeholders in the definition of standards (through ICANN and the IETF, for instance).

In the hardware layer, industries have been instrumental in defining governance and regulations. At the end of the day, the economic actors in an industry want to have business done. Imagine a world, for instance, in which each mobile operator used a different standard to communicate, in such a way that a customer of network A could only talk to other customers of the same network. Certainly, this fragmented network would not be as useful to the customer as the actual current model. The current model is possible because economic actors in the mobile industry cooperate to create common regulations which are shared by all. They leave competition to the sphere of product and service creation and provision, agreeing that for the good of all that it is better to have a common communication standard. Some would see this model as the best way forward in terms of reaching proper regulations for the hardware layers: the industries should define the regulations of each aspect of the digital infrastructures, avoiding involving governments. This consensual model among industry parties may work well for some aspects, but may also end in irreconcilable disagreements. For instance, in some countries, mobile operators had a ferocious dispute with customers for years regarding not allowing people to keep the same mobile number when changing service providers. This sort of disagreement is not in the interest of customers, and thus governments have been helpful in forcing mobile operators to change their behaviour.

The consensual model also works for some aspects of the software layer – for instance, agreement over using HTML language and the standards for adopting WWW infrastructure. However, code is also about creating filters to prohibit content or to control how people use the Internet. Thus, some elements of the software layer can be easily standardised in accordance with technical needs, while others are very controversial. The consensual model is also not going to work in the content layer of digital infrastructures, considering the infinite variety of interests we may have in any topic. The most probable outcome is that the current trend becomes more established over time: regulations are to be defined by each country, which is going to align these rules with the national legal framework. This fragmentation is a source of conflict for global corporations that provide services and products as part of digital infrastructures.

For instance, cloud services are affected by local legislation. Technically speaking, data could be moved to any place allocated in the cloud considering the capacity and proximity of servers. However, national laws protect the privacy of citizens and corporations in different ways. For this reason, cloud-service providers need to adapt their offering to each client considering the local legislation for that particular client. This means that the same cloud-service provider is offering many different services, depending on the country where each customer is located. We can see then that local laws that affect only the content layer have an impact on the hardware aspect, for instance, defining the level of investment in data centres in each country. This shows again the strength of the hourglass architecture model (discussed in chapter 4), which shows that each layer influences the others. The same logic applies to the governance and regulations of digital infrastructures.

A new area of governance concern is the use of advanced artificial intelligence, particularly machine learning and deep learning, which creates complex mathematical algorithms based on massive datasets. The bigger the datasets, the more reliable the algorithms will be in modelling patterns from the data. However, the problem is that even the more skillful computer scientists may not be able to explain the mathematics behind the algorithms. In a regular piece of software, programmers and developers code the algorithms, telling the machine how to execute a process (as discussed in chapter 14). With machines creating the algorithm, humans may not understand exactly how the AI model has proposed a solution.

What is the consequence of this? One could say simply that if the match is good enough and if people are happy with the result, there is no need for concern. We do not need to understand the calculations behind the results. However, this means that we cannot guarantee the rules of good governance are properly embedded in such an AI solution. If we cannot explain how the machine has reached an answer, then we cannot guarantee this answer is legitimate considering the laws and norms of a society. Two examples below can help us to understand the complexity of the topic.

The first example shows that some AI algorithms used in recruitment have discriminated against women, particularly in environments in which traditionally women have not been employed in the same numbers or conditions as men. Analysing these algorithms, it has been discovered that models were reproducing the same bias observed in previous recruitments, as per the datasets (Black and Van Esch, 2020). However, the problem now is bigger than before. If we know that humans have biases, we may try to reduce these biases through mechanisms such as also having women in recruitment panels. But if we think that the AI solution is not biased, then we may ignore these risks and accept the recommendation from the algorithm. In this example, it becomes very difficult to guarantee good governance.

The second example is about the difficulty that AI algorithms demonstrate in identifying with precision the faces of individuals of some ethnic groups (Buolamwini and Gebru, 2018). In this case, research has demonstrated that the problem is in datasets, which have a smaller representation of some ethnic groups. If more photos and videos are provided with a broader set of characteristics, the AI solutions will learn to identify any individual with the same level of precision (or equal error). Thus, the solution is to increase the representation of more ethnic groups in databases. However, what do we do while this problem is not corrected? Should we still allow AI applications to be used to recognise faces? If such a technology is used to give or withhold access to services, the implementation of a faulty technology means that some ethnic groups will have difficulties in accessing services. Even worse, if this algorithm is used to identify potential criminals, some ethnic groups would face a higher risk of being wrongly identified. An error in the algorithm may have serious consequences, undermining the fairness of a society.

Herzog (2021) discusses the problems of algorithmic bias from the perspective of access to opportunities. Although mainly invisible to most of us, algorithms are shaping the options we are offered everywhere. For instance, if a search engine offers better jobs to men, this means women looking for jobs through this search tool will not see the opportunities offered to men. Thus, a problem from the past is reproduced systematically by new algorithms undermining societal efforts to implement structural justice. Similarly, a credit score algorithm which considers residential address could easily affect the capacity of people living in a poor neighbourhood to get a loan, despite their good behaviour in paying back loans, thus creating a structural mechanism which limits their opportunities.

An increasing number of scholars, entrepreneurs, and experts are becoming concerned about further risks of AI diffusion in an uncontrolled manner. Some fear AI may bring existential risks for human beings when these technologies are used for making decisions not controlled by humans or controlled by evil agents (as discussed in chapter 14). For some experts, the only way to avoid this scenario is through strong regulations defining how AI can be developed and deployed. Following this increasing perception of risks, the European Union AI Act (2023) is one of the first comprehensive attempts at regulating the use of artificial intelligence, and it may become a starting point for other countries' discussion of their own legislations for the domain. The EU AI Act lists, for instance, what constitutes unacceptable risks for humans, such as the manipulation of people, the use of AI for scoring social behaviour, and real-time and remote biometric identification of people. This list of risks shows clearly the strong concerns experts have about how authoritarian governments may control citizens. The legislation thus aims to protect individuals and citizens against abuses from companies and governments.

Privacy and data protection

Within the broad scope of governance, we can add the discussions on privacy and data protection – topics which have become increasingly more important the more we understand how our data is used by companies and governments. Information about individuals and groups has always been used in one way or another by governments, organisations, and societies, and the idea of defining boundaries between what is private or what is not has also occupied the public debate since antiquity. As discussed by Solove (2008), the definition of privacy goes from the freedom of thought and freedom from surveillance, to the control of personal information and protection of reputation, crossing even the perspective of one's right to control their own body.

The more recent concerns about privacy, though, are fuelled by the increasing use of digital technologies to capture and process the data of individuals and groups, with aims of obtaining more information about the ways people think, act, and feel about as many topics as possible, and the way people are related to each other and to institutions, organisations, and groups. In exchange for services and convenience, most of us have accepted that to use digital services means to give the providers access to our data. Most of us, though, expect that these service providers will use our data in a legal manner, respecting our privacy.

Cases such as the scandal of Cambridge Analytica (see chapter 12) are perceived as being exceptions to the rule. However, the use of data about us is a fundamental part of business models on the Internet. All free services which depend on third-party advertising use our data for a better match between advertisers and potential buyers. The better the match, the higher the chances of converting a potential customer into an actual customer. This is a trade-off most of us accept, although some of us may become uncomfortable about the dimensions we have reached in terms of surrendering too much of our personal data (and privacy) in exchange for services and convenience.

Discussing this issue, Shoshana Zuboff (2019) coined the concept of 'surveillance capitalism', claiming we live in an age in which our experience as humans has been translated into behavioural data through the means of having digital technologies intermediating our interactions. These pieces of information are then processed by algorithms, which more recently have been further empowered through the adoption of machine learning techniques (AI). With these processed pieces of information about individuals, one can much better forecast behaviour, and to some degree induce the behaviour one wants, empowered by what is known about each individual. We can also extend this rationale to governments, which may not be interested in profiting from advertisement, but may very much be interested in controlling behaviours and political views of individuals.

Considering the way digital technologies make visible what was before invisible in terms of human interactions and individuals' characteristics and profiles, we can recall here the concept of the Panopticon, developed by Jeremy Bentham (1791) (see 'Panopticon', on Wikipedia, 2024). The author proposed an architectural design for a prison in which prisoners would be potentially watched day and night, although they would never know in a given moment whether they were. Bentham proposed that this system would facilitate the disciplining of individuals through the constant fear of being observed. Michel Foucault (1977) revived this concept of the Panopticon, also connecting the idea of surveillance to disciplining. This very same argument may be expanded to our contemporary societies, in which digital technologies have created a virtual Panopticon, which may be abused (or not) by companies and governments. In theory, an authoritarian government could metaphorically 'imprison' the whole population through means of controlling their behaviour through digital surveillance technologies.

Despite discussions on the limits of privacy, there is a certain level of understanding that privacy is an essential pillar of our freedoms and democracies, as well as of our wellbeing, psychological individuality, interpersonal relationships, and even capacity of being creative, and should as such be protected by laws and regulations (Solove, 2008). From this perspective, democratic countries develop laws and regulations which aim to protect the privacy of their citizens. Solove (2008) lists some of these laws. For instance, in the United States, the Supreme Court defined that governments must not conduct searches in domains in which individuals would expect a reasonable amount of privacy. The courts in Canada, France, Germany, Japan, and India have recognised the rights of privacy, meanwhile other countries have added the concept to their constitutions (e.g., Brazil, South Africa, and South Korea).

A good example of such a legislation is the European Union's General Data Protection Regulation (GDPR) (2016), which regulates information privacy in European Countries. The GDPR has enhanced the control individuals have upon their own personal data, also regulating how their information is transferred inside and outside of the European Union. This legislation has become a model for many other countries around the world, such as Brazil, Turkey, Japan, South Korea, and South Africa. Also, the California Consumer Privacy Act (CCPA) has relevant similarities with the European GDPR. Companies with global businesses who want to operate in markets such as the United States and Europe must implement digital interfaces and data processing to respect these legislations. In many cases, it is cheaper for companies to implement higher standards of data privacy across the world rather than trying to have a patchwork of local processes. In this direction, the GDPR and the CCPA have positively influenced a change in behaviour among companies and governments in the realm of data privacy and protection.

Issues on net neutrality

Net neutrality is the term used to define a particular form of distributing information through the Internet. In this model, ISPs, telecommunication companies, and governments are supposed to treat all pieces of information in the same way during transmission through the Internet, neither discriminating against them in terms of speed and priority of transmission, nor charging for any sort of content in a different way, nor censoring or blocking any sort of content that two parties legally share. The same principle used for information should be applied to users, websites, platforms, applications, access devices, and forms of communication, which should not be discriminated against or charged differently. With net neutrality, any two parties can interact on the Internet without the interference of a third party. Without net neutrality, a third party (ISPs, governments, mobile providers, etc.) could interfere in interactions, reducing our degrees of freedom.

Net neutrality is a fundamental principle of the Internet to guarantee equality among users and content providers, transparency in the process of transmitting data on the Internet, and an environment which favours innovation. One of the ideals of the Internet is that the network is open, meaning that Internet resources should be available to any person, company, or organisation (including governments). Anyone should be able to use the Internet in the same conditions as others with similar resources. Naturally, the information distributed by broadband has more speed than the information distributed via a dial-up connection, but this difference comes from the features of the technical infrastructure, rather than from someone (a gatekeeper) deciding that one user should get more speed on the Internet than others.

There are many ways of breaking the net neutrality principle, allowing companies and governments to become gatekeepers between content providers and users. For instance, a service provider can block or reduce the speed of a particular communication protocol, prohibiting videos in its network. In this case, a particular sort of protocol is penalised. For example, the service provider could slow down the speed of transmission of videos and force content providers of videos to pay more for having the normal speed back. A second model could block particular Internet Protocol addresses or treat these addresses in a different way. ISPs may use this model to impose fees on content providers which demand more bandwidth or which have more users.

For instance, an ISP may decide that either Google Search pays part of its profit to the ISP or the ISP blocks Google Search in its network. Some governments use this approach to filter those websites they consider to be opposed to their political interests. Similar mechanisms could be used by the owner of an ISP to favour a political view of a candidate, blocking or reducing the speed of access to the content of rivals.

Some ISPs and telecommunication companies argue they have invested lots of money in building their networks, thus the way they distribute content in their infrastructure is their own businesses. From their perspective, the ISPs would have the right to decide which pieces of information could be distributed (and the price that content providers and users would have to pay to get these pieces of information). If a user is not happy with an ISP, just contract another service provider. The invisible hand of the market would regulate the access to information. However, there is no such competition in the market. In any locality, we do not have many service providers to choose from, just as we do not have too many electricity, telephone, gas, and water suppliers. In many places around the world, a household has one service provider. Even if some places have five or six service providers in rich countries, the argument favouring market competition is fundamentally flawed because it ignores the discussion on who has the power to control the Internet. Today users navigate the Internet without gatekeepers. They pay for the ISP access, but they decide what to access. Why would a user be interested in having less freedom?

Those who defend net neutrality regulation argue that societies cannot allow some economic actors to have such power in defining Internet traffic. Digital communication is too important a right for societies to delegate to market forces and private companies the power to make decisions in the name of all. The argument goes that societies should guarantee by law and regulation the right to net neutrality in order to avoid situations in which gatekeepers maximise their profits instead of maximising the benefit for users and society. From this perspective, the lack of regulation goes against the principle of net neutrality and allows abuses to happen.

Those who opposed net neutrality regulation argue that the market should decide who will be the gatekeepers of the Internet. They argue that if service providers cannot make as much money as they would like (for instance, charging extra fees from Google, Amazon, Netflix for the use of their networks), they will not build better networks. This argument is logically flawed: the service provider may charge the final user in the way they wish, finding the right price to maximise profits. This is a fair use of price mechanisms, without making the service provider a gatekeeper of Internet traffic. The revenue would come from users, not content providers. If there are other obstacles to investing in Internet infrastructures, the government may need to step in to provide Internet infrastructure to speed up the digital development of a country.

Indeed, there are strong arguments that net neutrality favours innovation, reducing the entry barriers of those who want to challenge incumbents. Today, if an innovator offers a better service, anyone can choose to use this better option. Once upon a time, Facebook was a start-up, challenging incumbents such as MySpace and Orkut. Facebook could not be viable in a world in which incumbents could make deals with ISPs to block the access of new companies to the network. Without net neutrality, the Internet would become a place for those who have the means to get better deals, instead of being the place for better innovations from the perspective of users.

Of course, a country may regulate by law that different types of data should be treated differently in accordance with the order of priorities. For instance, emails and voice data could have priority over videos and games. This would imply that every time a network is very busy, games and videos would need to wait till the emails and voice messages have passed through nodes. This is a sort of discrimination by type of data, which attends to the needs of users to maximise the benefits for society without empowering the service providers as gatekeepers.

From the discussion above, it is implied that any attempt to protect or reject net neutrality depends on national legislation and regulations. As discussed in this chapter, it is a big challenge to try to define governance and regulations for digital infrastructures which are, technically at least, global structures with pieces which are regulated by national governments. When the matter is really technical, such as a communication protocol, it is easier to get an agreement (although it may take a long time to reach a consensus), considering all parties are interested in keeping the communication flow. However, when the matters are more political or affect business interests, there are more conflicts and disputes. In our example of net neutrality, it is clear that we have stakeholders with very different perspectives, and that national legislations can either empower the people, society, and most businesses, or serve small but powerful groups which control critical parts of the Internet infrastructure.

References

Benkler, Y. (2000). 'From consumers to users: Shifting the deeper structures of regulation towards sustainable commons and user access', *Federal Communications Law Journal*, 52(3), pp. 561–579.

Bentham, J. (1791). 'Panopticon – or the inspection house', in *Online Library of Liberty: The Work of Jeremy Bentham*, Vol. 4. Available at: https://oll-resources.s3.us-east-2.amazonaws.com/oll3/store/titles/1925/Bentham_0872-04_EBk_v6.0.pdf (Accessed: 24 February 2024).

Black, J.S. and Van Esch, P. (2020). 'AI-enabled recruiting: What is it and how should a manager use it?', *Business Horizons*, 63(2), pp. 215–226.

Buolamwini, J. and Gebru, T. (2018). 'Gender shades: Intersectional accuracy disparities in commercial gender classification', *Proceedings of Machine Learning Research*, 81, pp. 1–15.

Constantinides, P. and Barrett, M. (2015). 'Information infrastructure development and governance as collective action', *Information Systems Research*, 26(1), pp. 40–56.

DeNardis, L. (2010). 'The emerging field of Internet governance', *Yale Information Society Project Working Paper Series* (17 September 2010). Available at: https://www.researchgate.net/publication/228199379_The_Emerging_Field_of_Internet_Governance (Accessed: 17 March 2024).

European Union (2016). *European Union General Data Protection Regulation (GDPR)*. Available at: https://gdpr-info.eu/ (Accessed: 7 August 2024).

European Union (2023). *European Union AI Act (EU AI Act)*. Available at: https://artificialintelligenceact.eu/the-act/ (Accessed: 25 February 2024).

Foucault, M. (1977). *Discipline and Punish – the Birth of the Prison*. New York: Vintage Books.

Herzog, L. (2021). 'Algorithmic bias and access to opportunities', in Véliz, C. (ed.), *The Oxford Handbook of Digital Ethics*. Oxford: Oxford University Press, pp. 413–432.

Lessig, L. (2004). *Free Culture: How Big Media Uses Technology and the Law to Lock Down Culture and Control Creativity*. New York: Penguin Press.

Lessig, L. (2006). *Code Version 2.0*. New York: Basic Books. Available at: http://codev2.cc/download+remix/Lessig-Codev2.pdf (Accessed: 17 March 2024).

'Panopticon' (2024). *Wikipedia*. Available at: https://en.wikipedia.org/wiki/Panopticon (Accessed: 5 August 2024).

Solove, D.J. (2008). *Understanding Privacy*. London and Cambridge, MA: Harvard University Press.

Zuboff, S. (2019). *The Age of Surveillance Capitalism: The Fight for a Human Future at the New Frontier of Power*. London: Profile Books.

16 The future of digital infrastructures for business innovation

Introduction

This book aims to provide a broad understanding of digital infrastructures and their role in processes of innovation and change, balancing technical, societal, and business perspectives. Our point of departure is that while we all need some technical knowledge, it is not worth much without the other two aspects. Throughout the book, we have tried to add details gradually to build understanding. This may at times make the book a bit repetitious, but it does serve a pedagogical purpose of cultivating emerging understanding rather than announcing truths. Digging deeper into the subject is relatively easy by reading more and using the myriad online resources that are at our fingertips thanks to digital infrastructures.

Innovation in digital technologies and how we use them continues, showing no signs of coming to an end. It is good to keep up, but the more difficult and interesting the issues raised by these novelties, the more elusive are Thoreau's 'improved ends' (as discussed in chapter 4). We can easily get lost if we focus only on the technical aspects of innovation and uncritically accept the latest gizmos or hyped-up business models.

In such a rapidly changing domain, models and theories can help you understand more, see further, and make better judgments along the way. The theories and models introduced in this book can give more depth and nuance to our analysis, and help us know when to focus on the forest (macro view) and when to focus on the trees (micro view). But still, our theories and models remain contestable: they help us see but they do not tell us the truth.

In this spirit, this last chapter summarises key ideas discussed in the book and introduces some emerging topics for further research and reflection. These topics are chosen because they are being developed and first put to use now.

From infrastructures to innovation: What we know

We have adopted the layered model as our most fundamental conceptualisation of the architecture of digital infrastructures, and in particular the simple three-layer hourglass architecture (Zittrain, 2008). We have chosen this model as a good representation of the way digital infrastructures of all kinds evolve and how they enable innovation. Our focus on the Internet in the early chapters reflects first its importance as the bedrock of almost all other digital infrastructures, platforms, and digital business models, and second, the powerful influence that the 'DNA' of the Internet (its logic, architecture, and governance) has upon other digital infrastructures.

In the hourglass architecture, each layer contains elements which can be adapted as necessary over time to support data, information, and business processes (application). The elements of all layers are based on some installed base – this is clearest perhaps in the lower layers (physical),

DOI: 10.4324/9781003385578-16

but equally true in the application layer where the use of existing services is fundamental to almost all innovation. The middle layer (protocol) then provides a powerful and adaptable articulation between data transmission and diverse uses and users. As the core articulation, the stability and the incremental development of the protocol layer are critical features. The hourglass architecture also helps us understand that we do not need to have a big design plan to achieve a big digital infrastructure. Both the Internet and the WWW show how something initially used by a few research institutions can become quite quickly an infrastructure for the whole world. In both these cases the middle layer (protocol) has been able to provide a powerful and adaptable articulation between data transmission and diverse uses and users.

The most significant dynamic aspect of the architecture of infrastructures is how their layers evolve over time through a process of agreeing to standards and agreeing to upgrade them. This cultivation process is in part technical, but also social and political. There are multiple interests invested in the future of any infrastructure, and these different interests want evolving standards to reflect their needs. Infrastructures are then institutions where different interests and social actors negotiate and (we hope) come to some common understandings.

Layered architectures, the installed base, and standards may lead to path dependency – a constraint on future action. All technical and institutional developments made in the past might influence the way infrastructures evolve today and the way they are able to evolve in the future. There may be developments that are just not possible because of the installed base. On the other hand, the layered architecture and the use of new standards give us a level of flexibility to develop innovations, improvisations, and workarounds. So the installed base and path dependency are offset by digital generativity and the potential for innovation.

Indeed, innovation is an important concept in this book from two perspectives. The first is the innovation of digital infrastructures themselves – for instance, when faster networks allow the streaming of videos on the Internet on a massive scale, or when computer science allows the creation of cognitive computing (artificial intelligence). These innovations can be added to all layers of digital infrastructure, sometimes becoming digital business platforms (DBPs) which can enable new business activities. The second perspective is innovation in business models and platforms, and the creation of digital products and services within new market structures following new digital business strategies.

Discussion on digital innovation tends to focus on or drift back to the technical aspects – Thoreau's 'improved means' – but we also need to think of innovation in terms of new users and uses, and new digital business models – Thoreau's 'improved ends'. The most powerful innovations come from the way people and organisations appropriate digital technologies into their improved lives.

This book introduces some economic, managerial, and institutional perspectives to better understand why and how digital infrastructures evolve. These theories focus on the logic of growth, for instance positive network externalities, reducing transaction costs, building competitive advantages, and also the institutional influences from society. We also discuss some strategic perspectives on investing in digital technologies, such as the resource-based view (RBV), reconnecting the strategic view with the economic and technical rationales necessary to build robust competitive advantages.

Lastly, we have discussed the importance of governance and regulation of digital infrastructures and how different bodies and interests are drawn into maintaining their coherence as they evolve. Some of this is in the realm of governments, laws, and regulatory bodies, but many lie beyond in independent institutions such as the IETF or W3C or with the owners of digital platforms or digital infrastructures. The evidence we see is that just as the technical aspects of any infrastructure are varied and heterogeneous, so too are the governance structures. Governance is a mosaic of bodies and responsibilities, rather than achieved by a formal set of structures. In particular, we have discussed the case of net neutrality to exemplify the difficulties of building consensus on controversial issues.

New frontiers for digital infrastructure innovation

In this final chapter we turn to consider some aspects of where and how digital technologies will evolve in the next decade or so. We do not intend to propose futuristic projections, but to focus on infrastructural innovations that are already underway, and which may promise significant consequences in a ten-year time horizon. In other words, we follow today's installed base and its ongoing cultivation. Of course, in five or more years, our choices may seem rather dated, and so they should, and perhaps we are plain wrong, but that is the nature of prediction in any fast-moving and evolving field.

There is probably no controversy in saying that communications, work and social activities, entertainment, education, getting information, and buying/selling have migrated to a significant degree to the digital sphere. Depending on where you live this will be to differing degrees, but few places are untouched by such shifts. The more digital infrastructures are available, the more people join them to get the benefits, as discussed throughout this book. This pervasiveness of digital infrastructures and positive network effects changes the way we behave and the way we understand ourselves and our behaviour. From a macro perspective, economists and strategists have used the term the Fourth Industrial Revolution to express the scale of the impact of advanced technologies in the economy, particularly digital technologies (Internet of Things – IoT, big data analytics, artificial intelligence, quantum computing, robotics, etc.) (WEF, 2016).

The more we are online and interacting, the more data are generated about us and our activities. In the past, getting such data about large populations would be very costly or impossible altogether. Today, a great part of our communication patterns, location and travel, financial transactions, and purchases are observed and recorded. Our digital interactions leave traces. Every time we navigate the Internet, there is one or more algorithms registering our behaviour, such as Google, Facebook, Amazon, WeChat, or any other company which has placed cookies in our computing interfaces. Every time we send an email, we leave a trace to be analysed by the service provider or the company which receives the email. Every time we collaborate or interact online, we leave a trace of our contribution to a project and our way of thinking, as well as our mistakes and emotions. Every time we use our smartphones, the service provider knows with whom we are talking to, what information we seek, and where we are when we want it.

This phenomenon of generation of digital data on a vast scale has been called datafication and the result is resources of big data. Generating data, however, is not very useful per se. Big data is a resource but needs to be mobilised, which is the work of big data analytics. It is this that makes the mountains of data we generate have consequences. The promise is that big datasets and analytics can reveal new information that we could not know without data on this scale and at this level of granularity. For instance, we can know more about patterns of behaviour, unknown correlations and influences, customer preferences, public opinion trends, productivity, and levels of collaboration, to cite a few examples. When big data is available, organisations that exploit it gain knowledge of their processes and their markets and competitive advantages in relation to those which do not. There are direct economic benefits from big data analytics for businesses. Equally, there are direct implications for people which may not be seen as unalloyed benefits.

The potential of big data increases with the advance of other digital infrastructures. The IoT adds digital sensors with network connectivity to objects, allowing the communication of these objects between themselves and with the Internet in a broad sense. For instance, with this infrastructure in place, people start to be able to manage their home devices through the Internet. They can tell the heating system or air conditioner to start when they are on their way home. Other possibilities are to turn on the oven to warm food, or a food dispenser to release food to pets. Such IoT infrastructure changes the way we interact with our homes and offices, objects, living beings, and ourselves (e.g., fitness apps enabled by smartwatches).

On a bigger scale, the IoT can (or might) create, for instance, smart electrical grids, intelligent transport systems, and smart cities, changing the way governments and private companies manage urban spaces. Imagine an electrical grid in which all devices are connected to the same network, and the grid itself can decide which time is the best to do certain tasks at home – for instance, washing clothes or heating water – when there is excess of energy in the system. Or an intelligent transport system which automatically directs passengers, cars, and buses to the fastest routes in accordance with the information received from other vehicles in the network, avoiding traffic. Or an IoT infrastructure helping a city to manage schools, hospitals, services, power plants, water supply, and waste management. These activities, individually and integrated together, might be better managed using the information from diverse sensors including sensors carried by people (e.g., mobile devices). The result could be seen in many benefits – cost and waste reductions, improvement in air quality, and improvement of the quality of services, through better productivity, less pollution, fewer greenhouse gases, and happier people!

IoT has other potential applications, for instance in self-driving vehicles and electric-powered cars, buses, and trucks. Vehicles can quite easily understand maps to go from point A to point B without a human driver, and petrol engines can be changed to electric motors. But how to do it safely and reliably? For that we need to understand many material elements in the external context – such as other cars, bicycles, buildings, people and animals, weather, charging points, journey plans, etc. This needs a lot of data to be collected and then processed, probably remotely by multiple dedicated cloud services. The development of electric vehicles and self-driving cars calls attention to another familiar phenomenon: all infrastructures evolve and grow, drawing on an installed base. The new digital transport infrastructure builds on and extends existing transport infrastructures (roads, gas stations, maps) and blends this with mobile digital communications. We can foresee a new transport infrastructure built on top of digital infrastructures – including smart electric vehicles, more responsive public transport, street bicycles, and transport integration.

A second development which is going to affect the future of computing and with implications for businesses is artificial intelligence (AI). The day when computers will be able to fully match the human brain, i.e., when we are able to create a fully operational artificial general intelligence (AGI), is still far off, we believe. However, there are a growing number of narrower and specific areas in which computers are already better than humans, for instance, in managing massive volumes of data and finding unknown patterns in them (associations between data points), and playing games such as chess or Go. In addition, computer scientists have learnt that one successful way to build AI is through mechanisms which mimic the process of human learning. Instead of trying to develop software which 'knows' everything about X, better to have a program which can learn from past experiences of X – e.g., from databases of X in the past and from interactions with humans who know about X – the machine learning (ML) approach, discussed earlier in the book. To a good degree, using ML, AI services can interpret natural language (spoken or written) and answer questions on relevant topics, looking for a good match or anything meaningful within a range of probabilities, in the same way human beings do.

The fast diffusion of generative AI solutions has demonstrated not only that scientists and developers have advanced in their quest for AI, but also that we as societies are eager to embrace the new ML AI. For sure, there are still weaknesses and risks in AI products and services; however, it seems that the time has now come for these technologies. As infrastructures, we know that in use they will be improved and adapted to serve a wide range of activities and operations in the personal, business, and governmental realms.

By combining big data with ML techniques, artificial intelligence has become a very viable digital service. It is not about 'knowing' everything, but learning how to learn in specific domains and making better estimations of probabilities to match answers to questions. Even better, the developed general models of learning can be applied to the learning of any topic that has a suitable body of data to be analysed. Once an AI algorithm is trained for a task, the cost of reproducing that algorithm (AI as a Service, AIaaS) is close to zero. If an AI algorithm is more precise than humans at driving cars, it may be possible to substitute all drivers in the world with a single algorithm! But only if we reach a high level of confidence in it. A similar logic may apply in other areas such as the diagnosis of diseases from scans and X-rays, decision-making about investments, or even the teaching of some subjects.

An area which is fast harnessing AI is robotic process automation (RPA), combining software robots with AI agents. RPA learns from users (humans) how a task is done and then automates the processes with the tasks done in the same way (or better). The promise of RPA is to help businesses and governments be more efficient, faster, and more secure in regards to those processes which depend more on human interventions. For instance, banks may use RPA to evaluate documentations and credit scores of new customers, and even to open new accounts once the paperwork is approved by the system. For banks, automating such a process is advantageous: the knowledge for doing the task is standardised (there is an established process), the tasks are repetitive, and the volume of similar operations across a year is massive. Thus, there is a business case for the automation with the expectation of return on investment (ROI) with gains of efficiency, time, and precision (fewer human errors). Another example of RPA that we can see emerging everywhere (sometimes with disastrous results) is the use of intelligent chatbots, in which the AI interface is trained to give responses to customers, or even to solve problems related to customer services. However, these tools are still limited and need further development in order to have a higher level of correct output.

Increased roles for AI are probably inevitable. However, they still require a broad discussion in society to understand the advantages and risks of the use of AI. AI using ML depends on access to a large volume of data (big data) that captures some causal relationships. Those with access to relevant datasets have competitive advantages in relation to others. We also face the problem that the data we use to train an AI algorithm may be (actually, almost certainly is) significantly biased, leading to systemically biased AI services. If we are pessimistic, AI will actively create an increased gap between the haves and have-nots in society. The advancements in technology so far have not been revealed as being synonymous with better distribution of wealth in society; indeed, there are plenty of examples of the opposite (McAfee and Brynjolfsson, 2017).

Advances in the practical application of AI make possible the identification of patterns of behaviour, language, voice, and images that we could only imagine a few decades ago. This has enabled enhancements to products and services. For instance, you can use your voice or face image to open your mobile and have access to financial services through applications. It is safer to use biometric information than passwords. But it is also the case that the same technology can be used to identify and control people. The more digitalised our lives become, and the more information is gathered about our characteristics, behaviours, and beliefs, the higher the risk is that this can be used against us. Does this mean we should set limits? Do we need to build stronger governance structures and mandate powerful regulators? Or do we take the benefits and acquiesce, accepting this is the price we pay? The latter, you might argue, has been the default behaviour in the past two decades as our personal data has been mined and monetised by big digital businesses.

Technology is also going places. The enthusiasm for AI in the last few years is predicated on access to new and more powerful hardware architectures for high-performance computing (HPC). HPC uses a combination of supercomputers and vast computer clusters organised for parallel programming – a highly refined version of cloud service. And to make the digital game more interesting, we can add a small introduction to quantum computing. Instead of relying on the traditional computing world of binary information (each element of data in the computing process is either a 1 or a 0), the quantum computer processes information by considering the quantum states of a whole system.

This is not the place to discuss such a complex technology, and we are not the right people, but the expectations are that quantum computers will be able to tackle much more complex problems using more data, and much faster. Problems that today we cannot address in a feasible amount of time will be attainable by quantum computers. When or if quantum computers become fully operational, as per the theory, their speed to calculate things will be so fast that current technology will not be competitive anymore (at least in the processing of big data). We can only try to imagine the advances in AI algorithms, for instance, using quantum computing. Companies like Google and IBM are focusing on developing commercial applications for quantum technology. We are not yet there commercially, but it is good to pay attention to a development, which may radically change the way we experience computing, for the good and for the bad. For example, quantum computing may be able to break cybersecurity codes and processes as we know them today, making our current digital security useless; like using bows and arrows against fighter aircraft.

The future is a foreign country

In this final section, we explore a few implications and concerns deriving from our broad discussion of the future of digital infrastructures. We emphasise two aspects: one is about the survival of businesses and economies, and the other is about the need for change in education systems to equip us with the necessary skills for this new era. We are not giving answers because we do not have them, but want to call attention to things that will require more care in the future. You can read more about the theme in Brynjolfsson and McAfee (2011, 2014), McAfee and Brynjolfsson (2017), Zahidi et al. (2020), and Silva et al. (2022).

From the perspective of businesses and economies, there are not many alternatives to embracing the adoption of digital infrastructures and the enhanced services they deliver. Naturally, there are some niches which can survive or even thrive with less digital technology. But the great majority of businesses and public sector organisations are dependent on digital infrastructures now, and will become more so. Having more connections to buyers and sellers, more access to information and AI services, and the capacity for processing information at a higher speed, gives a competitive edge to individual companies and national economies. As discussed throughout this book, digital infrastructures help to drive innovation, potentially bringing more creativity, more productivity, better business models, and new digital products and services. And digital infrastructures mean that the product or service is potentially available across the whole world.

From the perspective of educational systems, the scale of the challenge is dramatic. The problem here is seen by some experts as the mismatch between traditional education systems, which were preparing people for living and working in economies before the emergence of digital infrastructures, and the future needs of countries and societies. Seen narrowly, many industries face difficulties in recruiting engineers, computer scientists, data analysts, programmers, and business professionals who are able to lead innovation with and through digital infrastructures. The situation becomes more serious if we believe that AI is going to substitute many professional roles partially or fully. Those potentially affected by AI solutions cut across professions and roles – including all kinds of knowledge workers such as bankers, doctors, teachers, accountants, and lawyers. Many people will need to reinvent themselves to some degree and orient towards areas where AI solutions do not fit or in areas in which they will be capable of using AI solutions for augmentation of their skills and performance (see the discussion on the topic in the report from the UK Department of Education, 2023).

There is no easy way out of this situation. Educational institutions cannot change as fast as the needs of economies and societies require: their architectures just do not allow quick and responsive change, let alone welcome innovation. One possible route is to be more focused on the process of 'learning how to learn'. Again, infrastructures may help to discern some steps in this direction – where the institution becomes more like a platform, and individual users pursue varied uses. We all need to learn how to do our own research to find our own answers to our problems. Instead of trying to present 'all that you need to know', this book tries to tells you a story to foster your interest in looking for more information, for example, through recommended readings and through your own (online) research.

Generative AI tools such as ChatGPT, Gemini, and Copilot may not be very helpful in this journey in their current form. However, if you learn how to ask interesting questions (prompts) and how to discern when the answer is credible or not, or even wrong (AI hallucinations), and if you learn how to check responses, then these tools gain greater value. Even more important: these tools are improving by the day, thus gradually generative AI interfaces are going to be more helpful and present in our self-learning processes. The best results from generative AI and AI personal assistants come from the way we interact with the interfaces. They are already improving productivity in many subtle ways, and will become more pervasive in all our activities.

We live in interesting times and alas there are no silver bullets for our challenges. We need to work hard to build bridges towards the future. With the addition of some human wisdom, digital infrastructures may, or dare we say *will*, help us to get there.

References

Brynjolfsson, E. and McAfee, A. (2011). *Race Against the Machine*. Lexington, MA: Digital Frontier Press.

Brynjolfsson, E. and McAfee, A. (2014). *The Second Machine Age*. New York and London: W.W. Norton.

McAfee, A. and Brynjolfsson, E. (2017). *Machine, Platform, Crowd: Harnessing the Digital Revolution: Harnessing Our Digital Future*. New York and London: W.W. Norton.

Silva, A., Elhussein, G., Leopold, T., and Zahidi, S. (2022). *Catalysing Education 4.0 – Investing in the Future of Learning for a Human-Centric Recovery*. World Economic Forum (WEF), Insight Report, May 2022. Available at: https://www3.weforum.org/docs/WEF_Catalysing_Education_4.0_2022.pdf (Accessed: 25 February 2024).

UK Department of Education (2023). *The Impact of AI on UK Jobs and Training*. UK Department of Education. Available at: https://assets.publishing.service.gov.uk/media/656856b8cc1ec500138eef49/Gov.UK_Impact_of_AI_on_UK_Jobs_and_Training.pdf (Accessed: 17 March 2024).

WEF (2016). 'The Fourth Industrial Revolution: what it means, how to respond.' Available at: https://www.weforum.org/agenda/2016/01/the-fourth-industrial-revolution-what-it-means-and-how-to-respond/ (Accessed: 22 March 2024).

Zahidi, S., Ratcheva, V., Hingel, G., and Brown, S. (2020). *The Future of Jobs Report*. World Economic Forum (WEF). Available at: https://www3.weforum.org/docs/WEF_Future_of_Jobs_2020.pdf (Accessed: 24 February 2024).

Zittrain, J.L. (2008). *The Future of the Internet – and How to Stop It*. New Haven and London: Yale University Press.

Index

Note: pages of content into **tables are in bold**; pages of content into *images are in Italic.*

Printed in the United States
by Baker & Taylor Publisher Services